Italian American
Ballplayers

Italian American Ballplayers

Major League Profiles, 1920–1980

OTTO BRUNO, JR.

McFarland & Company, Inc., Publishers
Jefferson, North Carolina

Library of Congress Cataloging-in-Publication Data

Names: Bruno, Otto, 1964– author
Title: Italian American ballplayers : Major league profiles, 1920-1980 / Otto Bruno, Jr..
Other titles: Thirty-five major league profiles, 1920-1980
Description: Jefferson, North Carolina : McFarland & Company, Inc., Publishers, 2025 | Includes bibliographical references and index.
Identifiers: LCCN 2025022836 | ISBN 9781476695570 print ∞
ISBN 9781476655130 ebook
Subjects: LCSH: Italian American baseball players—Biography | Major League Baseball—History—20th century | BISAC: SPORTS & RECREATION / Baseball / History | LCGFT: Biographies
Classification: LCC GV865.A1 B78 2025 | DDC 796.357092/2—dc23/eng/20250711
LC record available at https://lccn.loc.gov/2025022836

ISBN (print) 978-1-4766-9557-0
ISBN (ebook) 978-1-4766-5513-0

© 2025 Otto Bruno, Jr. All rights reserved

No part of this book may be reproduced or transmitted in any form or by any means, electronic or mechanical, including photocopying or recording, or by any information storage and retrieval system, without permission in writing from the publisher.

Front cover image (left to right): New York Yankees shortstop Frank Crosetti, Brooklyn Dodgers first baseman Dolph Camilli and Yankees center fielder Joe DiMaggio (National Baseball Hall of Fame Library, Cooperstown, New York)

Printed in the United States of America

*McFarland & Company, Inc., Publishers
Box 611, Jefferson, North Carolina 28640
www.mcfarlandpub.com*

For the Schnozz, the Little Professor,
Campy, the Reading Rifle, the Rock, Rico,
and all the rest of the men contained herein
who inspired multiple generations
and made this project a joy to undertake

For Frankie, Nick, and Jennie

And always, for Mary Beth

Table of Contents

Preface   1

Introduction   3

1. Babe Pinelli (1918)   9
2. Tony Lazzeri (1926)   15
3. Ernie Orsatti (1927)   21
4. Tony Cuccinello (1930)   27
5. Ernie Lombardi (1931)   32
6. Frankie Crosetti (1932)   38
7. Dolph Camilli (1933)   44
8. Cookie Lavagetto (1934)   50
9. Zeke Bonura (1934)   56
10. Phil Cavarretta (1934)   62
11. The DiMaggio Brothers: Joe, Vince, and Dom (1936, '37, '40)   68
12. John Berardino (1939)   79
13. Phil Rizzuto (1941)   85
14. Ralph Branca (1944)   90
15. Carl Furillo (1946)   95
16. Joe Garagiola (1946)   101
17. Yogi Berra (1946)   107
18. Vic Raschi (1946)   113
19. Sam Mele (1947)   119
20. Roy Campanella (1948)   125
21. Johnny Antonelli (1948)   131
22. Joe Altobelli (1955)   137
23. Rocky Colavito (1955)   144
24. Frank Malzone (1955)   150

25. Jim Gentile (1957)	155
26. Joe Torre (1960)	160
27. Ron Santo (1960)	166
28. Jim Fregosi (1961)	172
29. Dave Giusti (1962)	178
30. Rico Petrocelli (1963)	184
31. Tony Conigliaro (1964)	190
32. Sal Bando (1967)	196
33. Gary Gaetti (1981)	202
34. A. Bartlett Giamatti	208
35. Others of Note	214
Epilogue	229
Acknowledgments	231
Bibliography	233
Index	235

Preface

For over 20 years, I've been happily associated with an Italian American publication called *Fra Noi*, headquartered near Chicago, Illinois. I was introduced to its editor-in-chief, Paul Basile, via email by Professor Fred Gardaphe, a renowned writer, teacher, and expert on Italian American literature whom I met in the 1990s through another legendary writer named Jerre Mangione.

Initially, my writings for *Fra Noi* were strictly about Italian Americans in show business history, but after a few years, I suggested that during the summer months I could write some profiles on legendary Italian American baseball players. Happily, Paul Basile liked the idea and encouraged my efforts.

I never realized, until I went to put these pieces together as a book collection, just how many players I'd covered through the years. In fact, there were so many that some had to be "cut from the roster" just like players vying for a spot on a team in spring training.

This leads to the question of how these particular players were chosen for this collection. While I tried to write these pieces objectively as befitting a respected publication, this book ultimately is a personal one. First of all, the most recent ballplayer included in the collection broke into the majors in 1981. I fell in love with baseball in the early '70s and the first decade of my fandom is still the one that resonates with me the most. Our childhood memories and experiences are the ones that seem to stay with us forever and influence the way we view the world. In my case, it also influenced how I view the game of baseball. Therefore, the choices of who I profiled had everything to do with the author's interest and not the player's stats.

When I became a baseball fan in 1971/1972, I almost immediately began collecting baseball cards. Those cards, along with my monthly *Baseball Digests*, and a copy of a massive 1974 tome titled *The Baseball Encyclopedia: The Complete and Official Record of Major League Baseball Revised and Updated*, were my most relied upon teachers when it came to the history of the game. For those who may be quite a bit younger than me, I used the *Baseball Encyclopedia* back then the way I use the *Baseball Reference* website today.

The choices made for this book have a great deal to do with my initial interest in the classic ballplayers who played the game long before I was alive. I was always fascinated with history and the fascination for baseball history was particularly pronounced right from the start. I read as many of the historical accounts of the game as I could. There was a series of books published by Random House in the late 1960s and early 1970s under the imprint "Major League Library" with titles like *Heroes of the Major Leagues* by Alexander Peters, *Strange but True Baseball Stories* by Furman Bisher, and *Greatest World Series Thrillers* by Ray Robinson, to name a few. These books could always be found on the shelves of our school libraries. I read every one I could get my hands on.

When it came to choosing subjects for my *Fra Noi* profiles, the selection was based on my personal interest in the subject, the story their lives and/or careers had to tell, and—this was important—the amount of information I could find on an individual ballplayer in order to make an interesting enough profile for my readers.

Books were helpful—books are always helpful and necessary—but in this case, I also made numerous trips to the Baseball Hall of Fame in Cooperstown, New York, and combed through the player files stored at the A. Bartlett Giamatti Research Center. There they have files on just about every player who has spent any time in the Major Leagues. I never knew what I'd find in a player's profile. It might be a long, well-written story or interview done with the player for a major publication or it might be snippets of reporting about specific games and/or box scores from small town newspapers. Some clippings were identifiable as to who wrote them and for what publication but many were not. As you read through the profiles contained herein, rather than using endnotes or footnotes, I identify the writer and/or the source of a quote within the body of the story, when those writers or sources could be identified.

The profiles making up this collection are arranged chronologically by the first Major League season of each player. The rookie year of the first profile was 1918 (Babe Pinelli) while the last season of the final player in the collection was 2000 (Gary Gaetti). That's more than 80 years of baseball from within the Italian American community. It's a long, proud, and entertaining history. I hope you enjoy reading about these wonderful players as much as I enjoyed researching and writing about them.

Introduction

For nearly an entire century, baseball was called America's game. Few disputed its claim as our country's greatest contribution to the world of sports and one of the most wholesome, enjoyable, and unifying pastimes in our culture. It is not insignificant that baseball rose to national prominence at the eve of the 20th century, the century that thanks to American innovation and ambition would inspire Henry Luce to call it "the American Century." Further, it is also significant that Major League Baseball's nascent years coincided with decades of intense migration to the United States from foreign cultures. One of the most significant of those migrations consisted of millions of Italians who came to "l'America."

I once read a quote about how my Italian ancestors came to this country expecting to find streets paved with gold and instead found the streets not paved at all. What's more, *they* were expected to pave them.

It's a humorous but insightful anecdote. The immigrants who came to this country faced many hardships and overcame many obstacles. Most of them had very little, if any, education. Nevertheless, they packed up all their belongings, took a 20- to 30-day boat trip across the ocean in the hold of a ship—in conditions more disgusting than you or I would even want to imagine—and settled in a foreign land where they were unable to speak or understand the native tongue. Sounds crazy, doesn't it? In the book *Unto the Sons*, writer Gay Talese tells the story of returning home to America after visiting his father's hometown in Italy for the first time many years ago and asking his dad how he could have ever left such a beautiful place. He received this pragmatic and telling reply: "We couldn't eat the scenery."

Little wonder, then, that many of our Italian grandparents and Italian American parents were so intent on their children making the most of America's opportunities. This meant hard work, education, and discipline with little time left for fun and games. The immigrant mothers and fathers who worked so hard for little else but the advancement of their children's stations in life were at a loss when it came to understanding America's obsession with entertainment and games. The movies, the music, the sports of America, all were pastimes that many of the immigrants saw as frivolous and sacrilegious.

Their children, however, saw these activities as something quite different. They were more than just escapes from the daily grind of dreary chores, schoolwork, and part-time jobs. They were manifestations of the American dream. To the little girl who stayed up late at night sewing buttons on cards with her mother, the glamour of Carole Lombard was her American dream. To the little boy who got up at 4:00 a.m. to help his father deliver vegetables to the market before he went to school, Babe Ruth's home run exploits were the inspiration for his American dream.

As an Italian American writer and historian, I would posit that the three most important Italian American icons of 20th-century America were Fiorello La Guardia, Frank Sinatra, and Joe DiMaggio. All emerged on the national scene at roughly the same time during the 1930s and 1940s. All three had their initial and/or greatest successes on or around the island of Manhattan. Yet, during the middle of the 20th century, the one who was likely the best known and recognized all over the world was Joseph Paul DiMaggio.

An introverted son of a Sicilian fisherman in San Francisco, Joe DiMaggio captured the hearts and minds of his country in 1941 with his record-setting 56-game hitting streak, an achievement that still stands as arguably the most impressive and invincible record in all of sports. In 1941, baseball represented America to the rest of the world. DiMaggio's grace under pressure in that anxiety-ridden summer before America entered World War II propelled him to the position of baseball's most recognizable representative.

If Joe DiMaggio was that important to America as a cultural ambassador then what do you think he meant to Italian Americans? Certainly far more than any young person can imagine today. For our fathers and grandfathers, Joe DiMaggio was a literal example that anything was possible in America. The kids down the street might call you a "Dago" or a "Wop" but if you could hit like DiMaggio no one cared what your last name was. On the baseball field, nothing mattered but your skill and determination (of course, that wasn't exactly true because in 1936, when DiMaggio was a rookie, the color of your skin still needed to be white for you to be a Major Leaguer, but thankfully that injustice would be corrected during DiMaggio's tenure in baseball).

In his book *The Summer of '49*, journalist David Halberstam acknowledged the reluctance of immigrant parents to accept the idea of their sons wasting their days playing baseball. Of DiMaggio's father he wrote, "Giuseppe DiMaggio at first frowned on baseball as too frivolous. Only as Joe became a major star did his opinion change, and he came to enjoy his son's success." Halberstam went on to say that Phil Rizzuto's parents, natives of Calabria, also thought of baseball as a foolish choice for a career. It was Rizzuto's mother who had to convince his father to let him try baseball, saying that if he didn't make it he could always go out and get a real job.

Following World War II, thanks in large part to the successes of Joe DiMaggio, Tony Lazzeri, Ernie Lombardi, Tony Cuccinello, Frank Crosetti, Phil Cavaretta, and other sons of Italy, more and more young men from the immigrant tradition broke onto the baseball scene. In fact, many came from the San Francisco area, DiMaggio's hometown. Even with the example set by the great DiMaggio, Italian American parents were still reluctant to allow their sons to pursue a child's game as a career. Nevertheless, in a 1952 book simply titled *Yogi Berra*, about the New York Yankee Hall of Fame catcher, Joe Trimble wrote, "Sports presented just about the only outlet for the poor kids growing up on 'Dago Hill'" (the Italian section of Berra's native St. Louis). He might have said the only healthy outlet.

Berra's childhood pal, Joe Garagiola, expressed what baseball ultimately meant to him and the rest of the Italian American community in his 1960 book, *Baseball Is a Funny Game*. In Garagiola's rookie year of 1946, his friends and neighbors from "The Hill" (aka Dago Hill) sponsored Joe Garagiola Night at Sportsman's Park in St. Louis. Garagiola recalled the night as his greatest in baseball: "It will always be a top thrill to me because that night I saw many people there like Mama and Pop—people who didn't know what baseball was but wanted to be there because 'this is one of our boys.' It was best expressed by the vegetable peddler who in his best English told me a few days later, 'Gioi, you the firsta boy what comes from The Hill, witha name witha ends a, e, i, o, getta name in the paper and no killa somebody.'"

* * *

Like all children, I grew up hearing from my parents and their contemporaries just how wonderful the world was when they were young. With a fraction of the spending money kids have today they were able to use their ingenuity to create fun out of the simplest things. The movies were better, radio was wonderful, and an ice cream cone cost a nickel. I listened to these stories and regretted not being born in my parents' era. I was sure that I would never be able to look back on my childhood and say, "those were simpler and happier days." Of course, I was wrong. Looking back on my own youth, it seems so much simpler and more relaxed than what my own kids experienced 30 years later. For better or for worse, I'm sure my kids will think the same thing about their own childhood 20 years from now.

I grew up listening to Joe Garagiola swap baseball stories with Tony Kubek every Saturday on the game-of-the-week baseball telecasts on NBC. I also remember Curt Gowdy and Dizzy Dean as baseball sportscasters. Those Saturday games, along with the one eventually added on Monday nights, were the only baseball games I could see every week. There was no cable TV, there were no satellite dishes—at least not in my world. We were decades away from the MLB Network or Internet streaming. My children think I'm teasing them when I tell them I had my choice of but four television channels when I was their age. And yet, somehow, only being able to see one or two games a week made the games more special, more magical. In addition to watching the games on TV, I loved listening to ballgames on the radio in the darkness of my room at night. In fact, I still do. These days I listen to old broadcasts of Vin Scully, Lindsay Nelson, or Ernie Harwell on summer nights. No game has ever lent itself better to broadcast over the radio than baseball. My childhood constituted the waning years when baseball was truly the national pastime.

In addition to listening to the stories of Garagiola, Gowdy, Vin Scully, and others of their ilk, I learned everything I could about baseball history and the great players who were legends before I was born. Most of what I learned about baseball history came from books. However, my parents and their peers loved to regale us kids with stories of their youth and I was always an avid and interested listener. While most of my uncles and cousins talked of DiMaggio there were always those who would mention other *paisani* like Carl Furillo, Sal Maglie, or Rocky Colavito.

This was 15 or 20 years after these guys had retired and yet the eyes on these adult men would light up with a sense of excitement and pride I rarely saw from them. That's how strong the connection was to these sports heroes. Part of it was the typical child worshiping the great sport star. However, for these men much of the admiration and idolization came from the fact that these heroes had come from the same kind of Italian American families and neighborhoods in which they had grown up.

Influenced as I was by my elders, I always felt a special pride in the Italian American ballplayers of my own time. I loved Rico Petrocelli of the Red Sox. I rooted for Jim Fregosi, Ron Santo, Kurt Bevacqua, and Gene Tenace. Remember Dave Giusti, the crafty Pirate pitcher? Then there was the local minor league manager of our Rochester Red Wings, Joe Altobelli. I thought that he was the greatest manager in all of baseball. A decade later, so did everyone else when he led the 1983 Baltimore Orioles to the World Championship. I shared a special pride in them all but it was a much different kind of pride than my dad's generation experienced. And even with my awareness and fondness for the Italian American ballplayer, it didn't override the fact that my first baseball heroes were Roberto Clemente and Brooks Robinson, two men with no connection to Italian America.

It's quite difficult for the children of my generation and younger to understand the importance of Joe DiMaggio and the other Italian American baseball stars of the pre–Baby Boomer era. It's impossible, really. Those of us who grew up in the late '60s, '70s or '80s felt little, if any, real discrimination from classmates or teachers, or society in general, growing up as Italian Americans. Our parents came to our Little League games, school plays, and any number of school and community events and mixed comfortably and confidently with their non–Italian American peers. The thought of changing our names to get a job would never have occurred to any person of my generation. For kids my age, baseball and football heroes represented what we all wanted to be—professional athletes. For our fathers and grandfathers the baseball hero or boxing champion represented what they could, and would, eventually become—Americans.

Ballplayers like DiMaggio, Tony Lazzeri, Phil Cavaretta, Ernie Lombardi, Frank Crosetti, Roy Campanella, Joe Garagiola, Carl Furillo, Yogi Berra, Dolph Camilli, Rocky Colavito, and countless others meant so much to our fathers, grandfathers, and the Italian American community as a whole because their success mirrored and inspired our quieter daily victories in the new world. While their success provided immediate economic and societal advancement for them and their families, the rest of Italian America vicariously shared in the joy of their achievement and acceptance into the middle class, and upper middle class, society. Many Italian Americans would eventually get there themselves but by much longer and more circuitous routes. Finally, the positive image that Italian American ballplayers were able to convey to the nation as a whole through their participation in America's game also helped to pave the way for a more universal acceptance of their Italian American brothers and sisters throughout society.

* * *

This book does not pretend to be a general or comprehensive history of any sort. It is more akin to a love letter to a number of the men who made their fellow Italian Americans proud and etched their names not only in the annals of Major League Baseball but also in the hearts and minds of baseball fans of Italian ancestry as well as many more who were not.

♦ 1 ♦

Babe Pinelli
(1918)

Third time's the charm! After two false starts with the White Sox and the Tigers, Babe Pinelli became a valuable outfielder for the Reds from 1922 to 1927 (National Baseball Hall of Fame, Cooperstown, NY).

He suited up and was on the field for more than 3,400 straight baseball games—more consecutive games than Lou Gehrig or Cal Ripken. In fact, he participated in a total of more than 4,000 Major League games from 1918 until the last game of the 1956 season. His name was Ralph Pinelli but he was better known as "Babe" Pinelli, one of the most colorful and well-respected umpires in all of baseball history. Prior to his 22-year umpiring career, Pinelli spent 16 years as a professional ballplayer in both the Pacific Coast and Major Leagues. He was a fast and competitive little infielder with a fiery temper and a passionate love for the game. Most who knew him thought that umpiring would and should be the last possible career choice for a man with his disposition. However, he proved them wrong just as he had done all his life when he was told he could not achieve something.

He was born Rinaldo Angelo Paolinelli on October 18, 1896, in San Francisco, California. His father, a successful vendor, was killed in the devastating earthquake of 1906. Following his father's death, the young boy quit school to help earn money for his family. Unfortunately, his temper and his fists got him into trouble with the law on more than one occasion. Eventually, he began to focus his proclivity for fisticuffs on amateur boxing matches to earn some extra money.

In August of 1916 he married his Irish sweetheart, Mabel McKee. Before the spring of 1917, Pinelli and his new bride decided that he should pursue a career in baseball. He tried out and made the team in Salt Lake City but was with them for just a month before he was picked up by Portland of the Pacific Coast League. He went to Sacramento for the 1918 season and played in 94 games for the minor leaguers until being summoned to the majors by the Chicago White Sox. He played in 24 games at the end of the 1918 season with the Chisox but failed to impress. It may have been the luckiest demotion of his long career as he was far from Chicago and the White Sox when the Black Sox Scandal threatened to destroy the national pastime the following season.

Instead, 1919 found Pinelli back with the Sacramento team of the PCL where he hit a mediocre .252 but stole 51 bases for the third best mark in the league. At the end of the season the Detroit Tigers purchased his contract. He played in 102 games for the Tigers in 1920 but batted only .229. Early in the season Pinelli had a run-in with the iconic Ty Cobb. Both players had legendary tempers, and once it was announced that Cobb would be the new Detroit manager in 1921, Babe Pinelli was on his way back to the Pacific Coast League with the Oakland ball club. Teammates and friends of Pinelli's felt that after his experience with Cobb, Pinelli was even more determined to prove to "the Georgia Peach" (Cobb's nickname) and others that he could play in the Major Leagues.

In most of the articles and press releases of the 1920s, Pinelli is lauded for his toughness and determination. A 1926 press release from the Cincinnati Reds contains the following passage: "This small Italian person has something just as valuable as a batting eye or as defensive skill. He has an indomitable spirit. He loves baseball. The game is meat and drink to him." The press release goes on to describe Pinelli by saying, "His reverses had only served to make him more determined to win." The observation was made that "it was … his spirit and energy and courage as much as anything [that] carried him back from the field of defeat to get his third big league trial." The story concludes: "[the] main thing is his cockiness and his deep-seated and glowing love of the game from which he gains his fame and fortune." While the prose is certainly saccharine, the assessment seems to have been a universal opinion among those who played with and against Babe Pinelli.

He had a tremendous season with the Oakland Oaks ball club in 1921, hitting .339 and stealing 50 bases. That startling season got him a job with the Cincinnati Reds in 1922. He stayed with the Reds for the remainder of his Major League career until 1927.

His first season in Cincy was another banner year at the plate for Pinelli, who batted .305, knocked in 72 RBIs and stole 17 bases. The Cincinnati team was known to be a rough bunch of guys and Babe Pinelli fit right in. The team was known for fights in its own locker room as well as scraps with opposing teams. Unfortunately, while they won the fights they didn't win the pennants.

Pinelli once recalled for a newspaperman one of the more memorable battles in his career with the Reds. As Pinelli remembered it, Art Devlin, a coach for the old Boston Braves, started riding the Reds' players. "We were touchy," Pinelli said, "because things had been going very badly. We were blowing our pennant chances. Then Devlin started in on us. As we took the field, I bumped into Devlin and stepped all over his feet with my spikes. He howled like a coyote—and, of course, started swinging."

The benches cleared and the brawl was on. Devlin and Pinelli were both hurt in the melee. Pinelli was fined $100 and thrown out of the game. He watched the next day's festivities from the press box with an injured hand. "I knew there would be trouble the next day," said Pinelli. "The word was around that the first Boston player who had a chance to score was to give the works to Val Picinich, who was catching for us."

The retaliation began precisely as planned and Pinelli remembered that it turned into a riot with cops coming onto the field. In the confusion, Frank Wilson, a Boston outfielder, swung and hit the first guy he saw in the face. Unfortunately for Wilson, it was a policeman and he was taken into custody and brought to the jail still wearing his uniform.

The fiery Pinelli was thrown out of more than a few ballgames in his eight-year Major League career. In fact, he was thrown out of the second game he ever played as well as the very last game. Ironically, when he became a Major League umpire he was known to have a "soft thumb," ejecting an average of only two or three players and managers a year. He was tough but fair and highly respected.

The years 1922 and 1924 were Pinelli's two best seasons in the majors, hitting .305 and .306, respectively, but when he returned to the Pacific Coast League during the 1927 season, he left the big leagues with a .276 lifetime average.

He played professional ball for another five years, four of those with his hometown San Francisco Seals of the Pacific Coast League. He averaged .310 with the Seals for the 1928, 1929, and 1930 seasons. On July 4, 1929, Pinelli drove in 12 runs in one ballgame by hitting three home runs, two of which were grand slams. Pinelli once wrote about that memorable game, saying, "It wasn't that I'd improved as a hitter, I was stealing the signals of the Seattle catcher. When we played Seattle again, I couldn't buy a base hit. I heard the catcher laughing and, as I turned, he said: 'We changed the signals, wise guy.'"

He played on through 1932 in the Pacific Coast League and finished his career with the Oakland Oaks. Following his decision to retire, Pinelli asked Hi Baggerly, president of the Pacific Coast League, for a job as an umpire. Baggerly told him he needed some experience before he could consider hiring him. Pinelli immediately went out and bought a complete outfit and went down south to the Winter Leagues and called as many games as he could. He did the same in the spring and by the beginning of the 1933 season he was back on the field but in a much different uniform.

Pinelli claimed to have had ambitions for many years to umpire. During his playing days, he would sometimes visit the umpires' locker room and grill them with questions about their jobs. He'd study each umpire and pick up habits and tricks that he thought made a certain umpire stand out among the rest. There were many who discouraged Pinelli from pursuing the new career because they felt his disposition was too volatile to handle the strain of the job. He was described in a 1934 newspaper account as "a genial, likeable fellow, with innumerable friends, but he always was a hot-tempered, cocky young fellow whose Latin blood boiled over easily."

As always, Pinelli refused to be discouraged from trying something that people told him he couldn't do. He felt that he was fast enough to keep up with the swift plays on the basepaths, had keen eyesight which would benefit him behind the plate, and the discipline to control his temper when the situation called for patience and calm. History shows that he apparently knew his abilities and limitations better than anyone else.

He spent only two years in the PCL before being hired to umpire in the National League prior to the 1935 season. He quickly established a reputation for toughness and fairness in his new role as an arbiter in the big leagues. In a 1942 column called "Three and One," J.G. Taylor Spink notes, "Pinelli is usually on the tough assignments in Ford Frick's loop. [At the time, Frick was President of the National League]. For instance, he and Al Barlick and Lee Ballanfant have been in charge of most of the series played between the Giants and Dodgers. And last fall, when a firm hand was needed to handle what promised to be a tough World Series—Brooklyn's first in 21 years, featuring the rowdy Dodgers—Pinelli was picked."

Umpire Pinelli had quite a few tough assignments over the years. In a 1938 game at Braves Field in Boston, a St. Louis hitter knocked a soaring fly ball to Vince DiMaggio in center field. DiMaggio waited for the ball but it just hung up there.

Suddenly the wind kicked up and the ball started soaring back toward the infield and past the pitcher's mound. Years later Pinelli described the scene, saying, "Catcher Al Lopez, dashing backward, made the catch against the Boston dugout. I couldn't believe it. I turned to my umpiring partner, Beans Reardon. Beans was desperately clutching his pants and coat and 20,000 fans were running for cover. The game was over. A howling hurricane had struck New England."

The 1938 hurricane was the worst hurricane ever to hit the Atlantic Coast north of the Carolinas with wind gusts up to 120 miles per hour. What made it worse, there was little meteorological warning of the event.

In an article in *This Week* magazine in April of 1957, the newly retired Babe Pinelli told Al Stump about his first time behind the plate with the mighty Babe Ruth at-bat. "For rookie umps to set down the Babe [on a called strike] was practically suicide," Pinelli remembered, "So in my very first game behind the plate, I twice waved Ruth away on a called third strike. The second time all hell broke loose; he bawled, paved dirt, threatened to start a riot in the Boston confines. 'There's forty thousand here that know that last one was a ball, tomato-head!' roared Ruth. 'Maybe so,' I replied, 'but mine is the only opinion that counts.'"

In addition to the mighty Ruth, Pinelli also tamed two of the National League's most argumentative players and managers, Leo Durocher and Eddie Stanky. Durocher was like a rabid dog when it came to umpires. Pinelli recalled how during Durocher's playing days with the Cardinals, he tossed "Leo the Lip" out of two games for questioning the umpire's integrity: "After the second incident I told his manager, Frankie Frisch, 'Keep an extra infielder warmed up all summer.' 'Why?' asked Frisch. 'Because I'm bouncing your wisenheimer shortstop every time he opens up. He's going to learn to respect me or else.'" Pinelli said that throughout Durocher's managing days he rarely had any trouble with him.

Eddie Stanky was a student and disciple of Durocher's. One night in the dining car of the train, Stanky walked in and saw Pinelli reading a menu through a pair of horn-rimmed reading glasses. The young manager popped off with a sarcastic remark about how he'd always thought umpires were as blind as a potato with a thousand eyes. A short while later Pinelli was behind the plate for a game between the Cardinals and the Phillies. Stanky's Philadelphia club was leading 8–1 as the sun was setting. Back in those days, before all stadiums were equipped with lights for night baseball, games were often called on account of darkness. But Stanky began stalling so the game would be called after the top of the fifth and his Phillies would win the "official" game. Stanky questioned every call behind the plate, changed pitchers, called a conference with his catcher and even instructed his catcher to start a phony fight, all the while nursing an 8–1 lead.

Pinelli had enough and approached Stanky with the remark, "I won't need glasses to read the papers tonight." With that, Pinelli ruled the Cardinals the victors due to Stanky's stalling. Pinelli later said, "It was the first time a big-league game was forfeited short of legal length. Incidentally, Stanky never again mentioned my eyesight."

Pinelli's final game behind the plate came in Game Five of the 1956 World Series. A young pitcher by the name of Don Larsen took the mound for the Yankees. When Pinelli called the final strike on Dale Mitchell's checked swing, the history books had a new chapter written about the first and, to this day, only, no-hit, perfect game in World Series history.

When I mentioned to a colleague of mine that I was writing about Babe Pinelli, he looked at me and said, "I'm sure he was a good ump but the last strike on Mitchell was a ball." Such is the memory of true baseball fans and the legacy of unloved umpires.

Pinelli retired following the 1956 Series. He was only 61 years old but he had always been a devoted family man to his wife Mabel and sons Roy and Ray. He cited wanting to spend more time with them and his 11 grandchildren as his reason for retiring.

From his rough and tumble beginnings on the streets of San Francisco, Ralph Paolinelli had achieved his dream of being a big league ballplayer. Once that dream had been realized he set a new goal for himself and excelled in his second career as well. In the spring of 1957 he looked back on his days in baseball and said, "I couldn't have found a more exciting and happy career...."

♦ 2 ♦

Tony Lazzeri
(1926)

(From left) Joe DiMaggio, Frank Crosetti, and Tony Lazzeri. The three *paisans* of the Bronx Bombers (National Baseball Hall of Fame, Cooperstown, NY).

Years before a young San Francisco native named DiMaggio was drawing Italian American fans into Yankee Stadium, there was another San Francisco Italian that was introducing the game to his immigrant paesani in the Bronx and his name was Tony Lazzeri of the fabled Murderer's Row Yankee team of 1927. Lazzeri actually made his debut in pinstripes in 1926, a full ten seasons before Joe DiMaggio. Sportswriter Donald Honig wrote, "With a face out of a Caravaggio canvas, the quiet, hard-hitting second baseman had a reputation for on-the-field intelligence, and it was he and not Ruth or Gehrig who was looked upon as the team leader."

Tony Lazzeri was one of the greatest players of his generation who, for too many years, was remembered best for one failed at-bat in his rookie year. His post-baseball life was cut prematurely short and his tremendous accomplishments on the baseball diamond were forgotten for decades. His induction into the Baseball Hall of Fame 45 years after his death seemed to ignite a spark of renewed interest in the great second baseman but not nearly as much as he generated with his exciting play during the heyday of the first New York Yankee dynasty.

In his 2011 book, *Beyond DiMaggio: Italian Americans in Baseball*, Lawrence Baldassaro quotes from an October 3, 1926, edition of *Il Progresso Italo-Americano*, the nation's largest Italian-language newspaper of the day, as they reported on the ensuing World Series between the St. Louis Cardinals and the New York Yankees: "Even Italians, especially those of the second generation, are following with interest the shifting events of the American national game which, for some time now, outstanding players of our race have been participating." According to Baldassaro, "a major reason for the growing interest in baseball among Italian Americans was the appearance in the Yankee lineup that season of a rookie second baseman from San Francisco."

That may be true. *Il Progresso* had stated that there had been other Italian American ballplayers before Lazzeri, namely Ed Abbaticchio, Ping Bodie, and Babe Pinelli. Lazzeri, however, was the first to really flourish in the Big Apple. In 1926, New York City was not only one of the major media outlets of the United States but the one with the single largest population of Italian Americans.

In his rookie season Tony Lazzeri hit 18 home runs, which was the third highest total in the American League, while also driving in 117 runs. He was a star almost the minute his spikes hit the infield. The only event that dimmed his celebrity that first year was his final at-bat of the year.

In the seventh inning of the seventh game of the 1926 World Series, Tony Lazzeri came to bat with the bases loaded and the Yankees trailing 3–2. Cardinal manager Rogers Hornsby pulled starting pitcher Jesse Haines and called for 39-year-old future Hall-of-Famer Grover Cleveland Alexander from out of the bullpen. Having pitched a complete, nine-inning victory the day before, Alexander had gone out and celebrated well into the night, not expecting to be called upon to work the next day. Nevertheless, when Hornsby called for him, Alexander made his way to the mound. It was a classic showdown between aging veteran and anxious young rookie. The count was one and one when Lazzeri ripped a line drive down the left field line landing foul. The next pitch was a low, outside curve that had Lazzeri reaching and missing. The scoring threat was over. Many history buffs remember that seminal showdown as ending the series but it did not. There were two more innings to play. Alexander shut down the Yankees to seal the victory for the Cardinals but Lazzeri would always be remembered for striking out against the great Alexander to "lose" the 1926 World Series. Such are the selective memories of baseball fans. Luckily for Lazzeri, he had a thick hide. It was in his nature to be tough.

Anthony Michael Lazzeri was born on December 6, 1903, to immigrant parents in the Cow Hollow section of San Francisco. According to Lazzeri, his neighborhood "wasn't one in which a boy was likely to grow up a sissy, for it was always fight or get licked, and I never got licked." The toughness he learned on the streets originally translated into a desire to be a prizefighter but he loved baseball as well. He had no interest in school and was happy to be expelled at the age of 15. He went to work in a foundry while playing shortstop for a local semi-pro team. Eventually, the dreams of being a prizefighter faded but baseball presented new and exciting opportunities for the young Lazzeri.

In 1922, at the age of 18, he signed his first professional contract with the Salt Lake City Bees of the Pacific Coast League. He played most of the 1923 season with Peoria in the Three-I League before finishing the season back in Salt Lake City. Interestingly, he struggled at the plate in the Peoria B league and then started to flourish once he returned to the tougher PCL Salt Lake City team at the end of the season. The following season he split right down the middle spending half the year with Lincoln in the Western League before returning to Salt Lake City. It was a breakout season for Lazzeri as he clubbed 44 home runs and compiled a .307 batting average. Even so, those impressive numbers were nothing compared to the record-setting campaign that was to follow in 1925.

Tony Lazzeri's 1925 PCL season with the Salt Lake City Bees may be the single greatest minor league season in the history of modern professional baseball. He played in 197 games, scored 202 runs and added 222 runs batted in. On top of that, he put together a whopping .355 batting average and belted 60 home runs. It should be noted that no one had ever hit that many home runs in a single baseball season up to that point in time. Babe Ruth had hit 59 in 1921 and would, of course, hit 60 for the Yankees in 1927 but in 1925, Lazzeri was the first and only person to have done so. In *Beyond DiMaggio*, Baldassaro notes "All three records [runs, RBIs, HRs] remained unsurpassed throughout the history of the PCL, which was active until 1957."

It was in Salt Lake City that Lazzeri acquired his nickname of "Poosh 'Em Up Tony." According to Baldassaro, "Cesare Rinetti, co-owner of the Rotisserie Inn in Salt Lake City, was a big fan of his fellow Italian American. One day, when Lazzeri was at the plate, Rinetti reportedly shouted out, 'Poosh 'em up, Tony.' The next day, May 24, 1925, sports editor John C. Derks ran the following headline in the *Salt Lake Tribune*: 'Poosh Um Up, Tone,' Yella Da Fan, an 'Tone She Poosh.' From then on Lazzeri was known to the fans as 'Poosh 'Em Up.'"

The condescending tone of the *Salt Lake Tribune* headline was fairly common for the time. As insulting and politically incorrect as it seems today, it endeared Lazzeri to the fans in 1925 although it certainly made very clear that he was "foreign" as well. The truth is that newspapers continued the same kind of demeaning "dialect" reporting all the way through the 1950s when quoting Latin American players like Roberto Clemente and Minnie Minoso.

While Lazzeri put up incredible numbers in 1925, there weren't a lot of Major League teams beating a path to his doorstep. Many clubs were afraid to take a chance on Lazzeri because he was an epileptic. He would eventually go on to have a successful career in the big leagues without ever having an incident on the field, but at the time, management was wary.

The Yankees, however, took a chance, paying $50,000 to the Bees for Lazzeri's contract although they then turned around and paid Lazzeri what in comparison was the paltry sum of $5,000 a year. Even so, the contract was big news and it put additional pressure on Lazzeri. In addition to Lazzeri's jump to the big leagues, his epilepsy, and the scrutiny of the press and the fans, he was also being asked to switch positions from shortstop to second base. In the end, he handled it all with aplomb and had a tremendous rookie season, save for the Alexander strikeout at the end.

As an indication of Lazzeri's toughness, he came out in 1927 and showed no lingering effects of the season-ending strikeout as he turned in another stellar season, increasing his run production, stolen bases, and on-base-percentage. He contributed 18 home runs and 102 RBIs, as he became an important member of the famed Murderer's Row. In fact, Lazzeri was the only player besides Ruth and Gehrig to hit double-digits in home run totals and was one of four Yankees to drive in more than 100 runs. He was also one of only three to score more than 100 runs. Lazzeri was, along with Ruth, Gehrig, and Koenig, the heart and soul of the 1927 World Champion New York Yankees.

Tony Lazzeri would go on to have five more seasons in his career with more than 100 runs-batted-in, an incredible statistic for a second baseman, especially in the 1920s and 1930s. In May of 1936, Lazzeri became the first player in Major League history to hit two grand slams in a single game. In that same game he hit a third home run and a triple to drive in a total of 11 runs for an American League single game record that still stands to this day. In fact, the game before he knocked in four runs and the 15 RBIs in two consecutive games is still a Major League record.

Poosh 'Em Up Tony was also an excellent base runner, often finishing near the top of the statistical ladder in stolen bases every season. He finished up his career with 869 walks, 864 strikeouts and a healthy .380 on-base percentage. In *Beyond DiMaggio*, Baldassaro states that most baseball historians rate Lazzeri as an average defensive player but Frank Graham, the legendary sportswriter who covered the Yankees for the *New York Sun* wrote in 1927 that Lazzeri "stands out as the league's best second baseman only because he plays second base most of the time. He is just as good at short or third base as he is at second."

The greatest years of Lazzeri's career stretch from his rookie year in 1926 until about 1933. However, in the six World Series he played in as a member of the Yankees, his best performances came in 1932, 1936, and 1937. In those last three series he racked up four home runs, 14 RBIs, a .308 batting average and a .413 on-base percentage. While the '37 series was arguably his best statistically, it came after a season when his average fell to just .244 and his slugging percentage fell below .400 (by one point) for the only time in his career. Following the Yanks' five-game victory over the Giants in the 1937 World Series, Tony Lazzeri was released after 12 years in pinstripes.

Lazzeri signed with the Cubs for the 1938 season but only saw action in 54 games with Chicago's north-side team. He played a handful of games with both the Dodgers and the Giants in 1939 before the Giants released him midway through the season and his Major League career was over.

Following his release by the Giants in 1939, Tony Lazzeri managed some minor league teams and played one more season in the PCL with his hometown San Francisco Seals in 1941 before buying into a local tavern. Sadly, he died alone in his home of a heart attack in 1946 at age 42. His obituary in *The Sporting News* said, "He had half the league afraid of him" while the *New York Times* stated that he was "one of the most popular men in modern baseball."

In a December 1927 article in *Baseball Magazine*, F.C. Lane wrote, "Italians are noted for their volatile nature and excitability. In the main they are a joyous race. Lazzeri, however, moves in an atmosphere of settled calm, verging upon melancholy." Despite the gross stereotyping, the image of Lazzeri no doubt came from the slugger's stoicism and quiet demeanor.

There is a well-known story written about in a number of books and magazines about the road trip taken by Lazzeri and teammate Frankie Crosetti to spring training in 1936. They took along rookie Joe DiMaggio who was headed to his first Major League camp. All three were Italian Americans from San Francisco so the similarities seemed numerous and they figured they'd share the expenses and the driving from California to Florida. The trio drove almost the entire way with barely a word being spoken among them, not because of any animosity but because each one was, by nature, more close-lipped than the next. Each was intense on the field of play but at a loss when it came to small talk. Writer Frank Graham once wrote, "Trying to interview Tony Lazzeri is like trying to mine coal with a comb and a nail file."

He may not have been a conversationalist but Lazzeri was known to enjoy clubhouse practical jokes; the occasional hotfoot or lighting a teammate's paper on fire while he was reading it was standard hijinks of the day. Generally speaking, it was all in good fun except perhaps for one instance.

In an article titled "A Special Breed" in the collection *Reaching for the Stars: A Celebration of Italian Americans in Major League Baseball*, compiled by Larry Freundlich, Donald Honig writes of Lazzeri that "Like most Yankees, he took immense pride in his pinstripes; consequently, when the club let him go after the 1937 season (to make way for the gifted young Joe Gordon), Tony was deeply hurt."

Honig goes on to tell of a spring morning in 1939 when Lazzeri was trying to break in with the Dodgers. He took a young Pete Reiser with him and drove to the Yankees' camp in St. Petersburg before anyone was at the park. He got into the clubhouse by telling an old guard he'd been traded back to the team and once inside immediately started nailing shoes to the floor and cutting uniforms to shreds.

Reiser recalled, "Every so often I looked over at Tony. He was going at it with a vengeance, muttering under his breath, still sore at the Yankees for letting him go." Honig writes, "When they [Lazzeri and Reiser] went back outside they found the old man [guard] watering down the infield.

"'We're leaving.' Lazzeri called to him.

"'I'll tell them you were here,' the old man said.

"'I think they'll know,' the old Yankee said, walking away, suitcase in hand. 'But you tell them anyway. Tell them Tony Lazzeri was here.'"

♦ 3 ♦

Ernie Orsatti
(1927)

Discovered by Buster Keaton, the under-utilized Ernie Orsatti (National Baseball Hall of Fame, Cooperstown, NY).

How can a baseball player play in 700 Major League games, compile a .306 lifetime batting average, be an integral member of one of the most famous World Championship teams in baseball history, and still barely be remembered by the baseball loving public? It could merely be the passage of time but particularly for Italian Americans, the story of Ernie Orsatti is one that should be remembered and celebrated.

Growing up in America in the early part of the 20th century, Orsatti's dream was not to become a baseball player. His was the dream that belonged to all the other kids: he wanted to be in the movies. He was born and raised in Los Angeles and became enamored of the picture business early on in his life.

He was born on September 8, 1902, to Morris and Mary (Manze) Orsatti. He was the sixth of what would eventually be seven children born to the couple. Orsatti's parents would divorce in 1920 after 30 years of marriage. His father was an entrepreneur involved in banking and transportation. His mother and oldest brother, Frank, were quite successful in the real estate business.

Orsatti started hanging around the motion picture studios as a young boy. "My interest as a boy, was in motion pictures and not in baseball," Orsatti once said. "I wanted to be an actor, a director, a camera man—anything that would identify me with motion pictures."

He was still in grammar school when he began to pick up odd jobs on the various studio lots. After grade school he began at Manual Arts High School but eventually quit to enroll at the University of Southern California Preparatory School. While he played a little baseball here and there, he spent most of his free time at the studios, according to Orsatti, "doing work as an extra, carrying cameras and electrical effects, doing errands and doing anything that anyone would let me do."

In 1920 Orsatti quit school and went to work full time as an assistant to film director Chester Bennett. Orsatti had a variety of duties but eventually became a stunt double for film star Antonio Moreno. He also did stunts for Leatrice Joy and a number of other stars.

In 1922 Orsatti went to work for Buster Keaton as a property man. Keaton was a big baseball fan and had his own indoor team made up of people who worked for his company. Legend has it that you either needed to know baseball or film to work for Keaton. If you were a good enough ballplayer, he'd hire you to play and teach you film. According to Orsatti, "I was given a tryout as a catcher and as a first baseman and played those positions in 1922, '23, '24 and '25. We won three straight championships, and during this period, I got an education in the movies...."

Mike Donlin was a former big league ballplayer and friend of Buster Keaton. When Donlin saw Orsatti play he told Keaton that the kid could, and should, be playing baseball professionally. At the time, Keaton owned the Vernon team of the Pacific Coast League in partnership with Lou Anger and Fatty Arbuckle. In the spring of 1925 Keaton walked up to Orsatti on the set one day and said, "You're going to play baseball with Vernon," and showed Orsatti a contract to which Keaton had already signed Orsatti's name.

Orsatti played with Vernon for just a few games before he was sent to San Francisco and soon thereafter, to Cedar Rapids, Iowa. In Cedar Rapids he batted .347 and hit 12 triples. The '26 season was spent primarily in Omaha where he hit .386. He was soon spotted by Branch Rickey, who purchased him and put him into the Cardinals' farm system, which was the largest and most organized in all of baseball at the time.

The 1927 season saw him in Houston where in 122 games he hit a solid .330 and slammed out 16 triples. He so impressed the Cardinals that they called the 24-year-old up to St. Louis to finish the season. In his first at bat, he knocked out a double against Cubs ace Charley Root. He played in a total of 27 games for the Cards in his initial visit to the big show, batting .315, scoring 15 runs and driving in 12 more.

In 1928 he went back to the minor leagues, spending most of the year with Minneapolis of the American Association. This time in 123 games he batted .381 and smashed 15 triples and 15 home runs. In his 1932 interview with sportswriter Harry T. Brundidge, Orsatti claimed that his greatest thrill in baseball came while playing for the Minneapolis ball club in a game against Indianapolis. There were two outs with the bases loaded and Indianapolis at the bat. As Orsatti remembered it, "Spencer Harris, our center fielder, misjudged a fly. I had started running toward center with the crack of the bat, and when I saw that Harris could not get the ball, I charged, saw that it was going to hit the concrete wall, rushed on top speed and, using my picture stunting experience, made a dive for the ball, hit the concrete, but came up uninjured with the ball in my hand. I'll never make another catch like that."

Once again, he was called up to the Cardinals for 27 games in the fall of '28 and once again he hit over .300 and helped the Cardinals capture the National League pennant. Unfortunately, the Cards lost the series in four straight games to the Yankees but Orsatti had proven himself an important asset to the big club. So much so, his teammates voted him a half share of World Series prize money. He would spend the next seven seasons as a member of a dominant Cardinal team.

In 1929, his first full season in the majors, Orsatti played in only 113 games but impressed the fans by batting .332 and scoring 64 runs. He was a tough, hustling outfielder with a strong throwing arm. In a press release from the National League offices, he was once described as "supple as a hazel twig, [with] a keen eye and fleet foot and a tremendous amount of energy." The same release went on to say that. "Probably no player in the big leagues today made more friends than this earnest, ambitious and most likeable young Italian."

He was, by all accounts, a popular guy among all of his teammates. He was a renowned cook and loved to entertain his friends with elaborate Italian meals. He was a car lover and raced during the off-season. He once helped start a West Coast pro hockey minor league. Ernie Orsatti was a doer, a bundle of energy who was always in motion.

One of his closest friends on the team was Leo "The Lip" Durocher. Orsatti was Durocher's best man when Durocher married Grace Dozier in 1934. Orsatti was the uncontested "Dapper Dan" of the Cardinals' clubhouse until Durocher came along. Orsatti once admitted, "We bought our clothes together. Neither of us could afford them, but if Leo had something, I had to have it, too."

Orsatti got into only 48 games in 1930. The Cardinals were top heavy in talented outfielders. One is impressed to look back on the records of that 1930 season and discover that the three starting outfielders all batted .300 or better: Chick Hafey, future Hall-of-Famer, .336, Taylor Douthit, .303, and George Watkins, .373. However, even more astonishing is the fact that the other three reserve outfielders that season also batted over .300: Showboat Fisher, .374, Ray Blades, .396, and Ernie Orsatti, .321, on a club that finished with a .314 team batting average! Even with those incredible figures, the Cardinals lost the 1930 World Series to the Philadelphia Athletics in six games.

Orsatti was once asked about his trials busting into the Cardinal lineup. "In one way, I came along at the wrong time," Orsatti said, "The Cardinals were loaded with outfielders. Every year I'd go to camp thinking I finally had a regular job wrapped up when some phenom would come along—like Joe Medwick or George Watkins."

Orsatti was right, of course. At the time, the Cardinals had the largest farm system of any team in baseball. Many a fine ballplayer languished in the Cardinals' farm system for seasons on end, never truly getting a fair shot at Major League stardom. Eventually, Major League Baseball would break up their oversized system of teams around the country in an effort to create a more competitive balance throughout the league. Unfortunately for Orsatti, that would all occur after his departure from baseball.

The year 1931 wasn't much different from 1930. Again, Orsatti got in to about 70 games but this time his average dipped to .291—still very good but his first season below the magical .300 average. On the brighter side, the Cards would get a rematch against the same Philadelphia A's and this time they'd come out on top, winning the World Series four games to three. Orsatti, however, only made it into one game and struck out all three times he came to the plate.

In 1932, Orsatti came into his own as a recognized star as he enjoyed his best season since 1929. The impression he made on the writers and management alike didn't come solely from his impressive numbers at the plate—a .336 average with 44 runs scored and 44 runs batted in. A short piece in an August issue of *The Sporting News*, proclaimed "playing a considerable part of the season with his hands taped up, frequently suffering from a twisted or swollen ankle, but always fighting, Orsatti has done a great deal toward keeping up the Cards' pennant hopes in the darkest season the club has had in years."

Ultimately, his efforts weren't enough as the Cards not only failed to make it to the World Series but also finished with the first losing record the team had seen in eight years.

The next season, 1933, Orsatti played more games—120—than in any single season of his Major League career. He finished the season just under the .300 mark with a .298 average but, again, the Cardinals finished out of the money, coming in fifth place in the National League.

The following season would give birth to one of the most storied teams in all of baseball history, the 1934 Gashouse Gang. By this time, Orsatti was one of the veterans on the team at the age of 31—only Frankie Frisch, 35 years old, the player-manager who replaced Gabby Street halfway through the season, was older than Orsatti among the team's starting players. Orsatti would play in 105 games and hit an even .300 while patrolling center field for the Redbirds.

One of the oft-told stories of that rebellious team has to do with Orsatti's intricate solution to avoiding Frisch's curfew. Orsatti rigged a plan with the hotel manager so that when Frisch called his room to do a bed check, the switchboard operator would put the line through to the nightclub where Orsatti was relaxing. Orsatti would answer in a sleepy voice and when Frisch would ask about the noise, Orsatti just assured him he had the radio up too loud.

Whatever their shenanigans off the field, on the field the Cards were a force to be seen. Orsatti played in all seven games of the '34 series, batting .318 and scoring three runs while driving in two more. He also contributed some sparkling plays in center field, including a fingertip grab to save Game Six for Paul "Daffy" Dean. He finished the 1934 season as a World Champion.

Ernie Orsatti had reached the pinnacle of his baseball success. In 1935, he suffered through a miserable season. Once again, he got in to less than 100 games and compiled a paltry .240 average. The Cardinals no longer had room for him on their roster. They wanted to send him back to the minors but he wasn't interested. He asked to be traded and the team refused. Back then the players had no recourse in trying to get a release. You were literally owned by the team until they decided otherwise.

On February 21, 1936, Orsatti sent the following telegram to the *St. Louis Post Dispatch*. It read: "Most definitely given up baseball and want you to hear it directly from me. For St. Louis fans, I am now vice president of Orsatti & Co., artist representatives, Hollywood, California."

He did return to baseball, briefly, for one season in 1939. He was 36 years old and he played for Columbus and Hollywood of the minor leagues. He hit a respectable .287 but his legs just couldn't hold up. He would continue to play in exhibition games and old-timers games but his professional career was over for good.

A 1961 "Where Are They Now" column by Bob Hunter would touch on the disappointments and trials of Orsatti's post-baseball career. He had lost a chunk of money when a patent he held on the blinking light used for construction projects was not properly protected. He had three heart attacks between 1956 and 1961. He had been involved in a retail gift shop that also didn't make it. Nevertheless, the writer concluded that Orsatti was "a happy man."

He had found contentment with his third wife Joyce, he continued to follow the fate of his beloved Cardinals and he kept in touch with old teammates such as

Frankie Frisch, Jack Rothrock and others. He had two sons, Frank and Ernie Jr., both of whom would become respected stuntmen in Hollywood. He finished his days as the proprietor of a small bail bond business in Van Nuys, California.

Orsatti died on September 4, 1968, just four days before his 66th birthday. He finished his career with a .306 lifetime average and two World Championships. He was a colorful star from a colorful era of America's most beloved pastime. He deserves to be better remembered than he is.

♦ 4 ♦

Tony Cuccinello
(1930)

Tony "Cooch" Cuccinello, one of the most stalwart second basemen of the 1930s.

In the 1920s and 1930s as the children of America's immigrants were attempting to enter the workforce, so too were these same immigrant children entering the larger American cultural scene in politics, entertainment, and sports. In the world of sports, boxing and baseball seemed to be the two most common destinations for the Italian American athlete. Among the earliest Italian American stars of the game of baseball was Anthony Francis Cuccinello.

Tony Cuccinello never finished high school because, according to newspaper reports, baseball was just too alluring. All of the young man's time was spent with either a mitt or a bat in his hand. He worked at some odd jobs but started playing semi-pro ball at a very young age. He began pro ball when he was just 18 with the Syracuse Stars of the International League. He played a few games with the club prior to being sent to Lawrence, Massachusetts, in the New England League. He spent most of 1928 with Danville in the Three I League as property of the St. Louis Cardinals. His average over 127 games was .310. Nevertheless, he was sold to Cincinnati before the year was up and sent to their Columbus farm team.

At Columbus, Cuccinello developed into a real prospect. In the last 14 games of the 1928 campaign he batted .396 and to prove it was no fluke he played the entire 1929 season in Columbus and posted a .358 average. A season like that warranted a promotion and Cuccinello found himself in Cincinnati in 1930. Even though he had spent most of his career at second base, the Reds played Cuccinello primarily at third base for the '30 season. It didn't help his fielding statistics as he committed 23 errors in just over a hundred games, but his prowess at the plate continued and he finished his first big league season with an impressive .312 average.

In his second season in the majors the Reds assigned him to second base for the duration and his fielding average jumped to .969 compared to his .920 average the previous year at the hot corner. His bat continued to be hot as he pounded out 181 hits and drove in 93 runs with another solid year at the plate hitting .315. Cuccinello's first two years in the big leagues not only made him valuable to the hapless Reds but extremely attractive to the other teams in the league.

In March of 1932, "Cooch" or "Chick," as Tony Cuccinello was sometimes called, was part of an important trade that sent Clyde Sukeforth, Joe Stripp, and Cuccinello to the Brooklyn Dodgers in exchange for Babe Herman, Ernie Lombardi, and Wally Gilbert. Many of New York's Italians were outraged to lose Lombardi but thrilled to have hometown boy Cuccinello within their ranks. Cuccinello had been born in Long Island City, New York, on November 8, 1907. As a boy he dreamed of playing for the Dodgers and after eight years of pro ball his dream had come true.

The year 1932 was an important one in Cuccinello's personal life as well. On October 29 Tony Cuccinello married Clara Garoselli in a quiet ceremony in Queens, New York. The couple would eventually have three children and spend nearly 60 years together as man and wife.

Cuccinello's years with the Dodgers were, to paraphrase Dickens, a mix of the best of times and the worst of times. In his first season in Flatbush his average fell below .300 for the first time in his big league career as he finished with a .281 average but still contributed 12 home runs and 77 RBIs. The next year was even worse. He struggled through the 1933 season, finishing with a .252 average—the worst of his career. Unbeknownst to the fans or the press at the time, was the fact that Cuccinello had hurt his foot. In favoring the sore foot, he caused problems with his other foot, as well. His speed diminished and he put on weight. Finally, in the winter of 1934–35 the Dodgers sent Cuccinello to a prominent orthopedic surgeon for treatments to his feet—and the therapy worked wonders. He was able to train throughout the winter, lose 10 to 15 pounds and subsequently regain much of the quickness he had lost due to his injuries.

Whether he was healthy or not, Cuccinello remained an inconsistent hitter throughout his career. Not necessarily in terms of talent but more in the type of results he'd get from year to year. He seemed to either hit for average or power but rarely both. The reason for that might be explained in an article that appeared prior to the 1935 season in *Baseball Magazine*. Cuccinello spoke with writer John J. Ward for a profile and discussing his hitting problems said, "I've been told if I didn't try to murder the ball I'd hit it more often. The advice sounded good, so I follow it now and then, but I must say that it didn't seem to produce results. I'm not a punch hitter and am convinced I never shall be. I take a good cut at the ball and hit hard, for that's the only way I know. It's disappointing, in a sense, because I haven't made a great record as a hitter. But that's merely because I am not a great hitter. I might as well admit it and get it over with." You can hear the frustration in Cuccinello's remarks after his two disappointing seasons at the plate. Although he played in only 102 games in 1935 Cuccinello raised his average up to .292 for the season.

While his hitting was occasionally lacking, his defensive abilities at second base were always steady and consistent. Cuccinello and Leo Durocher helped the Reds tie a National League double play record as a team in 1931 with 194 double plays. Cuccinello set the individual record for second basemen that year with 128 and then tied it again five years later. The record has since been eclipsed. He was also known to be one of the more successful practitioners of the hidden ball trick, using it to perfection at least four times in his career.

His improved health and bat only made him more appealing for another trade and by the time the 1936 season rolled around, Cuccinello and teammate Al Lopez were on their way to the Boston Braves of the National League.

One of the great benefits of Cuccinello's time in Brooklyn was his meeting up with Al Lopez. They played together for four years in Brooklyn and four years in Boston and developed a friendship that would last for the rest of their lives. Cuccinello spent many years as a coach under Manager Al Lopez with both the Cleveland Indians and the Chicago White Sox. Both men eventually retired to Tampa, Florida, and spent two or three days a week playing golf with each other and scouting young ballplayers.

The trade to Boston in 1936 breathed new life into Cuccinello as he played in

150 games (the most action he'd seen since 1932) and brought his average back up to a dangerous .308 clip while driving in 86 runs. The average fell off again in 1937 and 1938 but he continued to contribute with RBIs and consistent play at second.

A newspaper piece from August of 1939, under the headline "Little Man Swings Big Stick" reads "At the age of thirty-one and in his tenth season in the National League, the little Long Island City Italian, with his wrists of steel, is hitting at a higher clip this year than at any time in his major league career." Nevertheless, 1939 would be Cuccinello's last full season with Boston. He ended up playing in only 81 games but batted .306.

The same newspaper article from August of 1939 said that "Opposing managers would prefer to see a player with a gaudy .350 average ordered up in the pinch than Cuccinello.... They say that Bill Terry would rather have almost anyone in the league at bat than Cuccinello. He has been a thorn in the side of the Giants for a long time."

That may explain why in the summer of 1940 the Giants and Bill Terry brought him to the Polo Grounds. His time in the Giants' lineup, however, was short and at the end of the 1940 season he told the team that he was interested in managing. In December of 1940 the Giants announced that Cuccinello would manage their farm club in Jersey City in 1941. And so it seemed that after 11 years, Cuccinello's playing days were over.

Cuccinello managed the Jersey City ball club in 1941 but managing was not as appealing to him as he thought it might be. Then something happened in the winter of 1941–42 that seemed to change Cuccinello's retirement plans. The world went to war and so did many of Major League Baseball's brightest young stars. It's hard to imagine now but there were serious discussions during the winter of 1942 as to whether Major League Baseball should even play again until after the war was over. In a famous letter from FDR to Baseball Commissioner Kenesaw Landis dated January 15, 1942, President Roosevelt stated, "I honestly feel that it would be best for the country to keep baseball going." And so it was that in the spring of 1942 baseball returned to the diamonds and so did Tony Cuccinello.

Cuccinello rejoined the Boston Braves in 1942 and played in just 40 games. He began the 1943 season with Boston but struggled terribly and was traded, for the first and only time in his career, to the American League. He finished the 1943 season with the Chicago White Sox and regained his form somewhat, batting .272 in 34 games with the ChiSox. He played two more seasons with the White Sox and in 1945, his last year in the big leagues; he lost the batting title on the last day of the year by a fraction of a percentage point. He finished the season hitting .308 and he finished his career with a respectable .280 lifetime average.

When asked many years later about his greatest thrill in baseball, Cuccinello cited a game against the Phillies in 1931 when he knocked out six hits in six at bats. He was also proud of helping his younger brother Al get to the big leagues.

Cuccinello remained in baseball but never returned to managing. In May of 1966 while coaching for the Chicago White Sox he was forced to take over the managerial duties for a few days for the ailing Eddie Stanky. Cuccinello told reporters that he was anxious for Stanky to return to the dugout, saying, "I'm getting ulcers. I would rather coach third base."

In all the articles mentioning Cuccinello during his 40-plus years in professional baseball, two statements appear over and over again. One is that he was one of the nicest guys to ever play the game and the other, that he was "a ballplayer's player." In the *Baseball Magazine* article of 1935 the writer John J. Ward described Cuccinello in that way and then went on to explain, "Such players are seldom showy, for their good qualities are not superficial. Hence, they do not attract much public attention. But players, among themselves, recognize them as smart, resourceful and capable men who are particularly good in an emergency."

This was Tony Cuccinello's blessing and his curse. He was not a flashy player with gaudy lifetime stats—just a steady, reliable, hard-working ballplayer who loved the game of baseball. His reward was the respect and admiration of those who played with him and against him.

♦ 5 ♦

Ernie Lombardi
(1931)

Hard-hitting Ernie Lombardi, the first catcher to ever win two batting titles.

Ernie Lombardi was a man who deserved much better than he got out of baseball. One of the greatest hitters in baseball history, he won not one but two National League batting titles in his career. Prior to 2008 he was the only catcher in over 100 years of baseball history to win two batting titles. (The Twins' Joe Mauer matched the feat in 2008 and surpassed Lombardi with three batting titles in 2009.) Lombardi won an MVP award, caught Johnny Vander Meer's back-to-back no-hitters in 1938, and finished with a lifetime batting average of .306. Despite his gaudy offensive statistics, one of the strongest throwing arms a catcher ever possessed and a World Series ring, it took 40 years before Ernie Lombardi was elected to Baseball's Hall of Fame.

Unfortunately, the call came ten years too late. By the time the Cooperstown voters moved to undo the disgrace of their decades-old Lombardi snub, he was dead. Shortly before he died, a deeply hurt Lombardi had said he wouldn't have gone to Cooperstown even if elected.

As kids, we are taught not to judge a book by its cover but that's exactly the curse that plagued Ernie Lombardi. He didn't look like a star, he didn't look like an athlete of any kind. He was a big, lumbering, gawky guy with a large ethnic nose. One of his nicknames was "The Schnozz." Most of the guys he played with could walk faster than he could run. He was a shy, unassuming, humble man. Nevertheless, you'd think his actions and accomplishments would have been enough to earn him the respect he deserved. They were not.

Ernesto Natali Lombardi was born in Oakland, California, on April 8, 1908. As a kid he'd often disappear from his job at his family's grocery store. He would eventually be found at one of the neighborhood playgrounds playing baseball. His father bought him an accordion so his son could learn music and Ernie sold the instrument to get enough money to buy a baseball glove.

Ernie loved to play baseball but he never thought that he'd make his living doing it. As a teenager he began to play semi-pro ball. Soon, he was asked to join the Oakland Oaks of the Pacific Coast League. He initially declined the offer but the Oaks persisted. Interviewed in 1931 during his first year in the big leagues Lombardi recalled, "the Oakland Club wanted me to sign up but for two years, I didn't bother with it. I was having too much fun playing in that kid league. But finally I signed ... three years ago. I been doing okay. I hit .369 in 1928, .371 in 1929 and .370 last year."

He signed his first contract in the majors with the Brooklyn Robins. The Brooklyn team was managed by the legendary Wilbert "Uncle Robbie" Robinson. When Lombardi showed up for spring training he made an immediate impression on the legendary manager. He had the confidence of a veteran ballplayer. "Say, look at the way he walks up there," Robinson observed. "He's got all the nonchalance in the world. He don't care whether or not he's up in the big show. Look at him! Look at that swing!"

The young rookie proceeded to put on quite a show for his new manager. He hit the veteran pitchers to all fields and he threw out base runners with a cannon-like arm. He also made an impression on his teammates with his 42-ounce bat, believed to be the heaviest in the entire league at the time.

Despite his strong first impression, and a rookie batting average of .297, Lombardi was traded after his first year in Brooklyn to the Cincinnati Reds. It may have had something to do with the fact that Robinson wanted to make him into a pitcher and Lombardi wanted no part of it. Brooklyn already had a strong catcher in Al Lopez and they needed a second baseman. The Reds had a good one in Tony Cuccinello so a deal was made during the off-season that included the two Italian ballplayers.

Lombardi would spend ten very productive years in Cincinnati. In his first year with the Reds, the 24-year-old Lombardi caught 110 games and batted .303 for the season. He would eventually bat .300 or better in seven out of the ten years he played in Cincy.

Most observers agreed that Lombardi's average would have been substantially higher if it wasn't for the one physical gift he lacked—speed. He was unbelievably slow on the bases. He was known to turn triples and doubles into singles and singles into outs. In a June 12, 1945, article in the *New York Times* Arthur Daley described Lombardi as "one of the most remarkable batters of this generation—or any other generation." He went on to say that every hit Lombardi got was an honest one. "Ty Cobb probably beat out a thousand scratch singles in his day," wrote Daley. "But the unfortunate part about big Lom's running is that he does most of it in the same place. If he had been blessed with Cobb's speed, he'd probably have a batting average to match Ty's."

Legendary sports columnist Jim Murray once wrote that "Ernie hit more 400-ft. singles than any player in the history of the game. When he hit a home run, the manager had to worry for fear the umpire would throw him out of the game on the way to the plate for delaying the game."

Lombardi's fellow players also agreed that had he possessed any level of speed whatsoever he would have finished with one of the highest batting averages of all time. Hall-of-Famer and lifetime .341 hitter Bill Terry once said, "Lombardi would have been the only man capable of hitting .500 if he could only run."

Ironically, one of the factors working against Lombardi was just how hard he hit the ball, perhaps too hard for his own good. Opposing infielders were actually afraid to "play in" on Lombardi and thanks to his nonexistent speed they could, and did, play him deep. Most of the time the infielders played him on the shallow outfield grass while the outfielders played him on the warning tracks against the outfield walls. Teammate Bill Rigney remembers, "Pee Wee Reese played him so far back on the grass, he had trouble reaching Gil Hodges with throws ... the guy was an awesome hitter." And that was at the very end of Lombardi's career!

In that 17-year career, Lombardi caught over 1,500 games. Due to his lack of quickness, some thought he was a less than spectacular receiver. However, he was known to have a shotgun arm and could throw runners out at any base without ever getting out of his crouch. Hall-of-Famer Stan Musial once said of Lombardi, "He was a fine catcher. He handled Johnny Vander Meer and Paul Derringer, and he was the strength of the old Reds." Jimmie Wilson, a catcher who played for 18 years and managed for nine, once said that "Lom's the best man [I] ever saw picking runners off first base with snap throws."

In June 1938, the 23-year-old Johnny Vander Meer accomplished something that no other Major League pitcher has done since—he pitched back-to-back no-hitters. He immediately became the sensation of baseball. However, there were others in Cincinnati who felt Lombardi deserved some of the credit as well. Newspaperman Stanley Frank wrote, "There will be no notation for posterity to the effect that Lombardi was Vander Meer's battery partner on the day and the night the kid made pitching perfection come to life, but the big guy no longer can be denied fleeting recognition as the outstanding catcher of the year. All of a sudden people are beginning to appreciate the job Lombardi must have done to have steered a wild, inexperienced southpaw through two straight hitless performances."

Bill Stewart, the umpire behind the plate for Vander Meer's second no-hitter also banged the drums for Lombardi. "Give some credit to Lombardi," Stewart said shortly after the game. "Sure, Vander Meer had to pitch perfectly to get his no-hitter. But what about the guy who told the kid what to pitch? If Lombardi had guessed wrong on one hitter, if he had called for a fast ball when a curve was the smart pitch, Vander Meer never would have made it."

For the many years that Lombardi was ignored by the Hall of Fame, his former teammate Johnny Vander Meer was quite vocal about his belief that Lombardi belonged among the game's greatest. "Not enough seemed to remember just how great a catcher Lom was," Vander Meer said in 1986 after Lombardi was finally put into the Hall of Fame. "I'll tell you this, I never knew a greater one and I saw the best of 'em—Cochrane, Dickey, Hartnett. None of 'em could throw like Lom could and the hitting speaks for itself."

Harry Craft, a former teammate of Lombardi who went on to manage and scout in the Majors, remembered Lombardi as "an outstanding catcher [who] helped all our young pitchers. I remember seeing Johnny Vander Meer so wild, he'd throw a ball two feet to the right of Ernie, and Ernie would just reach out and catch the ball bare-handed."

Craft also remembered seeing Ernie take a foul tip off his finger and just shake it off, ignoring the pain. Regardless of whether the finger was broken, split or bleeding, Ernie would just put the hand under his arm and walk back to the dugout without complaint.

One on-field injury that Lombardi could not shake off was considered by some to be the chief reason for his long wait to be admitted to the shrine in Cooperstown. In Game Four of the 1939 World Series against the New York Yankees, the Reds were leading by two runs when Billy Myers dropped a double play toss from Lonny Frey that allowed the Yanks to keep the ninth inning alive and tie up the score. In the top of the tenth with Frank Crosetti on third and Charlie "King Kong" Keller at first, DiMaggio hit a single to right. Outfielder Ival Goodman let the ball get through his legs. Crosetti scored easily and as the throw was coming into the plate Keller crashed into Lombardi, knocking him flat on his back. DiMaggio came all the way around to score and the play was known forever after as "Schnozz's Snooze."

The problem is that it made no sense to blame Lombardi for the Reds' World Series loss. The team was already down three games to none to the mighty Yanks. The game would have been over in the ninth were it not for the error by Myers. Most importantly, the only run that Lombardi could have prevented was DiMaggio's, which was run number seven. They lost 7–4 so they never scored another run in the bottom of the tenth, which means that Crosetti's run was the only run that the Yankees needed. By the way, Reds pitcher Bucky Walters later admitted the DiMaggio run was actually his fault because he never bothered to back up Lombardi as he was required to do.

Nevertheless, "the Snooze" was one of the big reasons that many baseball experts felt the writers kept Lombardi out of the Hall of Fame for so long. It was a story that grew over the years with few people remembering the true facts about the game.

The Reds came back the next year in 1940 and won the World Series, defeating the Detroit Tigers. Lombardi had another solid year, batting .319, but he was injured for most of the last month of the season. He only got up to bat four times in the Series, walking once and ripping a double.

In 1941 Lombardi had an off year, batting only .264—it was one of only two years in his 17-year career that he batted below .280. He was traded in the off-season to the Boston Bees of the National League. He turned 34 as the new season began and many thought his career was over. Instead he bounced back, batting .330 and winning the second batting title of his career.

Lombardi finished off his Major League career with the New York Giants and retired after the 1947 season with a lifetime batting average of .306. The following year, 1948, he led the Oakland Oaks of the Pacific Coast League, managed by Casey Stengel, to victory in the PCL Championship. After that the Lombardi biography becomes sketchy.

He did marry but he and his wife never had any children. For whatever reason, he didn't stay in baseball. He may have been too proud to ask for a job. By the 1950s, he attempted suicide. He spent some time in a sanitarium before recovering and being sent home. In the early 1960s he turned up as a "gopher" in the press box at Candlestick Park. His wife died in the early 1970s and then Lombardi fell sick and died in 1977.

Following Lombardi's overdue election to the Hall of Fame in 1986, veteran newspaperman Harold Rosenthal gave yet another reason for Lombardi's Hall of Fame struggles, claiming that it was Warren Giles, former Reds executive and National League President, who kept Lombardi out of the Hall of Fame once the decision became the responsibility of the Veterans Committee. After Lombardi's .342 MVP season in 1938, Giles refused to give Lombardi a modest thousand dollar raise. As Rosenthal explained, "Ernie got into the wine at some dinner in Cincinnati and called Giles cheap. Giles never forgot and never denied that he was the obstacle in the way blocking Ernie's selection."

When Ernie Lombardi was finally elected to the Hall of Fame in 1986, his sister Lena Renhardt traveled to Cooperstown to accept the honor in her brother's name. Lombardi was one of baseball's most misunderstood and under-appreciated players but Lena Renhardt didn't want Ernie's story to be thought of as a tragedy. "Using a word like that ... is much too strong," Lenhardt said. "Rather, his is a bittersweet tale of a great who ached for appreciation during his years on earth, only to receive it long after he was gone."

Despite his Hall of Fame struggle, Ernie Lombardi was definitely appreciated. His teammates and his opponents knew just how great he was, not only as a player but also as a person. He was often described as sweet, kind, and generous. He was known to pass out five-dollar bills to his teammates so they could go out and have a good time.

The fans also appreciated him. In 1958, Reds fans voted him as the most popular player to ever wear a Reds uniform. In 1965 he was chosen as the catcher on the all-time Reds team.

Lombardi's is a story of deep irony. He was a man who never sought recognition during his playing career. He was content to play the game he loved with passion and dedication. In the years after his retirement he was desperate for the recognition that meant so little to him while he played and was then hurt when it eluded him, particularly in his election to the Baseball Hall of Fame. In the years since his death, he has been hailed as one of the most underrated players of his time and one of the greatest hitters in the history of the game. The recognition came a little late for Ernie Lombardi but at least it came. In the end, greatness cannot be denied.

♦ 6 ♦

Frankie Crosetti
(1932)

Frankie Crosetti. He spent his entire adult life in the game of baseball.

Frankie "The Crow" Crosetti had one of the longest, and most successful, careers in the history of Major League Baseball and yet few fans recognize the name. No one would be more thrilled with that anonymity than Crosetti himself. After all, he cultivated it during his entire career.

He earned seven World Championship rings as a player and another nine as a coach of the Yankees. His 37 years with the Bronx Bombers literally spanned the eras from Babe Ruth to Bobby Murcer. He appeared in 122 World Series games—all in a Yankee uniform as either a player or coach. It's a record that will almost certainly stand for all time.

It's also rather ironic that a guy they called "Mr. Yankee" was something of an enigma. In all his years with the Yankees, he rarely spoke with the press or the media. He was the epitome of the no-nonsense guy who believed his work should speak for itself. For all the 16 World Series Championships of which he was a part, he only stayed around to celebrate one of them and that was the first in 1932.

Frank Peter Joseph Crosetti was born on October 4, 1910, in a town that turned out Italian American ballplayers the way the Ford Motor Company turned out automobiles: San Francisco, California. He never even played the game until he was 13 years old. Whether it was his work ethic, natural ability, or a combination of the two, he quickly built a reputation and following on the sandlots of San Francisco so that by the time he was 17 he'd been signed by the local San Francisco Seals of the Pacific Coast League.

He struggled during that first year with the Seals in 1928, a boy among men. However, the next three full seasons with the Seals he was a bona fide star, playing in over 180 games a season and batting over .300 each year. In later years, as an established Yankee star, Crosetti acknowledged Jimmy "Ike" Caveney as having had a positive influence on his development as a player. Caveney had played for the Seals in the PCL, moved to the Reds in the National League and then returned to the Seals in Crosetti's first full season of 1929. "I played alongside Caveney for three years," said Crosetti, "and at all times found Jimmy not only a willing teacher but a severe critic and an able corrector of my faults."

Following three phenomenal years in the PCL for the Seals, the Yankees bought Crosetti for $75,000—a huge sum of money in the Depression era 1930s. However, the high price tag put considerable pressure on Crosetti to perform immediately. Subsequently, he struggled to secure the position of shortstop with Lyn Lary, Billy Werber, and Red Rolfe during his first few years with the team.

At the start of the 1935 season, Manager Joe McCarthy assured Crosetti that the position of shortstop was his own. Unfortunately, Crosetti injured his knee during the 1935 season and missed the last 62 games. The injury resulted in surgery to remove loose cartilage from the knee.

When he returned to the lineup in 1936 he was better than ever. He had a solid year at the plate, hitting .288 while knocking out 15 homers with 78 RBIs and 137 runs scored. He also drew 90 walks and stole 18 bases on his way to being named to the American League All Star team. The team went to the World Series for the first time since Crosetti's rookie season in 1932 and once again they brought home the championship.

That 1936 ball club had two other Italian American standouts from the sandlots of Frisco, Tony Lazzeri and a young rookie named Joe DiMaggio. Suffice it to say, three genuine Italian American stars brought a lot of Italian American fans into Yankee Stadium and helped to create a following for baseball among Italian Americans all over the country.

Lazzeri, DiMaggio, and Crosetti had more in common than just their stellar play and their Mediterranean roots. They were all famous for their silent, taciturn personalities.

In the spring of 1936, the three *paesani* drove from San Francisco to Florida for spring training. There was so little conversation between them that it wasn't until the second day when they asked DiMaggio if he wanted to drive that they discovered the kid didn't know how to drive! In David Halberstam's classic *Summer of '49* he relays a story from Jack McMahon, an old reporter from the International News Service, who once spent the afternoon observing the three Sicilian teammates. "I bought a paper and sat down near them," said McMahon, "and after a while became aware of the fact that none of them had a word to say to the others. Just for fun I timed them to see how long they would maintain their silence. Believe it or not, they didn't speak for an hour and twenty minutes. At the end of the time DiMaggio cleared his throat. Crosetti looked at him and said: 'What did you say?' And Lazzeri said, 'Shut up. He didn't say nothing.' They lapsed into silence and at the end of ten more minutes I got up and left. I couldn't stand it anymore."

Despite their silence off the field, they all made their presence known on the diamond, playing on three World Series winners together. Lazzeri and DiMaggio both ended up in the Hall of Fame. If it weren't for his lack of big offensive numbers, Crosetti would probably be there as well.

Crosetti never became the hitter in the Major Leagues that he'd been in the minors. He ended up with a lifetime .245 batting average and 98 home runs. And yet, despite his anemic hitting stats, he was thought of as an invaluable weapon to the Yankee teams of the 1930s.

Leo Durocher once famously described his scrappy second baseman Eddie Stanky by saying, "He can't hit, he can't field, he can't run—all he can do is beat you." While Crosetti was nowhere near as hapless as Durocher described Stanky, the fact remains he wasn't your typical Bronx Bomber. He didn't pound home runs but he got on base, scored runs, and kept opposing players from scoring through his prowess with the glove.

The legendary sportswriter Frank Graham once wrote of Crosetti, "He never could hit and he never was very fast but he was agile and he could bob around out there and come up with the ball, sometimes in a most unbelievable manner." He did have one offensive specialty and that was HBP—getting Hit By a Pitch. In fact, he led the league in getting hit by pitches on eight different occasions—at one point, for five straight seasons from 1936 to 1940.

New York Times sports columnist Arthur Daley said of Crosetti, "If Frankie was the weakest hitter in famed 'Murderers Row,' it was not always apparent to the naked eye." Daley remembered him as "one of the most annoying .245 batters that baseball ever had. An artist at drawing walks and getting himself nicked by slightly errant pitches, he was on base often." Hall of Fame pitcher Ted Lyons said that Crosetti was "the only [unprintable] who ever could get hit in the behind with a strike."

Ironically, his most famous hit was a home run in Game Two of the 1938 World Series off of Dizzy Dean and the Cubs. Crosetti came to bat in the top of the eighth inning with the Yanks trailing the Cubs 3–2 and belted a home run with Myril Hoag on base to put the Yankees on top for good and win the ballgame.

In an article from the October 7, 1938, edition of the *New York Journal*, Crosetti is credited with saving the Game One victory of the '38 Series as well when, according to the paper, "Willie Herman [got a] hit off Red Rolfe. Stan Hack was on second at the time and, when the ball got away from Rolfe, Hack continued on to home. But the Crosetti had backed up," reads the article. "He [Crosetti] pounced on the ball and threw it home. Hack, with the tieing run, was tagged out. Instead of the score being tied and a man on second base, the Cubs had been retired and were still behind." Those were the kind of intangibles that made Crosetti such a valuable member of the Yankee team.

A banner year for Crosetti was 1938, as he led the league in a variety of categories including, games (157), plate appearances (757), stolen bases (27), and hit by pitches (15). He also made a hit off the field, marrying his childhood sweetheart, Norma Divincenzi. As you'd expect from a man who valued loyalty and long associations the way Crosetti did, he and his wife would remain together for the rest of their lives.

In 1939 he led the league again in plate appearances (743), at bats (656), and his specialty, hit by pitches (13). He also made the All Star squad again.

By 1940, after four solid years as the Yankees stalwart shortstop, Crosetti had a young rookie breathing down his neck for the starting spot in the middle of the Yankee infield. A kid named Rizzuto was tearing it up in Kansas City, the Yankees AA affiliate. It didn't help that Crosetti had the worst year of his career at the plate, batting only .194 in 546 at bats. By the spring of 1941, the job belonged to Rizzuto, who made quite the impression, batting .307 in his rookie season.

Phil Rizzuto always praised and credited Frankie Crosetti for the help he gave to the young man who took his job away from him. In a 1986 article for *Yankees Magazine*, Rizzuto was asked if Crosetti was a good teacher. "He was the best," Rizzuto answered emphatically. "Without Crosetti…. I would never have made it as soon as I did. You've got to remember that when I came up Crosetti was idolized by all the Yankees. He wasn't one of the big sluggers, but Crosetti was the glue for that whole infield. And here I was, a fresh rookie coming up and trying to take his job.

And they resented me. Crosetti took the time before each ballgame to position me on every pitch. He made me look good—and here I am trying to take his job away. He not only taught me how to play the hitters defensively, but he also taught me how to get hit with the ball."

Crosetti's unselfishness and patience in helping Rizzuto were also a clear sign of his ability to coach. Ability the Yankee brass would wisely put to use in the years to come. But "The Crow" wasn't quite done flying yet.

From 1941 to 1944, Crosetti played in anywhere from 50 to 95 games a year. He never batted higher than .242 but he continued to be a clutch hitter and a steady and reliable fielder. Rizzuto missed the '43, '44, and '45 seasons in the Navy. The Yankees tried to fill his spot with guys like Snuffy Stirnweiss and Mike Milosevich but they always came back to Crosetti.

In March of 1945 Larry MacPhail, the new Yankee President, was quoted as saying "You can scratch Frankie Crosetti's name off our roster." MacPhail was angry about Crosetti's salary demands for the 1945 season. MacPhail might have been angry but he wasn't dumb. He eventually negotiated with Crosetti to secure his services for the season. Crosetti went on to play in 130 ball games that year—his most since 1940. He also led the league one last time in getting hit by pitches.

From 1946 to 1948, Crosetti played in only a handful of games each year. He was, in essence, a player-coach. By 1949, he was the full-time third base coach, a position he would hold for the next 20 years. He was considered by many to be the perfect coach because he never had any desire to manage. He was the most self-effacing character imaginable. He was happy to come in and teach the new recruits and help the manager in any way needed.

In a 1957 article in the *New York Times*, Joseph M. Sheehan wrote, "There's no more tireless contributor to the intensive, personalized player instruction that has been a key factor in the Yankees' continued dominance. If any Yankee wants extra hitting or fielding practice, Crosetti is always available."

In another article that same year by NEA Sports Editor Harry Grayson, it was pointed out that "The Yankees ... developed one superlative infielder after another under Crosetti's tutelage—Joe Gordon, Phil Rizzuto, George Stirnweiss, [Jerry] Coleman, [Gil] McDougald, Andy Carey, Billy Martin, Tony Kubek, Bobby Richardson and Jerry Lumpe." In the same article, Gil McDougald had nothing but praise for his teacher, saying, "Crow was a tremendous help to me. He urged me to play shortstop as he played it, to charge in and play the ball and not let it play you."

After the 1968 season, Crosetti made the difficult decision to leave the New York Yankees. The league structure was changing with the addition of new expansion teams and the new schedule was going to limit the team's trips to the West Coast to only two for the entire season. At 58 years old, Crosetti wanted more time with his family. He was offered a coaching job with the expansion Seattle Pilots and he accepted.

In an uncharacteristically emotional letter, Crosetti said his goodbyes to the

Yankee organization and thanked all who had supported him through the years including Joe McCarthy, Ed Barrow, Bucky Harris, Casey Stengel, and Ralph Houk among others, saying "There are no finer people in baseball—or on earth, for that matter." Crosetti coached for three more seasons before finally calling it quits at the end of the 1971 season.

In retirement, he kept a predictably low profile, preferring to spend time with his family or pursuing interests like hunting, fishing, and golfing. He'd occasionally take in a ballgame in San Francisco or Oakland. Marty Lurie, host of the Oakland A's pre-game show, said of Crosetti, "He sparkled when he was in the stadium. Derek Jeter would love to see him every time he came to town. Frankie would tease him about breaking all his records."

The shy, crotchety, no-nonsense Crosetti never did endorsements, never did autograph shows. His son said he'd always sign an autograph if asked but he'd never charge for it. Crosetti once said, "Why should people ask ballplayers or actors for autographs? What did they ever do for humanity? A ballplayer and an actor just happen to be fortunate enough to have ability in his line. A great scientist or surgeon should be asked for his autograph."

Even so, Crosetti did OK for himself in the financial department. He invested those 17 Winner's share World Series checks in California real estate and profited accordingly from his foresight and business acumen.

Crosetti died in 2002 at the age of 91. Perhaps the best way to describe Crosetti was the way in which he described himself upon his departure from the New York Yankees in 1968, "Once a Yankee, always a Yankee."

♦ 7 ♦

Dolph Camilli
(1933)

Camilli was not only one of the premier sluggers of his generation but one of the best first basemen.

Dolph Camilli was a gentleman and a tough ballplayer. He was a native of San Francisco, like so many of the great Italian American ballplayers of the pre-war years, but he made a name for himself in three of the biggest cities east of the Mississippi River. Camilli made stops in Chicago and Philadelphia before becoming a mainstay of the Brooklyn "Bums" of the late 1930s and early 1940s. He is remembered as being an integral part of the 1941 team that brought Brooklyn its first pennant in 21 years and his career was one of consistency and strength at the plate and in the field.

Camilli was born on April 23, 1907, in San Francisco, California. His parents came from the Italian province of Tuscany. He also had a brother who boxed under the name of Frankie Campbell. A promising heavyweight, Campbell died following a fight with Max Baer in August of 1930.

Camilli attended Sacred Heart College in California in 1924 and 1925. In the spring of 1926 he was invited to join the San Francisco Seals of the Pacific Coast League. He played with them for a few weeks before being sent to the Logan team in the Utah-Idaho League. He played with Logan again in 1927 and by 1928 had made his way to Salt Lake City where he drew some attention with his improving play. By the end of the season he was a member of the Sacramento ball club of the Pacific Coast League and would continue to play for the team for part or all of the next five seasons until being purchased from Sacramento by the Chicago Cubs in August of 1933. He once identified his purchase by the Cubs as his greatest thrill in baseball.

His first at-bat in the Major Leagues was a home run that won the game for the Cubs over the Philadelphia Phillies. He played in 16 games at the end of the 1933 season with the Cubs. In those 16 games he hit two home runs and drove in seven runs but compiled an unimpressive .224 average. Nevertheless, he did show his prowess at first base, handling 177 chances and making just one error. The year 1934 would see Camilli's first full season in the Major Leagues. Despite his ability to hit the ball hard and produce runs, the Cubs traded him to the Philadelphia Phillies after just 32 games of the 1934 season. The Phillies, and their manager Jimmie Wilson, were more than happy to obtain Camilli from the Cubs as he finished the season with 16 home runs and 87 runs batted in.

Over the next three seasons, Camilli pounded out 25, 28, and 27 home runs for the Phillies and averaged 88 RBIs per season. He also began to consistently improve his batting average, which was .261 in 1935 and then rose to .315 in 1936 and .339 in 1937. In the field, he was almost always considered to be one of the very best fielding first basemen in either league.

As solid a hitter as Camilli was throughout his career, he sometimes thought too much about what he was doing at the plate. In addition to his high numbers in the home run and RBI categories, he always posted high numbers in walks and strikeouts as well.

As early as 1935 there was discussion in the Phillies front office and in the press about Dolph Camilli's batting stance. According to a Phillies press release in April of 1935, Manager Jimmy Wilson had advised Camilli to open his stance, presumably to pull the ball over the right field fence for more home runs. However, in a newspaper article from May 18, 1936, it was reported that Wilson approached Camilli about returning to the change in stance that he suggested the previous season. Except this time it was suggested that the change recommended by Wilson was to straighten his feet to be parallel to home plate. Whatever the case, newspaper reports suggested that Camilli happily followed his manager's suggestion to not only change his stance but to begin swinging at the first or second pitch he saw in any given at-bat. The belief was that Camilli both struck out and walked as much as he did because he looked at too many pitches.

Whether it was a change in stance, first-ball hitting, or settling into his situation in Philadelphia, 1936 was Camilli's best year of his career up to that point. He hit 28 home runs and drove in 102 runs while hitting .315 and walking more than he struck out for the first time ever. It was a banner year for the 29-year-old Californian. The following year he raised his average 24 points to .339 for the highest total he would ever garner in a Major League uniform.

Camilli started off the 1938 spring training sessions with the Phils but once the season started he found himself in a Dodger uniform. Young Larry MacPhail, the extravagant front office executive of the "Bums," was bound and determined to bring a pennant to the long-suffering borough of Brooklyn, New York, and Dolph Camilli was part of that plan. Camilli came to the Dodgers and hit 24 home runs and drove in 100 runs. The next highest RBI total on the team was 79 from a young third baseman named Cookie Lavagetto. He also led the league with 119 walks. Unfortunately, he led the Major Leagues with 101 strikeouts as well.

Camilli, who would become one of the most popular Brooklyn Dodgers ever, began his career in a Dodger uniform as a goat of the passionate and boisterous Brooklyn Dodger fans. They were disappointed in Camilli's performance because his batting average dropped almost 90 points to .251 for the season. An article from September of 1938 by Dave Camerer stated, "Camilli has been subjected to much verbal abuse by Flatbush fans who expected his bat to cannonade the Brooks from their low position to baseball's pinnacle." However, Camerer defended Camilli by focusing on his run production and the fact that Camilli "is about the finest defensive first sacker in the business, with the possible exception of the Reds' Frank McCormick." Herb Goren, another New York baseball writer, wrote at the end of the 1938 season: "Camilli is one Dodger who will pack his trunk, knowing where he will be playing next year. He will again be the Dodgers' first baseman. No one can take his job away from him. He will be 31 next season, but he is one of the most powerful men in baseball and built for long years of service."

As was becoming the custom, in the spring of 1939 a newspaper dispatch by Edward T. Murphy reported from spring training that "Dolph is making changes in his batting. Under orders from Leo Durocher he is pulling all of his punches into right field and showing symptoms of becoming a more active home run slugger."

Murphy went on to report "Camilli has always been what is called a pull hitter. That is to say, he would pull some of his shots into the right field sector. But he wasn't a consistent pull hitter. Durocher wants him to be one."

For all the apparent changing of batting styles and stances through the years, four things remained consistent. Camilli could always be counted on to hit about 26 home runs a year and drive in 100 runs while striking out and walking about 100 times each. According to sports columnist Tom Meany, Camilli's precise consistency in his offensive numbers through the years earned him the nickname "The Machine" from his fellow players. (This was long before Albert Pujols was even born!)

As he became more of a fixture in Brooklyn his fielding earned him an increasing degree of respect as well. In a 1941 article, baseball scribe Edward T. Murphy wrote, "There are two plays at which Dolph is a marvel. He has no equal when it comes to catching a poorly thrown ball and tagging the runner approaching first base. He is tops also in picking up a grounder and tagging the runner who is whizzing past him."

His teammates particularly appreciated his skill in saving the errant throw. The young Pee Wee Reese once said that Camilli used to tell the infielders to just get the throws away and in his vicinity and he'd worry about the runner. Murphy wrote, "Time and again Dolph will prevent errors being charged to other Brooklyn infielders by making his uncanny catches of wild throws and completing the play at first base. Camilli's exceptional skill as a fielder is the main reason for its [the infield's] tightness. He is the fellow who holds it together."

By 1941 Camilli had become a team leader and cemented the deal with his best season ever, hitting the high water marks of his career in home runs with 34 and RBIs with 120. Once again, he managed 104 walks with 115 strikeouts and a .285 average but this time he was recognized as the National League's Most Valuable Player. It was a significant season not only for Dolph personally but for the Dodgers who, under manager Leo "The Lip" Durocher, captured their first pennant in over two decades for the Brooklyn team.

Unfortunately, Camilli's Brooklyn Dodgers lost the 1941 World Series to the New York Yankees in five games—a series that will always be remembered for Dodger catcher Mickey Owen's dropped third strike on Tommy Heinrich's ninth inning at-bat that ignited a Yankee rally and led to a Game Four Dodger loss. The error took the wind out of the Brooklyn sails and they proceeded to lose Game Five and the series to the mighty Yanks.

At the end of the 1941 season, journalist Tom Meany wondered how Camilli's MVP award might affect his upcoming contract negotiations with Larry MacPhail. Camilli had earned a reputation for showing up in spring camp at the last possible minute. By the early 1940s, Camilli owned a 1,000-plus acre cattle ranch out West. Meany wrote that "In 1940, Camilli held out so long, and the debate between him and MacPhail grew so acrimonious, that there was one particular day in Clearwater when the pair came close to blows."

According to Dodger manager Leo Durocher in his autobiography *Nice Guys Finish Last*, "Camilli was a quiet, gentle man but he was as strong as an ox." Durocher remembered the incident to which Meany referred but with a somewhat different conclusion. Durocher remembered that, "After that third-place finish [in 1939] we had high hopes going into 1940. Dolph ... wanted $15,000, which he richly deserved. But he also wanted $1,000 to cover the traveling expenses of bringing his wife and four children to camp from San Francisco. MacPhail immediately roared that he wasn't running any kindergarten here, and he wasn't responsible for Camilli's 'eight kids.'"

As the "conversation" continued, Camilli corrected MacPhail that he had four kids, not eight. MacPhail ignored Camilli and continued to scream about Camilli's "eight kids." Durocher recounted, "Every time he said 'eight kids,' Camilli corrected him, and every time he had to correct him you could see him get a little madder. The next thing I knew I heard the usual MacPhail screaming followed by gurgling, choking sounds. I went running in and the first thing I noticed, being exceptionally observant, was that Camilli had both of his hands under MacPhail's chin and MacPhail's feet were a foot off the ground." In the end, MacPhail paid Camilli the $1,000 but refused to concede defeat. He told Durocher to give Camilli the money but to let him think it had come from Durocher and not MacPhail.

Camilli had his typical 26 home runs, 100 RBI season in 1942 but it would be his last productive and full season in the majors. At the end of the 1942 season Camilli hinted that he was probably finished with his career. As the 1943 season neared, he was even more convinced that he was ready to devote his full time to his family and his Northern California ranch. Nevertheless, he was ultimately convinced to return as a patriotic gesture. The President of the United States had talked about the importance of baseball to the national morale and the Dodgers' front office used that argument to convince Camilli to return.

Camilli came back but his heart just wasn't in it. He struggled through July with only six home runs and a batting average below .250. In early August, the Dodgers released their prized first baseman on waivers to the cross-town rival New York Giants. The fans of Brooklyn were aghast and burned the new general manager Branch Rickey in effigy at Ebbets Field. In a column by Hy Turkin under the heading "Camilli Calamity" the New York columnist wrote, "Brooklyn is beefing because Dolph is gone ... but they'll never forget the countless thrills of his game-winning homers."

In a response that predated Jackie Robinson's same decision by 13 years, Camilli chose to quit rather than play for the hated Giants. Years later Camilli was quoted as saying, "I hated the Giants. This was real serious; this was no put on stuff. Their fans hated us, and our fans hated them."

By the following season he returned to play and manage in the Pacific Coast League. He was convinced to come back to the majors in 1945 but he played in only 63 games for the Red Sox and hit .212 before he hung up his spikes for good.

His post-baseball life consisted of time spent playing golf, working on his ranch and raising his large family of children which eventually did grow to number seven (not quite eight) with numerous grandchildren and great-grandchildren. He scouted for a few years for the Oakland A's and the California Angels and his son, Doug Camilli, spent some time catching in the Majors for the Dodgers and the Washington Senators. In his final years, Camilli was active in a group of former Major Leaguers who were trying to obtain pension payments for the players who retired before baseball's pension system was created in 1947.

In 1984 Camilli was inducted into the Dodgers Hall of Fame. During the festivities he remembered the fans of Brooklyn with fondness, saying, "All they cared about was their family, their job and the Dodgers. And I don't know which one was the most important."

Dolph Camilli died in October 1997 at the age of 90, one of the most beloved Brooklyn "Bums" of them all.

◆ 8 ◆

Cookie Lavagetto
(1934)

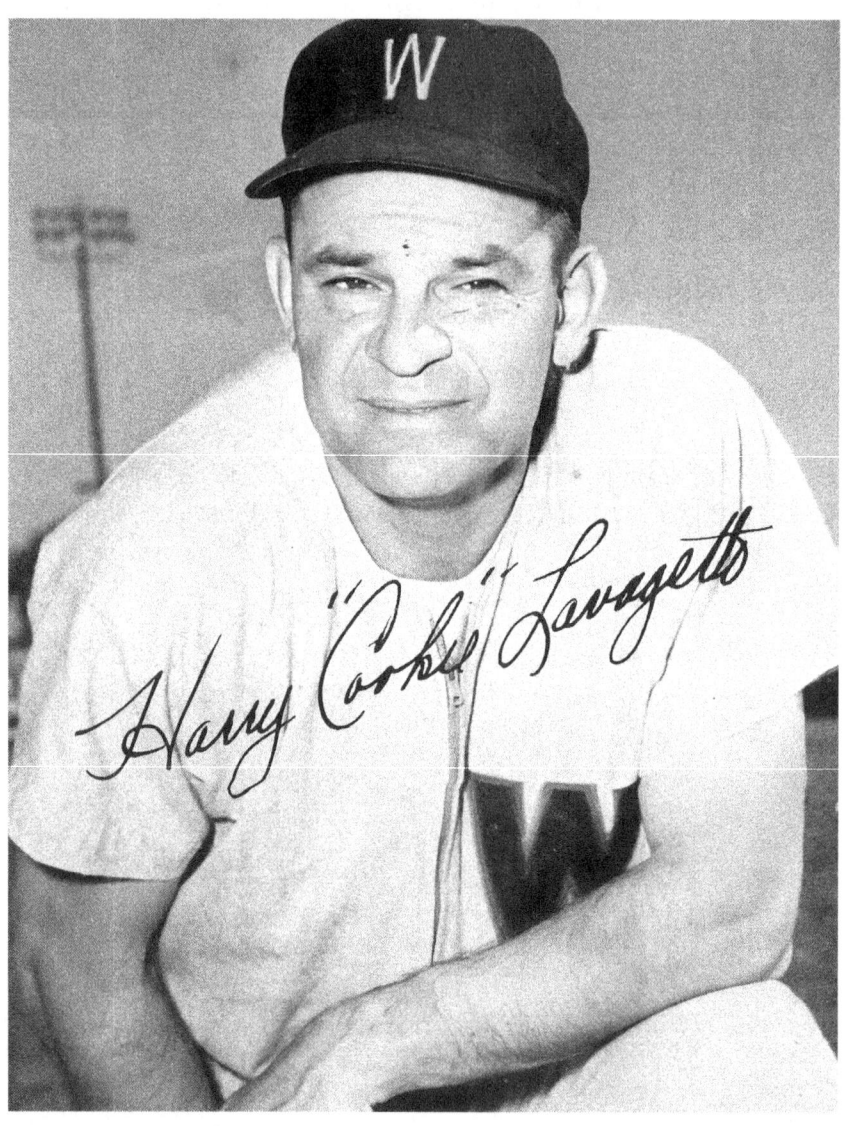

Cookie Lavagetto as the manager of the Washington Senators, circa 1959.

Leo Durocher was famous for saying "Nice guys finish last." That may be true in the baseball standings but not in the hearts of men. For example, when Cookie Lavagetto died in August of 1993, Durocher was bereft. "He was some kinda guy … some kinda ballplayer," remembered Durocher. "He just went about his business, never caused one iota of trouble. And a tough hitter with men on base. Hit .270-something for me in '41 and was one of my best RBI men. The tears are starting to come just talking about him."

"Leo the Lip" was not known for his outbursts of affection. Outbursts? Yes. Affection? No. And yet, he obviously felt deep affection for his old third baseman. In fact, almost all who played with and against Lavagetto remembered him as a nice guy. The fans, however, remembered him for providing them with one of the most memorable moments in Brooklyn Dodger history.

On October 3, 1947, with the Dodgers trailing 2–1 to the rival New York Yankees in the bottom of the ninth inning of Game Four of the World Series, Cookie Lavagetto strode to the plate with two men on base and delivered a game-winning double off the right field wall. It was certainly exciting but not necessarily unforgettable until you realize that the hit broke up Bill Bevens' no-hitter. Nobody had ever come that close to a World Series no-hitter before (one out away) until Yankee pitcher Don Larsen's perfect game nine years later. No single pitcher has pitched a World Series no-hitter since Larsen's in 1956. (Four Astro pitchers combined to no-hit the Phillies in Game Four of the 2022 World Series.)

In the mid–1970s there was a show on PBS entitled *The Way It Was*. The premise of the show was to reminisce about great sporting events of the past by bringing together many of the original participants. Legendary sportscaster Curt Gowdy was the host and the theme song was the Depression era anthem "Happy Days Are Here Again."

I watched a number of these shows during the four or so years it was on TV but after 40 years I remember only one—the episode that focused on the 1947 World Series between the New York Yankees and Brooklyn Dodgers. I remember the footage of Cookie Lavagetto knocking that double off the right field wall as Al Gionfriddo and Eddie Miksis scored the tying and winning runs. I also remember watching the film of Gionfriddo making the catch off DiMaggio as he reached into the bleachers to rob the Yankee Clipper of a home run in Game Six. Most of all, I remember the nostalgic joy expressed by the participants of those games as they talked about those glorious days gone by. While I can't exactly remember who the players were on the panel that night I do know I envied my dad and the other grown-ups I knew who had seen these diamond heroes play in their prime.

Regardless of the fact that he would always be remembered for that game-winning, no-hit busting double, Lavagetto would later contend that it was not his greatest thrill in baseball. Cookie was too nice a guy for that to be his high water mark.

In 1951 Cookie Lavagetto told columnist Harold Burr, "I felt kind of sorry for

(From left) Leo Durocher, Dolph Camilli, Pete Coscarat, and Cookie Lavagetto. The beloved Bums of Brooklyn (National Baseball Hall of Fame, Cooperstown, NY).

Bevens. I told him so the next day when the photographers posed us for our picture together." Cookie remembered that Bevens told him, "'It's all right Harry, that's baseball.' But he must have still been choked up over what had happened," said Lavagetto. "One pitch and I was the hero and he was the goat—that's sure baseball."

Harry "Cookie" Lavagetto was born Enrico Attilio Lavagetto on December 1, 1912, in Oakland, California. According to a 1961 article by Walter Bingham in *Sports Illustrated*, a teacher told Lavagetto on his first day of school that in English Enrico was either Henry or Harry. The young man went home and discussed the matter with his parents and came back the next day as "Harry." For better or for worse, that name would not stick once he found his place in baseball.

In the spring of 1933 Lavagetto desperately wanted to make baseball his career but there were no takers. He was receiving pressure from his father to take a full-time job as a trash collector. By chance, or perhaps destiny, a charity game was scheduled between a group of big leaguers from the area (and the San Francisco/Oakland Bay area produced many of them) and some of the local standouts from the neighborhood.

In the fifth inning, Lavagetto would punch his own ticket into the big leagues in the same fashion as he'd punch out 14 years later. He was put into the game in the fifth inning and in his first at-bat he came up with the bases loaded. He smashed a double that drove in all three runs and within 24 hours, he was swamped with offers from a number of pro clubs. Years later he would recall this double, and not the one in the '47 series, as his greatest moment in baseball.

According to the 1961 *Sports Illustrated* article, "He signed with Cookie DeVincenzi, owner of the Oakland team of the Pacific Coast League. Harry became known as 'Cookie's boy' and, eventually, just plain Cookie."

He spent the 1933 season with the Oakland club before being signed by the Pittsburgh Pirates. His rookie season of 1934 was a bit of a disappointment as he hit only .220 but he did drive in over 40 runs while playing 83 games at second base for the Bucs. In 1935 he came back as a 22-year-old sophomore and batted a solid .290. In December of 1936 he was traded to the Brooklyn Dodgers for a pitcher named Ed Brandt.

In his first season with the Dodgers he was finally made into a full-time player and responded by hitting .282 while driving in 70 runs. He played 100 games at second base and 45 at third. By the following season, 1938, he was Brooklyn's regular third baseman, starting over 130 games at the hot corner.

As the Brooklyn third baseman, he became the focal point of one of Brooklyn's legion of colorful fans. Jack Pierce owned a tavern in Brooklyn and held season's tickets behind the visitor's dugout near the third base bag. Pierce would bring a variety of banners, balloons, and signs to the ballpark. The signs and banners all had "Cookie" written on them and every time Lavagetto made a play or got a hit, Pierce would release helium balloons into the air. Throughout the game Pierce would chant "Cookie, Cookie!"

In the '61 *SI* story, Bingham relates one particular anecdote where "in one clutch situation with Lavagetto at bat, Pierce was yelling so much that Lavagetto had to step away from the plate and tell him to shut up. Cookie then lined out a hit to win the game. Everybody was happy, but when Cookie and some teammates returned to their Brooklyn hotel, there was Jack Pierce with tears streaming down his face. His feelings were crushed." That's about as good an example of what the Brooklyn Dodgers meant to their fans as any you will find.

Lavagetto suffered through a variety of bad luck injuries on and off during his career. When he was healthy, he was one of the best. In 1939, he hit 10 home runs, garnered a career-high 87 RBIs and batted a solid .300. In 1940, the injuries returned, culminating in an operation to remove his appendix. He played in 35 fewer games than in 1939 and his average fell to .257 while driving in only 43 runs. The year 1941 saw Lavagetto's comeback and he boosted the average to .277 while driving in 78 runs. His strong showing helped the Dodgers capture the National League pennant for the first time in over 20 years.

Unfortunately, Cookie Lavagetto was one of the many ballplayers whose career was interrupted and cut short by World War II. According to a 1990 obituary, "Lavagetto was the first Dodger to join the armed forces in World War II ... despite a 3A classification." He enlisted in the Navy in 1942 and missed four of the prime years of his career to the service. Once he returned home, he was 33 years old and just couldn't regain his previous form. As he said, "[I] was washed up."

He lasted two more years with the Dodgers, playing in 88 games in 1946 and 41 games in 1947. By '47 Spider Jorgensen was the starting third baseman for the Dodgers. Lavagetto got into just 18 games as a third baseman. In the series he came up seven times, struck out twice, and got just one hit—but that one hit has gone down in the annals of Brooklyn Dodger history as a franchise highlight. It was the last Major League hit Lavagetto would ever get. Before the start of the 1948 season, the Dodgers released him. He was angry and felt betrayed by the Dodgers' front office. He was 35 years old but he wasn't done yet.

He returned to the Oakland Oaks in the Pacific Coast League. During the 1948 season his manager was future Yankee field boss "Casey" Stengel. He helped Stengel win a PCL Championship and also helped out as an unofficial coach to some of the younger players. Columnist Art Rosenbaum recalled, "Lavagetto became a volunteer mentor of a twenty-year-old peppery infielder [named] Billy Martin. Lavagetto had Stengel's endorsement, and Lavagetto himself showed no jealousy in sharing his experience. One of his main acts was to make sure Martin was shifted from third to second—'The kid can be a star at second, but he doesn't have the build for a third baseman.' That decision stuck, to Martin's benefit."

In 1949, Stengel moved on to manage the Yankees and Charlie Dressen became manager of the Oakland ball club. Lavagetto played under Dressen during the 1949 and 1950 seasons until Dressen was hired by the Dodgers to manage. At that point, Dressen took Lavagetto with him to Brooklyn as a coach. Dressen thought Lavagetto still had a little gas left in the tank as well. In a 1961 interview, Dressen claimed the Dodgers would have won the 1951 pennant if he had been allowed to use Lavagetto. "I wanted to put him on the active list, but the brass said no. They didn't want to send a young fellow down. Hell, with Cookie to pinch hit down the stretch, I could have won easily."

Dressen managed the Dodgers from 1951 through 1953. When he was refused a two-year contract in 1954, he quit. In an act of loyalty, Lavagetto also quit. The following season, 1955, Dressen was back managing the Washington Senators and sitting right by his side was Cookie Lavagetto. When the team got off to a rough start in 1957 Dressen was fired. The job was offered to Lavagetto but his first inclination was to decline the offer. Dressen had to talk him into taking the job and convince him he was ready to be a manager.

He enjoyed life as a coach. He could voice his opinion when asked, hit fungos to the outfielders, and play cards with the players. He was part of the game he loved but without too much responsibility. Managing was something altogether different.

When he began to manage he was unsure of himself. He tried to be everybody's friend. He didn't like to chew out the pitchers. He took the losses too seriously. Pretty soon the stress began to affect his health. He broke out in hives, lost his appetite and had trouble sleeping at night. Eventually, over time, he began to relax and find his own style and his own voice as a manager.

In his three full seasons as the Senators' manager the team improved slowly but surely, each year winning more games than the year before. In 1961 the team moved to Minneapolis–St. Paul and became the Minnesota Twins. After 59 games and a 23–36 start, Lavagetto was fired.

In 1962 he became one of Casey Stengel's coaches on the first New York Mets team. Following a health scare during the 1963 season, Lavagetto longed to be closer to home so the Mets and the San Francisco Giants worked out a trade for coaches—Lavagetto went to the Giants and Wes Westrum came east to the Mets. Lavagetto remained with the Giants until his retirement in 1967.

The double to break up Bill Bevens' no-hitter in the 1947 World Series will always be the feat for which Cookie Lavagetto is best remembered. Nevertheless, it should not be forgotten that he was also a good, solid player in his day. In his five full seasons with the Brooklyn Dodgers he drove in an average of 71 runs per year and scored 70 runs as well. During his ten-year career, he walked 485 times while striking out only 244 times. He was a steady third baseman with a strong throwing arm. He was also known as one of the best clutch hitters of his time. "He was a great two-strike hitter," [recalled] Whitlow Wyatt, the ace of the Dodgers' pitching staff before the war. "With men on base he was about the toughest man to get out that we had on the club."

It's somewhat ironic that the three men most remembered for their exploits during the classic 1947 World Series between the Yankees and the Dodgers, Bill Bevens, Cookie Lavagetto, and Al Gionfriddo, never played another Major League game after that series. It's even more ironic that Cookie Lavagetto said to writer Walter Bingham in 1961, "I prefer to remain in obscurity."

Fortunately, that will never happen. The name of Cookie Lavagetto will be remembered for as long as World Series games are played. That's just the way the cookie crumbles. Sorry—I couldn't help myself.

◆ 9 ◆

Zeke Bonura
(1934)

Zeke "The Physique" Bonura, first-bagger of the Washington Senators, 1938.

My hometown minor league baseball team is the Rochester Red Wings of the International League—an old and storied franchise. I've been going to Red Wing games since 1972. When my sons were little I'd tell them that my first Red Wing idol was a player named Al Bumbry. Their first question was, "Is he in the Hall of Fame?" I had to explain that while he's not in the Hall of Fame, he was nevertheless an excellent ball player. He was an exciting, scrappy outfielder who batted over .300 three times in his career and was an important part of the 1983 World Champion Baltimore Orioles. They seemed to understand, but the next time I mentioned a baseball favorite from my childhood their first question was still, "Is he in the Hall of Fame?"

In some ways, I think the media are partly to blame for this. The sportscasters and sports talk show hosts tend to speak only in hyperbole and superlatives and if an athlete isn't among the elite of his/her sport, it's almost as if they aren't there at all. I suppose there's nothing new about this phenomenon. After all, how many people remember Gee Walker, Hal Trosky, and Barney McCosky? They were all premier American League outfielders during the 1930s and 1940s. They ended their careers with lifetime batting averages of .294, .302, and .312 respectively. Unfortunately for them they played in a league and during an era with two guys named Joe DiMaggio and Ted Williams.

The point is there are a great many excellent ballplayers who never made the Hall of Fame and never will. However, that shouldn't diminish their accomplishments or our memories of them. In addition to the solid players whose lifetime achievements fall just short of immortal recognition, there are hundreds, even thousands of others whose careers were cut short by injuries, war service, or social and labor injustices.

That brings us to the case of one Henry John Bonura, better known as Zeke Bonura—a jovial, hard-hitting first baseman whose Major League playing time was limited to just seven seasons from 1934 to 1940. While he's not in the Baseball Hall of Fame and never even played in a single postseason game, he left a rich and colorful legacy in the annals of Major League Baseball.

Bonura was born on September 20, 1908, in New Orleans. He was named after his paternal grandfather Enrico (Henry) and his dad Giovanni (John). Both of Bonura's parents were immigrants from Palermo, Sicily. He was their only son in addition to two daughters, Philomena and Rosina.

Henry Bonura was an athletic, bright, and energetic young man. At the age of 13 Bonura entered St. Stanislaus College as a seventh grader. It wasn't a college in the way we think of one today but more like a prep school with a more extensive curriculum than the average high school. He immediately caught the eye of a varsity coach by the name of Foster Commagre. The coach recruited Bonura to play sports and the young man eventually earned letters in football, basketball, track, and baseball.

Legendary Notre Dame football coach Knute Rockne once spotted the 6'2", 220 pound Bonura at a National Catholic Youth Tournament where the young athlete was playing basketball. After the game Rockne approached Bonura's Coach Commagre and commented that he wanted the young man "with that magnificent physique to play for him." From that moment on his teammates began calling him "Physique" which eventually got shortened down to "Zeke." The newspapers and sportswriters of the South noticed Bonura as well and called him "The South's Wonder Athlete."

On July 4, 1925, the U.S. Track team was competing against a number of foreign countries at a widely publicized track meet in San Francisco, California. The 16-year-old Bonura (he wouldn't turn 17 until September) was at the meet representing St. Stanislaus against powerhouse athletes like Finland's Jon Myrra, the world record holder in the javelin throw. It was a foregone conclusion that Myrra would return to Finland with his title.

On his very first attempt Zeke Bonura raced to the line and hurled the javelin nearly 214 feet for a new world's record. The crowd was stunned by the young man's achievement. After a few silent moments the crowd erupted in cheers. He not only won the event and set a world record (it would be broken in 1930) but he also became the youngest male athlete ever to win an event at the United States AAU Track and Field Championships.

In his years at St. Stanislaus, Bonura may have excelled in all sports but clearly baseball was his favorite. He could have easily made the 1928 Olympic team but chose instead to concentrate on baseball. In his years at school he hit .440, .420, .410, .425, and .520—unbelievable numbers and unbelievable consistency. He was the first team Varsity shortstop as a seventh-grader.

Starting in 1926 Bonura also began to play semi-pro baseball in various Louisiana leagues. In the course of three seasons he batted .400 or better every year. By the time he graduated high school, Bonura was a highly coveted prospect for both college and Major League baseball teams. Although Zeke Bonura most definitely wanted to play Major League Baseball, he also wanted to get an education. In 1928 he entered Loyola University of the South for a two-year program in Business. Once again, Bonura lettered in baseball, football, basketball and track.

Once he left Loyola, Bonura was offered a bonus to sign with the Cleveland Indians. Instead he chose to play for the New Orleans Pelicans of the Southern League. In those days, the minor league teams were independent of the Major League ball clubs. Bonura made a deal with the Pelicans that he would get half the selling price if and when the team sold him to another team. He played two seasons with the Pelicans and his manager Larry Gilbert called Bonura "The greatest natural hitter I ever saw." He played for the Dallas Rebels of the Texas League in 1933 and hit a solid .352 while being named the Most Valuable Player of the league.

In 1934 Bonura finally found his way to the Major Leagues when Dallas sold him to the Chicago White Sox. He also received half the sales price paid to the Rebels for his contract. He set a White Sox rookie record for single season home runs by knocking 27 balls out of the park. In 1936 Bonura set the single season RBI record for the White Sox with 138 RBIs. The record stood for 62 years until broken in 1998 by Albert Belle.

A colorful character, Zeke Bonura was a newspaper man's dream. He was portrayed in the papers as a little boy in a man's body. A small newspaper item from April of 1936 reads: "Just a big boy—forever talking about his 'Mama' and 'Daddy.' Occasionally throws a banana-shower for his mates—the bananas being shipped, charges prepaid, by 'Daddy' who deals in that commodity. Blushes when his mates swear at him in Italian."

In a feature article from that same year, Irving Vaughan of the *Chicago Tribune* touched upon some of those same topics while spotlighting how Bonura's childlike nature went over with his manager, Jimmy Dykes. According to the article, Bonura was a frequent frustration to his manager by ignoring or misreading signs. He was known to occasionally steal a base although he was never a base-stealing threat. Vaughan writes, "Periodically, Dykes flares up and launches forth on his favorite subject. Bonura always knows, of course, when the lecture is coming and Dykes never disappoints him."

Vaughan goes on to explain that Bonura's responses to Dykes' frequent tirades only exasperated his manager all the more. "Does Big Zeke wax indignant and threaten to go home to his mama in New Orleans?" asks Vaughan. "He does not. He simply tries to explain with the straightforwardness of a boy who isn't convinced he has done any wrong. Frequently his alibis are so high in the realm of imagination that Dykes, who is no bashful gentleman at the art of talking, can't find the appropriate words. He just has to stall for time by employing a few mumbled curses. But he never can make Bonura swear back. All that Zeke will say is 'Oh, gee whiz, papa.'"

In the bottom of the 14th inning in a game against the Yanks, Bonura came quite close to giving his manager a heart attack. The bases were loaded with Bonura on third. There were two outs and a 3–2 count on batter Johnny Allen. The pitcher, Whitlow Wyatt, had been struggling and it looked as though he would walk in the winning run. "All of a sudden," Vaughan wrote, "a cloud of dust started to raise between third and home. It was Zeke calling on his legs to carry out a Ty Cobb thought." Catching everyone in the ballpark by surprise, Bonura stole home and won the game for the White Sox.

Dykes' rage was alleviated only slightly by the fact that Bonura scored but he warned Big Zeke not to try it again. The best reaction to the play came from Yankee catcher Bill Dickey who was quoted as saying, "What's this game coming to? If a big lumberman like that can steal home, then we had best fold up."

Jimmy Dykes was also critical of Bonura's fielding and it was a claim that stuck to Bonura throughout his playing days. The statistics, however, tell a bit of a different story. He has a lifetime fielding average of .992 and he led American League first basemen in fielding average three out of his five full seasons in the league. Nevertheless, he was never recognized as a great fielder.

His sociability may have hindered his fielding. Bonura, by all accounts, loved to talk, tell stories, and generally have fun playing ball. In the 1936 *Tribune* article Vaughan explains that Bonura, "because of his good nature [is] always willing to listen to stories the enemy first base coaches like to tell him. This gets his mind off the work at hand and makes it easier to slip a batted ball past him."

In 1939 he was traded to the New York Giants who were managed by former first base legend Bill Terry. In a *New York Post* article from spring training of that year, Bonura's new skipper said, "If the guy can only hit like he talks." Terry went on to tell writer Jerry Mitchell, "He talked to me for five straight hours and my ears are bent. And my side's sore; every time he tells you a gag he has to drive home his point with a jab in the ribs."

In his four seasons with the White Sox, Bonura hit 79 home runs, had 440 RBIs, scored 392 runs and batted well over .300, yet he never felt fully appreciated by his manager and front office. He was traded to the Washington Senators in 1938. His batting average fell to .289 but he still managed to belt 22 home runs and collect 114 RBIs. It's important to note that in the old Griffith Park where Bonura played for the Senators the left field fence was 410 feet and the center field fence was 520 feet from home—a monster of a park for a right-handed hitter.

In Washington he gained a fan for life in the person of Vice President John Nance Garner. Apparently, Mr. Garner, who was a baseball fan, was thrilled when Bonura was traded to the Senators. On Opening Day of 1938 Bonura greeted the Vice President and took pictures with him prior to the game. He promised Garner that he would hit a home run for him and then, to the thrill of all who heard his bold prediction, went out and did it.

From the Senators he went to the Giants for a year and then split the 1940 season between the Senators and Cubs. In 1941 he went to Minneapolis, a minor league club where the fans loved him and he loved the town right back. He was hitting around .400 and received a couple of offers from big league teams but turned them down. He liked Minneapolis and he also knew that he would soon be called into the draft for World War II.

During the war, Bonura was sent to North Africa to establish baseball teams and leagues for the entertainment of the troops. He proved to be a master at the task and quickly became a favorite of the GIs with whom he worked and coached. In 1947, following a dinner to honor Bonura for his war service, sports columnist Frank Graham wrote this about Bonura's war record: "No day was too long for him when there was something he could do for somebody. No distance was too far for him to travel. No problem was too great that he couldn't wrestle with it and get it down." Al Schacht, "The Clown Prince of Baseball," whose comedic performances thrilled crowds in ballparks across America, went to North Africa to entertain the troops like so many of the entertainers of that era. While on tour, he was reunited with his old baseball pal Zeke Bonura. When he came home he said, "Nobody in baseball is doing a bigger job in this war. He [Bonura] is the idol of every kid in North Africa."

His days with Uncle Sam's team earned him a most valuable player award of a different kind when General Dwight D. Eisenhower conferred the Legion of Merit upon Colonel Bonura for his distinguished service to the U.S. war effort.

Following the war, the 37-year-old Bonura was too old to resume his playing career. He did some coaching and managing at the minor league level. He finally retired from baseball in 1952 and began to breed and train beagle hounds. He became world famous for his breeding and five of his dogs became "National Champions."

Zeke Bonura was a man of great humor and kindness. He was a positive symbol of Italian America at a time when immigrants were still fighting for acceptance into mainstream society. He was also one helluva ballplayer with a lifetime average of .307 and 704 RBIs in just seven seasons. His career was shortened by a world war but his positive impact on the game and its fans was felt for many years after he'd hung up his spikes.

♦ **10** ♦

Phil Cavarretta
(1934)

A Chicago favorite, Phil Cavaretta started with the Cubs at age 17.

For two solid decades Phil Cavarretta was a favorite of the Cub fans at Wrigley Field. He was the ultimate hometown boy made good. As a kid, he and his friends would sneak into Wrigley Field to get a look at their baseball idols. When he was still just a kid, he got a tryout with that very same Cubs team. In a matter of days he was playing on a minor league farm team and within a few months he put on the treasured Cubs uniform and kept it on for the next 20 years.

Phil Cavarretta was the original "Charlie Hustle" known for his "all out" style of play long before Pete Reiser or Pete Rose had ever seen the Major Leagues. He literally grew up on the diamonds of Major League Baseball and learned as he went along. He had some pretty great teachers like Charlie Grimm, his first manager in the big leagues, and Hall of Famers Kiki Cuyler and Billy Herman. He was a solid first baseman, a National League MVP, and one of the great clutch-hitting Cubbies of all time.

Philip Joseph Cavarretta was born on July 19, 1916, near North Avenue in the tough Little Italy neighborhood of Chicago's north side. In order to avoid the more negative elements of his surroundings, Cavarretta spent much of his time at the old Larrabee Y and Stenton Park playground. It was there that his dreams of a baseball career took bloom. In a 1993 interview with *Sports Collectors Digest* Cavarretta spoke of the positive influence of baseball on his childhood, saying, "I just love baseball. It kept me out of trouble. It's been my life and I still think it's the best game around."

He started out as a pitcher and proceeded to pitch his Lane Tech High School team to the City Championship. In 1932 he pitched his American Legion team to the State Championship and by 1933, he was on the mound, leading his American Legion club to a National Championship. Naturally, Cavarretta's skills began to turn a few heads. When Cavarretta decided to quit high school to help his family out financially, Coach Percy Moore from Lane Tech sent the young ballplayer to see his friend Charlie Grimm, manager of the Cubs.

On the day of his tryout, Cavarretta did not disappoint his coach or manager Grimm; he raced all over the outfield chasing flies, pitched 15 minutes of batting practice, and then belted a batting practice home run off Cubs star pitcher Lon Warneke.

Within a few weeks he was playing ball for the Peoria team of the B-level Central League. In his very first game, Cavarretta hit for the cycle collecting a single, double, triple, and home run. When the league folded in mid-season he was sent to Reading in the New York Penn League. By September, he was called up to the parent Cubs. He had just turned 18.

In his first full game as a Cub, Cavarretta hit a home run off Whitey Wistert to lead the Cubs to a 1–0 victory over the Cincinnati Reds. In the seven games he played at the end of the 1934 season, he impressed the team and the fans by hitting a triple and a home run, driving in six runs and batting .381—an auspicious debut indeed. He never returned to the minor leagues. When the 1935 season started, Phil Cavarretta was a Cub and after the first few games, Manager Charlie Grimm turned first base over to the young phenom.

At 18 years old, Phil Cavarretta, who had grown up down the street from Wrigley Field, was the starting first baseman for the Chicago Cubs. While some of the press corps and fans thought his .275 batting average that year was a disappointment, others felt his timely hitting helped propel the Cubs to the pennant. In a 1946 *American Legion Magazine* article, Herb Graffis wrote of that 1935 season, "When somebody had to get a hit, draw a pass or get hit by a pitcher to push a runner around, Cavarrretta made his .275 look like .750."

Considering his age and the fact that he drove in 82 runs, he proved to everyone that he was a Major League ballplayer. He also proved that he was always willing to learn and to work on his hitting and fielding. "Defensively, I wasn't too good, at least when I first came up," Cavarretta noted in the 1993 interview with *SCD*. "But, Charlie Grimm took me under his wing and helped me. He helped me on the throw from first to second, because I felt that was the toughest play for a first baseman. It seemed like I always hit the (runner) in the back because I released the ball too quick."

In a 2002 interview with *MLB.com*, Cavarretta also gave credit to Hall-of-Famer Billy Herman, who played second base on the '35 Cubs, for the time he put into teaching the young Cavarretta. "When I first came up, I was 18 years old and just out of high school and Billy was a second baseman," Cavarretta said. "Being inexperienced, I'd play first base and I played one position and that was it. I never moved. Billy said, 'I've been around a while. I'll communicate when we're out there and move you around.' This was a big plus for me. Later, he became my roommate. He was very, very intelligent."

In a May 1945 article from *The Sporting News* written by Edgar Munzel, Charlie Grimm is quoted as saying, "Cavarretta always was a willing workman. When he started, he used to come out early and I'd give him all the pointers I knew about playing the bag." Grimm had been one of the premier fielding first basemen of the 1920s and early 1930s. By the time Cavarretta was done, he played over 1,250 games at first base with an outstanding lifetime .990 fielding average.

As for his hitting, he got some valuable advice from Cubs coach, and eventual Baseball Hall of Famer, Kiki Cuyler. Cavarretta started out as a pull hitter. In the 1946 *American Legion Magazine* article, Cavarretta told Graffis, "Ki explained it to me so it made good sense. He told me that if I'd stand a little farther back in the box I'd hit outside pitches to left field and hit inside pitches between first and second instead of slapping them against the stands. He's a fellow who knows his business and I couldn't brush off that kind of advice."

That advice paid off for Cavarretta with a .293 lifetime batting average over the course of 2,030 games.

The amazing element of the Cavarretta story is the early success coupled with the steady progress Cavarretta made through the years. He had to have been an unusually mature 18-year-old to have maintained such an even keel in such a high-pressure business. Through the years he credited his parents, his high school coach Percy Moore, and Charlie Grimm with teaching him the things he needed to know about life as much as baseball.

In 1935, his first full year in the majors, the Cubs won the pennant by winning 21 games in a row in the month of September. Cavarretta has often cited that 1935 club as the best he ever played on. "We were able to win 21 games in a row against some good clubs—St. Louis, the Giants, the Dodgers, just to name a few," Cavarretta said in 1993. "I was only 19 years old at the time, but still I was on cloud nine."

Unfortunately, the World Series was a different story as the Cubs lost to a strong Detroit ball club in six games. Cavarretta had a disappointing series at the plate, batting only .125.

The Cubs returned to the World Series in 1938 under Gabby Hartnett but lost to the powerhouse Yankees in four straight.

In 1945 it was Cavarretta's turn to be the powerhouse as he earned MVP honors in the National League with a league-leading .355 average, .449 on-base percentage and .500 slugging percentage. After ten years, he literally led his Cubbies to the pennant and World Series as captain of the team. Unfortunately, the Cubs came up just short of victory, losing Game Seven to the opposing Tigers.

Almost 50 years after that World Series defeat, Cavarretta was still thinking about just how close they came to the ultimate victory. "Being just 19 years old in my first World Series, 1935, and then playing in another World Series 10 years later.... I think about it quite often, to be honest with you," Cavarretta said. "I try to figure out how we could have won that seventh game. I second guess everything, just like I do now [1993] when I watch the Cubs."

The one aspect of that '45 series he didn't need to second-guess was his own play. He banged out 11 hits, scored seven runs and drove in five more while compiling a .423 series average. (He had also batted .462 in the disastrous 1938 series against the Yankees.)

In an August 1954 *Sporting News* article Cavarretta cites being chosen to manage the Cubs in July of 1951 as another thrill in his long career. "It happened in Philadelphia," Cavarretta recalled. "We came back to Chicago and I made my debut in a double-header against the Phillies. I started and finished the first game. I hit a triple off Robin Roberts that drove in two runs. We won 4 to 2. I was coaching at third when the second game started. Late in the game, we started a rally and Roberts came in to relieve. When we loaded the bases, I came in as a pinch-hitter and knocked a home run on the first pitch. Beating Roberts twice in one day, both as a manager and a hitter is something I'll never forget."

Talking to Jerome Holtzman of the *Chicago Tribune* in 1992, Cavarretta spoke of that 1951 managerial debut and specifically the insertion of himself into the game with the bases loaded and the team down by three runs. "It was a stupid thing for me to do," he said. "In a spot like that you're either a hero or a bum." Cavarretta is anything but a bum so it all worked out for the best.

Unfortunately, the same can't be said about the rest of his managerial career.

His record as a manager for the remainder of 1951 was 27–47. In 1952 the Cubs finished at .500 with a 77–77 record and then posted a dismal 65–89 record for 1953. In spring training of 1954, Philip K. Wrigley fired Cavarretta shortly before the regular season was to start, for comments that Wrigley felt reflected a "defeatist" attitude on the part of his manager. In the 1992 interview with Holtzman, Cavarretta said, "A lot of people still think I was fired because I said we didn't have a good team. I didn't say that. What I said was we needed help at first base, third base and center field. Mr. Wrigley interpreted that as a defeatist complex, something like that. Actually, I always have had and still have the utmost respect for Mr. Wrigley. He was a wonderful man."

At 37, his managing days may have been over but his playing days were not. He eventually landed on the south side with the White Sox at Comiskey Park. In the August 18, 1954, *Sporting News* article he admitted, "It's too much to manage and try to play, too. I'm convinced of that. I've always been a hard loser and it took a lot out of me. But now it's just like starting out all over again. I have no worries except about myself."

There must have been something to what he said because in 71 games with the White Sox he batted .318—the first time he had batted above .300 since 1951. He played only six games of the 1955 season before he decided that it was time to retire. Retire from a playing career, that is. He remained in the game of baseball for many years after that as a coach and a scout and while he worked for a few different clubs, he considered himself a Cub—first, last, and always.

Throughout Cavarretta's career, he was recognized as a hustling, hard-nosed ballplayer. When asked about this in the May 1945 article in *The Sporting News* Cavarretta said, "Hustling was just born in me, I guess. To my way of thinking that's the very least you can do when you play ball and it pays off all around. By hustling you look good, you make your ball club look good and you make the fans feel like they're really getting their money's worth."

Strange, isn't it? To read a ballplayer talking about making the team look good and giving the fans their money's worth? Sadly, we can't go home again. Cavarretta's era was a lifetime ago and we must move on. However, the memory of great competitors like Phil Cavarretta gives us an even greater appreciation for the ballplayers that still play hard today. There may seem to be fewer of them but they're out there if you look closely enough.

For those willing to listen, Cavarretta's philosophy of the game is timeless and still speaks to today's ballplayers, both amateurs and professionals. Continuing on the subject of hustle, Cavarretta went on to say in the same 1945 interview, "If you want to look at it selfishly, even that should be good enough to make a fellow hustle. By running out every ball you hit, for instance, you get tremendous returns. I figure I can get from a dozen to twenty more hits a year simply by hustling. When you hit the ball right at somebody, many players just loaf to first taking it for granted they're going to be out. However, if you run your hardest every time, that infielder will know he has to make the play fast. And in hurrying he often just slaps the ball down and you may get a hit."

That's good advice for Little Leaguers of any generation. You're never too old, or too young, to learn lessons so basic and so valuable.

Phil Cavarretta died in December of 2010 at the age of 94. His legacy of hard work, good sportsmanship, and love of the game will live on. He will long be remembered not only in Chicago but wherever baseball fans remember the men, like Cavarretta, whose competitive spirit and respect for the game stoked the fires of our childhood dreams.

◆ **11** ◆

The DiMaggio Brothers: Joe, Vince, and Dom (1936, '37, '40)

The Yankee Clipper comes across again as catcher Roy Campanella looks on (National Baseball Hall of Fame, Cooperstown, NY).

11 ♦ The DiMaggio Brothers: Joe, Vince, and Dom (1936, '37, '40)

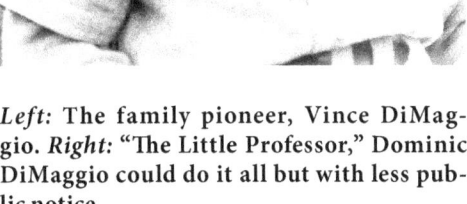

Left: The family pioneer, Vince DiMaggio. *Right:* "The Little Professor," Dominic DiMaggio could do it all but with less public notice.

Baseball may no longer be the most popular sport in the United States but it is still the national pastime. Baseball is America's game. In fact, many would argue that baseball and jazz are the only two truly American cultural institutions to evolve from our nation's history.

The idea of America may have been born in the minds of some erudite British ex-patriots with white wigs, but it was built on the blood, sweat, and tears of immigrants from all over the world traveling to our shores to find a better life for themselves and their children. Whether it was for economic, political, or religious freedom, America offered new hope to oppressed people elsewhere. To our Italian and Sicilian ancestors, it was thought to be a kind of Utopia where everything was possible and everyone had an equal chance. The truth was somewhat different; the American dream did not burn as bright for people of color (i.e. slaves), people who couldn't speak English, people whose religion was something other than Christian, or people who were something other than men. Nevertheless, they still flocked to America because at least here there was a chance, there was hope that talent and passion and hard work would eventually bring success ... and justice.

The early Italian and Sicilian immigrants believed that only hard work and sacrifice brought success. The more enlightened also believed that education was part of that equation. However, there were few who believed that a successful and respectable life could come from playing games or sports. In almost every story of a successful Italian American athlete from the first half of the 20th century there is a parent who scorned his/her son's idea of a professional career in baseball, boxing, football, or any other sport. Games were for children, not for men. In many of those cases, even when the son began to bring home good money for his "play," the father or mother still saw the whole exercise as "not respectable." It wasn't until an athlete's wealth and fame was able to transform the entire future of his family that his parents saw the power of sport in this new land. They never quite understood it, but they learned to respect it and appreciate it.

It's entirely possible that more than any other figure in the history of American sports, Joe DiMaggio helped to change the perception of professional athletics in the minds of immigrant parents all over this country. He was an example to all immigrants in America of what could be accomplished through sports. To Italians and Sicilians, he was more than an example; he was a hero, a saint, a savior.

In the mid–1930s, however, the reputation of Italian Americans was still more often questioned and mistrusted than it was respected. Despite producing great politicians like La Guardia, scientists like Marconi, or movie makers like Capra, they were still being more associated with the Al Capones or Lucky Lucianos of the world. If it wasn't the Italian American gangsters of the movies, they were forced to contend with the image of the arrogant strutting of Mussolini, Hitler's Italian lap dog. It was at just that moment that young Joseph Paul DiMaggio burst onto the national scene. In his rookie season with the New York Yankees he hit 29 home runs, drove in 125 runs, and batted .323 while leading his team to their first World Championship since a fellow named Ruth had led them to victory over the Chicago Cubs in 1932. In his 13 seasons with the Yankees, Joe DiMaggio would lead the Yankees to nine World Championships.

Those born after 1970 or thereabouts can't fathom the importance of Joe DiMaggio today. Italian Americans, while still often brazenly stereotyped in the media and in Hollywood, are nevertheless one of the more assimilated and successful ethnic groups. First of all, the color of our skin is not a hindrance. Those of us who are third- or fourth- generation do not speak with accents and many of us have college degrees and professional careers. It's much different from the pre–World War II generation of my parents. My uncle used to tell me that in his neighborhood the educated kids usually became teachers, lawyers, doctors, or civil servants. Those who were not as lucky or as good in school often ended up on the wrong side of the law and lived lives of constant struggle and disappointment. To those early Italian American citizens and their children, Joe DiMaggio was a man who brought them more than just thrills on the baseball field. He brought them respectability and hope.

In *Joe DiMaggio: The Hero's Life*, author Richard Ben Cramer writes of the young ballplayer's importance to his fellow Italian Americans after that rookie season: "He wasn't from Mussolini, or for Mussolini. Joe was everything the papers said and more. He played that clean American game ... on pristine grass. He was strong, but shy—a regular Joe—from a big family, working people, who'd made their way by honest labor. He played for a team whose very name stood for America. By his natural grace, he made them champions. (And whom did he invite to the World Series—brought across the country for that brilliant event? His mamma!) ... DiMaggio was their American story. Here was the face they could show in their new world."

And so, from the very beginning he was more than just a great baseball player. He was a symbol, a representative of his people and of all the immigrants. He was able to do things on the baseball diamond that others could only dream of doing. He wasn't just a ballplayer, he was a Yankee. He wasn't just a great hitter and fielder, he was a champion. He wasn't just the son of an immigrant Sicilian fisherman, he was the personification of Sicilians and Italians everywhere. Joe DiMaggio was a hero and it was a role he would continue to play long after his playing days ended. It was a role that, arguably, he played better than anyone before him or since.

Born on November 25, 1914, when he came up with the Yankees in 1936, Joseph Paul DiMaggio was a phenom. The New York press and their fans saw him as the man who could save their franchise. From 1920, when Babe Ruth had joined the Yankees, until 1932, the Yankees were in seven World Series and won four of them. In 1933 and 1934 Ruth was aging and slowing down and by 1935 he was gone; the Yankees not only didn't win the World Series during those three years, they weren't even in the mix. Then along came the young DiMaggio and right away he hit the ball like few others before him ever had and patrolled the outfield like a veteran. In DiMaggio's first year, the Yankees returned to the World Series and won it. Not only that, but they would go on to win the next three years in a row, all behind the spectacular play of their young center fielder.

Few figures in American history have been written about as often, and as endearingly, as Joe DiMaggio. Unlike the boisterous self-promoters of today's sports world, however, DiMaggio was a silent star. He was anything but a quote machine during his years in the largest media market in the United States. Nevertheless, he was the star of the team, the big story to all who followed the game, so the New York media had to create much of the legend that is and was Joe DiMaggio. To paraphrase an old saying, when the truth isn't as interesting, print the legend.

In DiMaggio's time, the newspapermen covering baseball actually traveled with the teams. Quite often, they became friends with the ballplayers they were assigned to report on. If they wanted the privilege of traveling with the team and the cooperation of the players, they had to be very careful about what they wrote. If they were too critical they might find themselves with a new assignment. Therefore, it was up to New York sportswriters like Dan Daniel and James M. Kahn to create an image of DiMaggio that was as fantastic on paper as were his feats on the field. Whether they were exactly factual or not was less important than whether they lived up to the image of this great new sports hero.

While DiMaggio seldom gave the writers any help in their myth-making endeavors, he realized fairly quickly that they had created a persona for him and that he then had to live up to it. In recent years writers like Richard Ben Cramer have suggested that DiMaggio was not a man who was obsessed with the game of baseball from his earliest youth, but rather just a guy who saw that baseball meant a way to fame and fortune and who used his talent to carry him up the ladder of financial success. Whether that's true or not, the reality is that he did understand the talent he had been blessed with and once given the opportunity to use it, he honed that talent and worked at perfecting his skills so that no matter what, he would be the absolute best that he could be.

Joe DiMaggio was, of course, only one of three Major League Baseball playing brothers. Joe debuted in 1936 and Dom, whom Boston Red Sox fans will always remember, came into the league in 1940. However, there was that other DiMaggio brother, the one who always gets "lost in the shuffle," as I see it. Vince DiMaggio, born on September 6, 1912, broke into the majors in 1937 with the Boston Braves of the National League. He was the oldest of the three brothers and the simple truth is, had it not been for Vince, we might never have even had the opportunity to see or hear of Joe and Dom.

There were even more DiMaggio brothers prior to Vince but those boys were expected to work on the fishing boat with their dad. In fact, Vince often said that his older brother Tom was the best baseball player in the family. Tom caved in to his father's wishes and became a fisherman on the wharf in San Francisco but Vince rebelled against his father's old world edicts and pursued a career in baseball, essentially paving the way for his two younger brothers.

Just as talented in the outfield as his brothers, Vince was alas not on the same level when it came to hitting as his younger brothers were. He enjoyed some impressive years with the bat in the minors and even a couple in the majors but he suffered from too many strikeouts. He led the league in strikeouts six times, four times accumulating more than 100 K's in a single season. It was the only offensive category in which he ever led the league. In the field, however, he was highly respected and led the league multiple times in putouts, assists, and double plays as a center fielder. He was also remembered as the most gregarious and social of the brothers compared to his taciturn (Joe) and shy (Dom) brothers.

"Joltin' Joe" as he was called also spent way more time in the headlines of the day. As everyone knows, he played in New York in the largest media market in the U.S., if not the world, at the time, while Vince spent most of his career in Boston (NL) and Pittsburgh and Dom played his entire career for the Red Sox. Joe DiMaggio played in 10 World Series while Dominic was in just the one in 1946 and Vince never made it to a postseason at all. Those things matter when it comes to recognition and legacy.

That said, there was never any doubt that Joe DiMaggio was a winner. He had all the trademarks of a successful competitive athlete; on the field of play he was ruthless, he was single-minded in his pursuit of victory, and he expected more from himself than anyone else. These qualities would solidify as the years went by and make him into one of the great leaders of the legendary Yankee franchise. He suffered with injuries throughout his career, but the pain he endured in his years after the war is what legends are made of.

11 ✦ The DiMaggio Brothers: Joe, Vince, and Dom (1936, '37, '40)

In *Summer of '49* by David Halberstam and *The Hero's Life* by Richard Ben Cramer, both writers tell a story that sheds light on DiMaggio the leader. It was late in the 1949 season and the Yankees were in a bitter fight with the Red Sox and the Indians for the pennant. DiMaggio had missed much of the first half of the season due to injuries; he was battling bone spurs in his heels and one had given way to an awful infection. When he finally did return to the lineup, he was hitting close to .400 and playing like a man ten years younger. The anger of having to sit out the first half of the season only stoked the fires of his competitiveness.

The Yankees were in Washington to play a doubleheader on an oppressively hot August afternoon. The Bronx Bombers won the first game of the doubleheader and Yogi Berra, the young second-year catcher, begged off catching the second game due to the heat. Instead Gus Niarhos caught the second game. Bucky Harris, the Yankee manager, asked DiMaggio if he wanted to rest in the second game but DiMaggio refused. The Yanks lost the second game and Niarhos had come up a couple of times with men on base but could not deliver a hit.

At the end of the game, DiMaggio was so exhausted from the heat and the pain that he was fighting in his legs and feet that Eddie Lopat and Allie Reynolds (two Yankee pitchers) had to practically carry DiMaggio off the field. When DiMaggio saw Berra in the locker room he exploded—he couldn't understand how a 20-year-old kid couldn't play both ends of a doubleheader in the heat of a pennant race. He berated Berra in front of the whole team. For Joe to say more than two words to anyone was rare—for him to show this kind of anger at anyone besides himself was extraordinary. The message certainly got through to the young catcher. From that moment on, Berra would become one of the most durable and reliable catchers in the league.

This story illustrates the leadership role that DiMaggio took in his later years but it also sheds light on the determination and iron will of DiMaggio. According to Cramer, after this game DiMaggio "confessed to his friends, back in New York, that his right heel felt 'like an ice pick was stabbing me.' He ran on his toes and his knees swelled up. Then he got a charley horse in his left thigh: after games, he couldn't lift his leg into a cab. But he'd be back the next morning, extra-early for extra tape. 'How's the leg, Joe?' 'Fine,' would be his monosyllabic answer."

And then there was "Min." That was Joe's name for his brother Dominic who became yet another successful Major League center fielder, for the aforementioned Boston Red Sox, the Yankees' American League rivals. Dom was also highly respected for his abilities as a defensive player although he was also a more successful hitter than Vince. Dom played 10 full seasons and never hit below .283, finishing his career with a .298 batting average and a .383 on-base-percentage. Nevertheless, as respected as Dom was among his peers, Joe DiMaggio became an icon of American popular culture while Dominic DiMaggio became "Joe DiMaggio's brother." Joe set the standard with which Dom was forced to compete. Since both were in the American League and played against one another often, the rivalry with Dom and Joe was more pronounced than it was with Vince and Joe.

The reality was Dom DiMaggio was more than just a capable baseball player. He was a stable, self-assured, hard-working man. He didn't live his life by the standards of others. He just went about his business and worked as hard as he knew how to overcome all the obstacles that were set before him, including his older brother's reputation. In the end, many would argue that, in the big scheme of things, he ultimately accomplished more than his brother Joe.

Popularity does not always breed success. It may bring fame, it may bring fortune, but neither fame nor fortune guarantees happiness. In the case of the two most famous DiMaggio brothers, Joe garnered fame and fortune; Dom found a lesser degree of fame and fortune but a much larger portion of happiness.

Dominic Paul DiMaggio, born on February 12, 1917, was the youngest of nine children born to Giuseppe and Rosalie Mercurio DiMaggio. As alluded to above, Papa DiMaggio didn't understand or appreciate the lure of baseball on his sons. He expected his boys to work hard and earn a living and the respect that came with it. The oldest baseball-playing brother, Vince, bore the brunt of Papa DiMaggio's disdain for the game. However, once Vince and his younger brother Joe showed that there were actually men willing to pay you to play ball, then Papa DiMaggio came around to the American game. In fact, by the time the youngest, Dominic, was in high school his father was asking him when he was going to play.

Dom DiMaggio didn't need too much encouragement. He looked up to his brothers and was happy to follow the path they'd paved for him. The problem was he wasn't born with the same physical gifts as his two older brothers. Dom DiMaggio was short as ballplayers go, only 5'9" tall. He weighed between 160 and 170 pounds and, worst of all for athletes in the 1930s, he wore glasses. There weren't more than a handful of professional athletes at the time that used corrective lenses.

Dom DiMaggio had to work hard for everything he achieved in baseball. He also used his brains. He had a very analytical mind and would never make rash decisions. He studied the game in a very scientific manner. That studious personality along with the glasses he wore, earned him the nickname "The Little Professor."

In *Teammates*, a terrific book by David Halberstam about the special friendship between Ted Williams, Bobby Doerr, Johnny Pesky, and Dom DiMaggio, Halberstam writes about Dom's baseball tryout. "The tryout was held in early 1937. There were, Dom could still recall even 65 years later, 143 boys who turned up, but he still felt optimistic about his chances. He weighed barely 140 pounds ... but he had recently seen an eye doctor, who fitted him for glasses. That had made a huge difference. He could hardly believe how poor his sight had been in the past, how vulnerable he had been in this game where vision was so critically important."

DiMaggio was the number one pick in the tryouts and got his chance to play for the hometown San Francisco Seals. It was a lucky break in more ways than one. Lefty O'Doul was his manager and hitting coach. O'Doul was a lifetime .349 hitter in the Major Leagues and had helped Dom's brother Joe when he was with the Seals. O'Doul recognized the desire in Dom DiMaggio to improve his game and especially his hitting. According to Halberstam, DiMaggio was lunging at balls, trying to put his weight into the pitches. O'Doul taught him that he was actually losing power that way and that he'd get more out of his swing using his legs and hips to greater advantage. Dom DiMaggio always credited Lefty O'Doul with having helped make him a Major League hitter.

Even as the Seals' first pick, DiMaggio had his detractors and doubters. In his own book *Real Grass, Real Heroes*, written with Bill Gilbert, DiMaggio remembers that *San Francisco Daily News* columnist Tom Laird was suspicious of DiMaggio's value. "He wrote a column called 'Looking 'Em Over,' and he kept telling his readers that the only reason the Seals signed me was as a gate attraction because I was Joe's brother."

Laird questioned DiMaggio's ability to play center field because of his unusual style. DiMaggio played center field facing towards left field with his back towards the right fielder as opposed to facing the plate like most center fielders do. He felt it gave him a better jump on balls hit over his head. He was such a strong center fielder that no one ever questioned his ability to get to a ball. DiMaggio remembers that shortly after Laird's column appeared suggesting DiMaggio was on the Seals roster under false pretenses, DiMaggio had a game in which he made a couple of impressive catches on balls hit over his head. After that game, according to DiMaggio, Laird wrote, "Anybody who says this kid can't play is out of his mind."

Years later, when DiMaggio was playing for the Red Sox he reminded Laird of his earlier column but Laird denied writing it. DiMaggio told him, "Tom, I know you did. I have the clippings. But I want to thank you for writing that stuff. You just made me that much more determined to become a success." A DiMaggio never forgets.

On the last day of the 1937 season, Dom DiMaggio was batting .297 and the Seals were scheduled to play a doubleheader against Los Angeles. In the first game, DiMaggio got three hits, pushing his season average above .300. DiMaggio desperately wanted to bat .300 to prove that he belonged in professional baseball.

Lefty O'Doul suggested DiMaggio sit out the second game. This would ensure DiMaggio a .300 season. Dom refused to take the easy way out. The pitcher in the second game had been tough on DiMaggio all season long. He couldn't hit him. He wanted to prove to himself he could hit the guy. DiMaggio got three more hits in the second game and finished the season with a .306 average.

Just four years later, his friend and teammate Ted Williams would be faced with the same situation, the same offer from his manager to sit out, and the same refusal to take the easy way out. The only difference was Williams's final at-bats were for a .400 season. He, too, played both games, got multiple hits, and ended up with a .406 season.

Dom DiMaggio followed up his rookie success with another .307 season in 1938. In 1939, DiMaggio hit .360 with 239 hits and won the MVP award as the top player in the Pacific Coast League. Shortly after that breakout season, he was sold to the Red Sox for $75,000.

In Dom's rookie season in the majors, he once again hit the magical .300 mark, batting .301 in 108 games and scoring 81 runs. He was quiet and observant, careful not to push himself on his teammates. Halberstam writes, "Because he seemed so reserved, almost shy at first, respect preceded intimacy."

In time, friendships grew out of that respect, particularly with the other young Bosox stars, Johnny Pesky, Bobby Doerr, and Ted Williams. The four men would all depart Boston in a short two years to serve their country during World War II. When they all returned in 1946, they led their team to a World Series, falling just short of winning the coveted championship, losing to the St. Louis Cardinals. They would come close, but the Red Sox of Pesky, Doerr, Williams, and DiMaggio would never reach the series again.

It must be remembered that along with Hall-of-Famers like brother Joe, teammate Ted Williams, and Hank Greenberg of the Tigers, Dom DiMaggio was another one of the countless ballplayers whose careers were altered by World War II. Dom was 26, 27, and 28 years of age during those three years he missed due to World War II. He almost certainly would have compiled more impressive numbers and, quite possibly, have been able to move his lifetime batting average above the coveted .300 mark, which, in turn, might have helped him get into Baseball's Hall of Fame.

Ted Williams was always very vocal about his belief that Dom DiMaggio should be in the Hall of Fame. In fact, according to a 2001 article in *Sports Illustrated*, there was even a pamphlet available at the Ted Williams Museum in Hernando, Florida, called "Why Dom DiMaggio Belongs in the Hall of Fame." The pamphlet explained that during the ten years of Dom DiMaggio's career, "only Williams scored more runs (1,144 to 1,046) and nobody had more hits (1,679) than Dom had." There's also a 1951 quote from Casey Stengel that read, "With the possible exception of his brother Dom, Joe is the best outfielder in the league." That's quite a compliment, especially coming from a Yankee manager about a Red Sox player.

In the same *Sports Illustrated* article Dom said, "Joe never expressed an opinion, not to me," when the conversation turned to Joe and the Hall of Fame: "I would have loved him to, but we're not that kind of people. I know that when people used to ask him who was the best defensive center fielder he ever saw, he would say, 'My brother Dom.' But he would never say, 'Dom belongs in the Hall,' because if he had said that and I had gotten in, he knew people would have said, 'Dom's only in because Joe pushed for him.'"

What's probably closer to the truth is that, on some level, Joe DiMaggio was a little jealous of his two baseball playing brothers. Dom became a very successful businessman through his hard work and keen intelligence. Vince, in the last 10–15 years of his life, was a salesman and he'd embraced Born Again Christianity. Dom DiMaggio enjoyed a long and happy marriage to his one and only wife, Emily, as did Vince to his wife, Madeline. Dom and Emily had three children, all successful and accomplished in their own right and by all accounts, they were very close to their parents. Vince and Madeline had two daughters with whom they remained close.

However, in his post-baseball life, Joe became "Mr. Coffee." He certainly didn't fare well in his family life. He was married twice, divorced twice. He had one son, Joe Jr., from whom he was estranged for the last 20–30 years of his life.

As for the brothers themselves, Vince and Joe drifted further apart as the years went by whereas Dom DiMaggio was able to maintain good relationships with both brothers for their entire lives. He was always respectful of the privacy that Joe so closely guarded. It's both ironic and fascinating that Dom DiMaggio was one of the few people in the entire world who was intimately close with both Joe DiMaggio and Ted Williams—two of the most legendary sports icons of the 20th century. The irony comes from the fact that Joe DiMaggio was a silent, introverted, sometimes sullen figure and Williams was at turns arrogant, bombastic, and temperamental. It's a testament to Dom DiMaggio that he found a way to support both men without losing his own identity and dignity.

In the end, it was an incredible accomplishment that three such talented baseball players would come out of the same family. There have been over 400 sets of brothers who made it to the Major Leagues but none accomplished as much collectively as the DiMaggio brothers did. There were 22 All Star appearances between the three brothers which is a record—Vince (2), Joe (13), and Dom (7). The brothers received MVP votes on 20 occasions—Vince (2), Joe (12; three wins), and Dom (6). Had the Gold Glove awards existed during their careers, it's not hard to imagine that every one of them would have won it at one time or another.

Dom brought the three brothers together one last time in the summer of 1986 for an old-timers game at Fenway Park. A short time after that Vince was diagnosed with cancer and died that October at the age of 74.

Dom DiMaggio, who died in May of 2009 at the age of 92, lived a life of accomplishment and merit and to the people who knew him best he was a loyal friend, a smart businessman, a loving family man, and a great ballplayer in his own right. He was the "Little Professor" who accomplished big things.

As for Joe DiMaggio, he will never be forgotten by the sports world. In 1941, Joe DiMaggio set baseball's single season record by hitting safely in 56 straight games. There have been just a handful of baseball records that were thought to be unbeatable; one was Ruth's record of 714 home runs eclipsed by Hank Aaron in 1974 and another was Lou Gehrig's 2,130 consecutive games played which was surpassed by Cal Ripken, Jr.'s, 2,632 games. DiMaggio's record still stands. It was that 1941 season and the phenomenal streak that took DiMaggio out of the lore of baseball culture and made him an icon of popular culture. The big band of Les Brown recorded a tune that summer entitled, "Joltin' Joe DiMaggio." A portion of the lyrics read "Our kids will tell their kids his name / Joltin' Joe DiMaggio."

Nearly 75 years after DiMaggio last played the game, I can assure you that my kids know his name. However, unlike their father who heard about the great DiMaggio from men who saw him play, they hear about DiMaggio from someone who grew up only hearing the legend and maybe that's all that really matters. After all, it was his legend that gave birth in a way to a whole new generation of Italian Americans. In fact, after the DiMaggio era we were all really American Italians as opposed to Italian Americans. "The Great DiMaggio," as Hemingway called him, paved the way for the assimilation of Italian and Sicilian immigrants and gave them a hero of whom they could all be proud.

In 1967, 16 years after his retirement and 26 years after the Les Brown recording of "Joltin' Joe DiMaggio," Paul Simon in his hit song "Mrs. Robinson" asked the question, "Where have you gone, Joe DiMaggio / a nation turns its lonely eyes to you." Well, he may be gone but nearly 60 years after that iconic lyric was written, his impact on the game of baseball and Italian American culture remains.

♦ 12 ♦

John Berardino
(1939)

Johnny Berardino, baseball star and television star.

Many kids dream of a career in professional sports while still more might dream of becoming a TV or movie star. Most never succeed in either pursuit. A very chosen few make it in both. Johnny Berardino was one of the chosen few.

Reading through the clippings of his combined careers in baseball and showbiz, there emerges a split personality seemingly at war with itself. In some articles, Berardino claims that acting was his first love while in others he expresses his devotion to baseball.

John Berardino's first taste of Hollywood was as a child actor in some of the early Hal Roach "Our Gang" comedies. His whole family got caught up in the hype to the point that his father invested a substantial amount of money in a movie starring his son. Unfortunately, the movie never panned out. According to a 1940 interview with Berardino, the actor stated, "My father lost a fortune in [the] movie production. He lost his shirt, in fact, so that ended my movie career—definitely," said Berardino. From that moment on, dad encouraged his young son to focus on sports.

John Berardino was born on May 1, 1917, in Los Angeles, California, to Ignazio and Ann Mussaco Berardino. Both of Berardino's parents were immigrants from the Italian region of Bari. They met in the old country but married here in America. John was one of three children. Growing up, his baseball hero was the Yankees' Italian American second baseman Tony "Poosh 'Em Up" Lazzeri.

The young Berardino excelled on the playing fields of his native southern California as easily as he had in front of the cameras. He played football, basketball, and baseball but it was on the baseball diamond where he felt most at home. Right down the street from where Berardino grew up was a city run park called Yale Playgrounds. It was there that he cut his teeth on the national game. Berardino had all the tools—he could hit, field, and run. He played on his Belmont High School baseball team during the week and made a little extra money on weekends playing semi-pro ball.

Berardino was able to secure a typing job in 1935 with the National Youth Administration at the University of Southern California. Through that position, he was allowed to matriculate as a student at the school. He was asked to try out for football but chose instead to put all his time and efforts into baseball. By the spring of 1937, the sophomore made the grade with the varsity team. Unfortunately, he soon broke his finger diving for a ball but the manager brought him back as an outfielder because he needed the young Berardino's bat in the lineup.

Late in the season, the USC team played an exhibition game with some professional players and at the game Jacques Fournier, a bird dog scout for the St. Louis Browns, spotted him. By evening, Fournier was at Berardino's home negotiating a contract for the young man with Papa Berardino. Initially, Berardino's dad was not enthusiastic about his son playing baseball for a living. Once it was explained to him that his son could make money from this game, he gave his consent. By the end of the school term, Berardino was playing for the Johnstown team of the Middle Atlantic League. His manager was none other than Jacques Fournier.

In 91 games Berardino batted .334 with 122 hits and 12 home runs. He impressed his bosses defensively in the field as well and by the next year, the Browns jumped him from the C Level Johnstown team up to the Triple A level San Antonio team in the tough Texas League. Once again, he hit a solid .309 while punching out 13 home runs in 141 games. He made 38 errors in the field but according to his coaches that was because he made attempts at balls others wouldn't have been able to get near. On the upside, he led the league at his position with 108 double plays.

While playing for San Antonio, he suffered an all too familiar injury. According to an article in *The Sporting News* he was "whanged on the hand by a bad bouncing ball in an early inning, but stuck to his job despite a finger that yelled for relief." Following an examination after the game, it was determined that Berardino had once again broken a finger.

After his one season with the San Antonio team, Browns scout Ray Cahill recommended the parent club bring him up to the majors. "Ordinarily," said Cahill, "the Browns would leave as young a player as Berardino in the minors for at least another year, as he is not subject to the draft and therefore cannot slip out of the organization. However, this boy showed such great class last season that it was decided to bring him up even though he has had only two years' experience in the minors."

Cahill went on to describe Berardino as "tall and rangy and exceptionally fast. He has the big hands a star infielder needs and he owns a strong throwing arm, especially suited for double plays."

"Besides all that," Cahill effused, "Berardino is a smart, scrappy ballplayer who has given every indication that he can stand up under any kind of competition. I don't know how he can miss stardom in major league baseball." So it was that by 1939 he was the second baseman of the St. Louis Browns. In less than two full seasons in the minors, he earned the call up to the big club.

Ray Cahill wasn't the only veteran of the game who recognized potential in Berardino. Berardino's first big league manager, Fred Haney, was also enthusiastic about Berardino's value when he was able to plug Berardino into three different infield positions during the 1940 season as three of his regulars all slumped or got injured.

In a 1940 article written by John Drohan, Haney praised Berardino after he stuck him in the shortstop position without any previous experience. "Of course," Haney continued, "he doesn't know all the tricks of the trade down there, you couldn't expect him to. But on a straight cash and carry basis he'll do as he is for the present and in a year I'm willing to wager all the water in the Mississippi that he'll be the boy the other clubs will want to talk about when they discuss trades with the Browns; something they're always willing to do."

Following the 1940 season, Berardino started acting again at the Community Playhouse in Pasadena, California. The acting bug had not only bitten him again but it would eventually define his future following baseball.

At this point, however, the young Berardino was still a ballplayer first and foremost. The 1940 and '41 seasons were Berardino's best at the plate, driving in 85 and 89 runs respectively. His .271 batting average in 1941 was the highest he ever earned in a full season of play. When you combine those respectable hitting stats with his steady glove and tough, on-field demeanor, Berardino was one of the most valuable players on the Browns' team.

Unfortunately, after December 7, 1941, the landscape and the attitude of America and baseball changed. The country was at war. Berardino enlisted first as an Army Air Cadet on January 19, 1942. He failed to make the grade and washed out as a pilot. He returned, temporarily, to the Browns for 29 games in 1942, hitting .284 before enlisting in the Navy. He spent all of the next three baseball seasons in the United States Navy. Near the end of his tour of duty Berardino was involved in a jeep accident and injured his back. That injury would cause him problems for many years to come.

When he returned from military service, Berardino had a solid year for the Brownies, hitting .265 while driving in 68 runs and scoring 70 more. Once again, he proved to be a dependable defensive weapon in the St. Louis infield. In 1947 he seemed ready to duplicate his performance from the previous year when his season was derailed on June 18 after being hit by a pitch by Red Sox pitcher Dave "Boo" Ferriss. Berardino suffered a fractured left forearm and he finished the season with only 306 at bats and a .265 average.

In the November following the 1947 season, the Browns traded Berardino to the Washington Senators. As soon as the trade was announced, Berardino issued a statement saying he had signed a seven year contract with Richard K. Polimar Productions and he was "through with baseball." The Senators immediately said they would ask the Commissioner's office to look into the trade and determine whether the Browns had prior knowledge of Berardino's decision when they put together the deal with the Senators. Baseball Commissioner "Happy" Chandler decided in favor of the Senators and nullified the deal. One month later, the Browns traded Berardino to the Indians for George Metkovich and cash.

It's difficult to determine exactly what happened during the winter of 1947–48. Berardino supposedly "gave up his Hollywood career" to go to the Indians. Some articles thought it was the showman in Bill Veeck that made him sign this second baseman with Hollywood aspirations. There was probably some truth to that as Veeck eventually insured Berardino's face/profile for $1,000,000 with Lloyds of London. At the time, Berardino was not an established star but the potential of future stardom was supposedly the basis of the policy.

One of the major reasons Berardino accepted the deal with the Indians was because Veeck apparently told Berardino he could make movies in the off-season. However, there were many sportswriters who reported that Berardino was obtained in order to help make a deal with the Tigers for a pitcher the Indians wanted. Whatever the case, no such deal was ever made. Berardino would be a Cleveland Indian for the next two seasons but in a role to which he was not accustomed.

In a March 1948 article Berardino acknowledged that the Indians were planning on using him as a utility infielder. He told sportswriter Ed McAuley, "Naturally I want to play. I'll be miserable if I am kept on the bench for weeks at a time. But I'm not a griper or a clubhouse lawyer. I won't make any trouble. If Lou [Lou Boudreau, the Cleveland manager] thinks the best possible infield is one which does not include me, I'll abide by his judgment."

Berardino went on to say, "But let me tell you this. If one of those fellows goes out of the lineup and I take his place, he'll have some difficulty getting his job back. I believe that I can step into any spot in the infield without weakening it."

Berardino never broke out of the utility role in 1948 but, in fact, played games at every infield position for the '48 Indians. His defense was as steady as ever but the lack of day-to-day play adversely affected his hitting as he finished the season with a .190 average while stepping to the plate only 179 times. Nevertheless, the 1948 Indians went on to defeat the Braves in the World Series and Johnny Berardino proudly wore his 1948 championship ring for the rest of his life.

There wasn't much difference between Johnny Berardino's 1949 season from the previous year except he didn't get a World Series ring. He got into only 50 games and, again, hit just below .200 for his batting average. Early in the 1950 season he was traded to the Pirates. In the 1950 season alone, he played on four teams—the Indians and the Pirates in the majors and Sacramento and San Diego in the Pacific Coast League.

His last full season with one team came in 1951 when he returned to the St. Louis Browns. William DeWitt, club president, announced the signing in January of 1951, saying "We feel very fortunate in getting Berardino. He is a veteran infielder with eight years of big league baseball behind him and should be a steadying influence on our young infield. He has played all four infield positions and always been a favorite with St. Louis fans. He is a family man and because of his age, and the fact that he has three years of military service behind him, should be valuable insurance against future draft calls."

It's obvious that the Browns were getting him for more reasons than what they felt he could do for them at the plate. They wanted a veteran in the young clubhouse and they were also concerned with losing players to the Korean War draft. It had, after all, been only six years since the last war that had decimated the big leagues.

He started the 1952 season back with the Cleveland Indians and finished the season with the Pirates. By now, Berardino was 35 years old and following an injury to his leg, he decided to call it quits on his baseball career.

After he hung up his spikes, there was no doubt that acting was Berardino's future. He took a number of uncredited roles in TV and small films before really starting to establish himself in Hollywood. Eventually, he slightly altered his name to Beradino, removing the second "r," because he said agents and producers had trouble spelling and pronouncing the name.

His first regular role on a television series came in 1954 on the series *I Led 3*

Lives. He played Special Agent Steve Daniels but the series lasted only one season. He continued with roles on shows as diverse as *The Cisco Kid* and *The Loretta Young Show.* In the 1961–62 season he played Sgt. Vince Cavelli in the series *The New Breed.* It was one of the actor's favorite roles but again, it lasted just one season.

Finally, in 1963 he appeared in the first episode of a new daytime serial entitled *General Hospital* as Dr. Steve Hardy. Beradino's portrayal of Dr. Hardy would become one of the most iconic characters in all of TV soap opera history. Berardino played the character for over 30 years until the actor's death in 1996.

Beradino was one of the people instrumental in establishing recognition for daytime programming for the annual Emmy Awards. In 1993 he received a star on the Hollywood Walk of Fame.

In the 1970s and 1980s, John Beradino was always willing and happy to attend old-timers games. It was clear that while he spent more years in front of the cameras than he did on the ball field, he never quite made up his mind as to which held his greater loyalty. Nevertheless, he definitely made his mark as a steady, reliable player in both arenas of entertainment.

♦ 13 ♦

Phil Rizzuto
(1941)

"The Scooter" led the A.L. in fielding percentage twice and double plays at shortstop three times.

Many years ago, my two baseball-crazed sons, then seven and ten, spent the spring and summer pestering me about taking a trip to the Baseball Hall of Fame in Cooperstown, New York. Our family first made the pilgrimage back in 2005 but now the boys were older and knew far more about the game and its history. Their desire to return to the Mecca of baseball history and memorabilia was at a fever pitch.

So it was that we found ourselves in the plaque gallery of the Baseball Hall of Fame on August 15, 2007. As we strolled through the gallery I noticed that one plaque had a spray of flowers draped over it. It was the plaque for Philip Francis Rizzuto, the famed Yankee shortstop, who had just died the day before our visit. As I paid my respects at Rizzuto's place in the Hall, I had to smile as I thought back on this colorful, crazy baseball character.

I was raised by my brother Joe to be a Yankee-hater. There's no real debating the love or the hatred that one feels for the New York Yankees. I could give you a long dissertation on why I feel I cannot root for the New York Yankees but what would be the point? It's enough that everyone knows it's got to be one way or the other—you either love them or you hate them.

That said, I am a lifelong resident of New York State and I've spent the majority of my 60-plus years in Rochester, New York. For as long as my memory allows, I have been able to listen to the games of only two baseball clubs on our local radio—the Rochester Red Wings (our Triple A club) and the New York Yankees. Even though I've always hated the Yankees, I spent decades listening to Yankee games in the hopes of hearing them lose. The first, and for me most memorable, trio of Yankee broadcasters I remember hearing were Frank Messer, Bill White, and Phil Rizzuto.

Yankee fans loved Rizzuto—never was there a more blatant cheerleader in the broadcast booth. However, if you were a guy rooting against the Yankees, as I was, Rizzuto drove you absolutely crazy. He was so biased in his passion for the Yankees that he made you sick. You often wished you could reach into the radio and strangle the little kibitzer. At the same time, you couldn't help laughing, both at him and with him. The truth is, like Howard Cosell, he was such a reliable source of controversial, and sometimes nonsensical, statements that he was a guy you just loved to hate! It didn't matter how boring the game might be on any given night—if Rizzuto was in the booth and the game was plodding along he'd just start talking about the most recent Sinatra concert he'd attended or about the best linguine and clam sauce he'd ever eaten or any other unrelated bit of trivia that popped into his mind. He'd drive the listener and his broadcast partners over the edge. And yet, when he wasn't there—well, we all missed him.

Phil "the Scooter" Rizzuto was born on September 25, 1917, in Brooklyn, New York. Like many of the children of immigrants, his father thought that baseball was a silly game for children and not a job a man could count on to support a family. It was Rizzuto's mother who convinced his father to give their son a chance to follow his dream. However, when he tried out for his hometown Brooklyn Dodgers he was told by the Dodgers' manager, a gentleman named Casey Stengel, that he was too small to play professional ball. He suggested to the young shortstop that he go get himself a shoeshine kit and pursue that as his profession. Little did the sarcastic Mr. Stengel know that years later Mr. Rizzuto would be a primary catalyst on the New York Yankee teams that would win five straight championships from 1949 to 1953. And don't think that Rizzuto ever let his skipper forget that earlier slight although Stengel always claimed to have no memory of the tryout.

For Rizzuto, nothing came easy. He was not given the athletic body that most would think necessary to play alongside some of the giants with whom he shared the field. And that alone may explain why you had to admire Rizzuto, whether you liked him or not. His official height and weight was listed at 5'6" tall and 160 pounds. Many athletes are known to embellish those numbers. That possibility for Rizzuto is a frightening thought. By comparison, consider that Ted Williams, a peer against whom Rizzuto played literally hundreds of games over the course of his career, weighed in at 205 pounds and towered above the diminutive Rizzuto at 6'3" tall. In a book co-written with Tom Horton in 1994 called *The October Twelve*, Rizzuto includes a quote from Ted Williams about Yogi and the Scooter: "Berra could move the runner, and move him late in the game like no one else I ever saw play the game. A lot of people said their shortstop Rizzuto was too small, but, damn, those two guys knew how to beat you. Makes me sick to think about it."

Rizzuto was the kind of player baseball people describe as "scrappy," or a "spark plug." Due to his lack of power in the hitting department, he learned to bunt. In fact, he became one of the game's best bunters and won many a contest for the team known as "The Bronx Bombers" by merely lighting the fuse. Rizzuto was a lifelong promoter of the bunt and the help it could provide to a ball club. He once said, "You can't learn speed or power, but you can learn to bunt."

Rizzuto was chosen to play on five All Star teams and started two of them. He also played in nine World Series between 1941 and 1955, playing in a total of 52 games. While his lifetime World Series batting average was a less than impressive .246, he actually batted over .300 in four of those series. His best stats came in 1942 against the St. Louis Cardinals when he batted .381 for the series. It was one of only two series losses Rizzuto would endure with the Yankees. He would win seven World Series rings and over the course of his full 52 World Series games, draw 30 walks, steal 10 bases, and score 45 runs.

For the fans that got to see Rizzuto play in his prime he may have been the best fielding shortstop of his time. He played the game before there were Gold Glove Awards given out for the best fielder at a given position. However, according to the men that played with him and against him, he would have surely won numerous Gold Gloves. His teammate, pitcher Vic Raschi, once said his best pitch was "anything the batter lines, grounds, or pops to Rizzuto."

But for those of us who only remember the "Scooter" who came to us via the broadcast booth, he was a character. Although the Messer, White, Rizzuto team is the one I remember most vividly, Rizzuto helped develop many broadcast partners over the years. Shortly after Rizzuto's death, all had something to say about his influence on their broadcasting careers and his importance to Yankee history and lore. Jim Kaat, who worked his first season as a broadcaster with Rizzuto, called him "a breath of fresh air in the booth. He always kept you on your toes because you just didn't know what he was going to come out with next."

The late Bobby Murcer also broke into the broadcast booth with Scooter by his side. "I've never met someone so lovable and so talented at the same time," said Murcer. "I never gained so much weight in my life, eating all those cannolis, salamis and cheeses we had each and every day." Former Major Leaguer and retired YES Network analyst Ken Singleton said Rizzuto's "enthusiasm and spontaneity were unmatched in broadcasting. His ability to connect with the fans was unparalleled."

Nearly every broadcast partner Rizzuto ever had recalled a prank that he liked to play, especially on rookie announcers. Around the sixth or seventh inning he'd get up between innings and ask his partner if he'd like a cup of coffee. He'd then walk out of the booth and not be seen again for the rest of the evening, leaving the rookie broadcaster all alone to call the last three innings of the ballgame. The next day Rizzuto would return to the park and enter the booth, cup of coffee in hand, and say "Here's your coffee."

Rizzuto was notorious for leaving the ballgame early to beat the traffic and return home to his beloved wife Cora. He spoke of his wife and family often during broadcasts and in the 1994 book *The October Twelve* he reminisced about how he and his wife first met. He had been asked by Joe DiMaggio to fill in for him at a speaking engagement in Newark, New Jersey, because DiMaggio's wife, Dorothy Arnold, had just given birth to their son. Rizzuto agreed to help out his teammate and showed up in Newark to speak to a church full of people expecting to hear and see The Yankee Clipper. Needless to say, the fans in Newark were disappointed. Rizzuto did his best under the difficult circumstances but later claimed "One priest told me it was the first time he had ever seen someone booed at a communion breakfast, or in church, for that matter."

One of the organizers of the breakfast was a Newark fire chief named Emil Elenborg who took pity on the Yankee shortstop and quickly took him out of the church and brought him to the quiet of his home to rest and have dinner. In his book Rizzuto explains, "He [Mr. Elenborg] told me how little it would all matter the next day and that in a week it would be a faint memory, and here I am writing about the details fifty years later. I heard some activity on the second floor—you could see the top of the stairs from my chair in the living room or parlor. I suddenly noticed two feet moving down the stairs. Then, dancing two steps at a time, appeared a vision in a red sweater and blue skirt. Their daughter, Cora. I didn't think about my reception at the church, Joe, Dorothy Arnold, Joe Jr., or my cake and coffee. All I could think about was I was in love. It has been that way for over fifty years."

When he died in August 2007, Phil Rizzuto was survived by his daughters Patricia, Cynthia, and Penny, his son, Phil Jr. and his beloved wife of over 60 years, Cora.

There are over two hundred men in Baseball's Hall of Fame and almost all of them are there because they were given physical and mental gifts that most of us do not have. Granted, they all worked hard to get the most out of their talent and they made the right choices about how they used those gifts but they were blessed just the same. While Phil Rizzuto entered the Hall of Fame in 1994 as a player, elected in by a Veterans Committee made up of men he played with and against, there's more than a little doubt in my mind that his playing ability alone is what motivated his admirers to elect him.

Phil Rizzuto, to put it mildly, was a force of nature. He was annoying, charming, humorous, opinionated, and he loved the game of baseball. He was both a cheerleader and an ambassador for his team, the New York Yankees, and for the game of baseball in general. He was also an ambassador for his beloved Italian American culture and countrymen.

In David Halberstam's *The Summer of '49*, he sums up Phil Rizzuto's legacy with quotes from his teammates and opponents. Billy Johnson, the Yankee third baseman, once told Ted Williams "…the key to our team [is] that little guy there. Without him we're just another team. You have to be with us to know, because what you see once in a while we see every day." Johnny Pesky, the Red Sox shortstop during those years called Rizzuto "the best shortstop I'd ever seen. He was so quick, with extraordinarily quick feet, he could always make the plays. He was the best shortstop of the era—he held that team together the way Pee Wee Reese held the Dodgers together."

For me personally, he was a member of the dreaded Yankee organization and yet his colorful personality and idiosyncratic traits, more often than not, made the game more fun. Pinstripes or not, he was one of the game's great characters.

♦ 14 ♦

Ralph Branca
(1944)

Ralph Branca. The young hurler won 21 games for the Dodgers in 1947 at the age of 21.

October is the cruelest month ... at least it is for the losers of Major League Baseball's yearly championship. Baseball players have one of the longest and most grueling regular seasons in all of professional sports. When you combine the regular season with spring training games and the amount of playoff games needed to win it all, you approach 200 games from March through October. (In recent years, the season often doesn't end until November.) The further a team goes into the playoffs, the more intense the pressure on all involved. That's why some of the saddest, and most tragic, stories in baseball's long history come from a loss that ends a team's season. The circumstances are that much sadder when the season ends on a bad call by an ump, a dropped ball, a wild pitch, or a walk off home run.

The ledger sheet of baseball's past is filled with good, solid ball players whose long list of positive accomplishments are overshadowed by one bad game or one missed play. There is Fred Merkle neglecting to touch second base after a walk-off hit that lost them the game and resulted in his Giants thereby ending the season in a tie with the Cubs. The Cubs beat the Giants in a one game playoff and moved on to their last World Series victory prior to 2016. While his manager, John McGraw, and his teammates didn't blame Merkle for the loss, just about everyone else did. Unfortunately, all anyone remembered him for was his "bonehead" play that blew the 1908 season for the Giants. He was forever referred to in the press as Bonehead Merkle. When his career ended he wanted nothing to do with baseball. Just a few years later Fred Snodgrass, also playing for the Giants, dropped a routine fly ball in the tenth inning of the final game of the World Series against the Red Sox. He never lived it down. And let us not forget Mickey Owen's infamous drop of the third strike that would have ended the fourth game of the 1941 World Series and led to a two games to two tie with the Yankees. Instead, The Yankees went on to score four runs and win the game and the series.

The names of baseball's goats, whether fairly remembered for their miscues or not (usually the ignominy is unfair) are many, from Bill Buckner to Johnny Pesky to Bob Moose to Donnie Moore. (Tragically, Moore killed himself three years after he gave up a home run that prevented his team from reaching the World Series.)

And there is one more very well-known name in this pantheon of players whose careers ended up being remembered for one fleeting moment instead of a lifetime of hard work. That man is Ralph Branca.

Branca, of course, is the victim of Bobby Thomson's "Shot Heard 'Round the World" on October 3, 1951. The home run that won the pennant for the New York Giants and left Branca as the most famous goat in baseball history. New revelations would come to light many years later about the Giants stealing signs but it did little to salvage Branca's unjust fate.

Branca was born into a large Italian American family, one of 17 children. Three of his brothers made it to Class B ball but only Ralph, the tallest of the group at 6 feet, 3 inches tall, made it to the big leagues. As a kid, his older brothers Ed and Julius would take him to games at the Polo Grounds and so he became a Giants fan. Mel Ott and Carl Hubbell were his heroes but especially Hubbell, the Hall of Fame screwball pitcher. In Fay Vincent's book of interviews with baseball stars of the 1950s and 1960s, entitled *We Would Have Played for Nothing*, Branca told the author, "Hubbell was a really great left-hander. I remember sitting in the bleachers in the Polo Grounds and watching his screwball go the other way and marveling at it."

As a 16-year-old in 1942, Branca went to open tryouts for all three New York teams. The Giants never even let him pitch. The Yankees watched him but thought he was too young. The Dodgers paid close attention and asked to see what pitches he had. When he graduated from high school in June of 1943, he signed with the Brooklyn Dodgers.

He wanted to join the Navy as a pilot. However, he'd had asthma and a punctured eardrum as a kid so he didn't pass the physical for the special Navy program he wanted to join. He still thought he might get drafted in January of 1944 when he turned 18 but again he was rejected. So in the summer of 1944, instead of pitching bombs for Uncle Sam, he was pitching baseballs for the Dodgers' farm club in Montreal.

By the end of the season the Dodgers brought him up to the big leagues to get a look at what he could do. In *We Would Have Played for Nothing*, he recalled his first appearance in the Major Leagues was June 11, 1944, in the Polo Grounds. "I remember walking from that bullpen," said Branca, "and it seemed like I was on a treadmill—I kept walking and walking. And believe it or not, I struck out the first three guys. I got Mel Ott to pop out. My boyhood hero. Threw a fastball inside."

He pitched 44 innings in 21 games for the remainder of the '44 season, compiling a 0–2 record with one save and a 7.05 earned run average. Not a very impressive beginning but he was only 18 years old.

In 1945 he started 14 games for the Dodgers' St. Paul farm team, earning a 6–5 record with a 3.33 ERA in 100 innings pitched. He again made the jump to the Dodgers and this time started 15 games and finished with a 5–6 record and an impressive 3.04 ERA in 67 innings pitched. He was now officially a Major Leaguer.

As a kid coming up to the big leagues he was surprised and a little shocked to see guys smoking and drinking. His first roommate was Hall-of-Famer Paul Waner. Branca remembered that on his first road trip to Boston Waner woke up in the morning and reached for a bottle under the bed. Branca said, "He takes out a bottle. They had these round tumblers, and he filled it about that high and said, 'This is my orange juice.' I said, 'Okay.' But he said, 'Don't tell anybody.' I said, 'No, I wouldn't say a word.' But that was a funny experience. The first road trip I took."

He would later room with Clyde King, Gil Hodges and others and learned a great deal just talking baseball with his teammates day and night. The Dodgers were a close group. He was a particularly good friend of Jackie Robinson, the man who broke the color barrier in baseball in 1947. Robinson appreciated the fact that Branca refused to sign the petition that some Dodgers sent around the clubhouse in 1946 saying they didn't want to play with a colored ballplayer. "I played with blacks my whole life as a kid," said Branca. "So when Jackie came along, it didn't mean anything to me because they lived next door to me."

In 1946 Branca went 3–1 with a 3.88 ERA with only 67 innings pitched. Brooklyn couldn't quite overcome the St. Louis Cards and finished two games behind the Redbirds for the pennant. The year 1947 would be very different for both the Dodgers and Branca.

Ralph Branca won 21 games in 1947 at the age of 21. He was one of the youngest pitchers ever to win 20 games in a season. He led the league in starts with 36 and was third in ERA behind only Ewell Blackwell and Warren Spahn with a 2.67 mark. He was named to the All Star team and pitched in two World Series games, losing a Game One start and then picking up the win, relieving Vic Lombardi in Game Six. Except for the Dodgers losing the series to the Yankees in seven games, it was the greatest year of Branca's career.

Branca seemed well on his way to back-to-back 20-game seasons as he breezed to the All-Star break of the 1948 season with a 12–5 record. However, in a game in St. Louis, Branca was behind home plate playing pepper when an errant throw from infield practice struck him in the leg and he fell to the ground. The team doctor looked at the leg and told Branca he was fine to continue his regular routine which included running before games. The result was that his leg got infected and the infection spread to his arm. He won only two more games and finished up the season with a 14–9 record. "I remember my leg got swollen up," Branca said. "They called it periosteomyelitis; the lining of the bone got infected."

Despite a 13–5 record in 1949, according to Branca the leg continued to trouble him. In 1950 he was used as much in the role of a reliever as he was a starter. Even though he won 20 and lost 14 during the 1949 and 1950 seasons, his earned run average did increase by an entire point. He started the 1951 season as a reliever. By the end of the season he had started 27 games and compiled a 13–12 record with a 3.26 ERA down from 4.69 the previous season.

In the second week of August the Dodgers were leading the National League by more than 13 games. They went into the Polo Grounds for a three-game series with the Giants and lost all three. It was the beginning of the end. When the season finished, the Dodgers and Giants were tied. This led to a three game playoff that finished on that fateful October day at the Polo Grounds.

Branca spent years denying that "the home run" defined his life. As time went on, he admitted to his understandable annoyance at constantly being asked about one pitch from a 12-year career. At dozens of Old-Timer Games for decades after the event, he was asked to pitch to Bobby Thomson, to essentially recreate the lowest moment of his professional life. That he even bothered to show up says something about the man and the sense of security he had as a person.

In 2001, an article appeared in the *Wall Street Journal* by Josh Prager that provided Branca with a taste of vindication. The story revealed that just before the Giants began their incredible 37–7 run to finish the season, they acquired a ballplayer named Hank Schenz from the Cubs. Schenz told one of the Giant coaches, Herman Franks, that he had a powerful telescope from his days in the Navy and he brought it in to show Franks. The Giants ended up planting the telescope in the Giant clubhouse, which was above center field at the old Polo Grounds. From there, they could focus it on home plate and steal the catcher's signs. They hooked up a buzzer into the bullpen and using a simple system of codes, the player in the bullpen would signal the hitter to tell him what kind of pitch was coming—fastball, curve, or changeup.

In *We Would Have Played for Nothing,* Branca tells Fay Vincent, "[Back] then, Bobby Thomson was reluctant to say that he got the sign on that pitch. He got them during the year, and he got them during the game, but that time up, he says his mind was elsewhere. Well, to be truthful, I find it hard to believe, because if you're used to doing it for seven weeks, you're going to do it in that situation. I'm not taking anything away from him. He hit what I thought was a real good pitch. I give him credit because he hit a tough pitch, but I say—and he's been a friend of mine for years—I say, 'I give him credit for hitting the pitch, but this should not have been a play-off.'"

History makes strange bedfellows and due to one pitch and one swing taken decades ago, Ralph Branca and Bobby Thomson will forever be inextricably linked together. And while Thomson probably didn't mind having his career remembered for a walk-off home run, Branca deserved better.

Branca hurt his back after that 1951 season and never fully recovered his pitching power. He finished his career with an 88–68 record and a 3.79 earned run average. He went on to have a very successful career in the insurance business. He and his wife had two daughters.

In 1986 he was asked to join the board of B.A.T., the Baseball Assistance Team, and was made the organization's first president. The organization helps out former ballplayers who are in need of financial, psychological, or physical assistance. While most ballplayers today make millions of dollars a year, there are thousands who participated in the game long before multi-million dollar paychecks were the norm. In an essay written by Branca in 1993 he talked about his experiences as a member of B.A.T. "I saw the case of a pitcher who spent ten years in the big leagues, and when his youngster died, B.A.T. had to pay for his funeral," said Branca. "There was an outfielder I had pitched against who was suffering from Alzheimer's and his wife couldn't pay the rent, so B.A.T. paid it. And there was a former pitcher and father of three young kids who suffered from such severe depression that he had been declared permanently mentally disabled. BAT helped him, too."

"B.A.T. has been a learning experience for me," said Branca. "I always knew that I had been lucky. But, until B.A.T., I didn't know how lucky."

Ralph Branca died in November of 2016. Those who knew him as a cherished teammate, a fierce competitor, a devoted husband and father, a successful businessman, and a caring, charitable human being recognized him as a man whose life was about much more than a single pitch. If only those plaudits could be heard 'round the world.

◆ 15 ◆

Carl Furillo
(1946)

Carl Furillo, "The Reading Rifle," one of the best outfielders of the 1950s and strong at the plate as well, winning the 1953 batting title with a .344 average.

When I began to fall in love with baseball in the early 1970s, I learned as much about the history of the game as I could—baseball fans, in general, are like that. For me however, as the late and last child of Depression-era parents, history was something more than dusty, inconsequential relics of the past. I was always fascinated by my parents' childhood and the culture in which they grew up. I spent many a day and night fascinated by the tales I'd hear from them and their peers. So as I began to follow the day to day adventures of players named Stargell, Bench, and Seaver, I also began to read and study about the day to day adventures of the players who had come before them—guys like DiMaggio, Williams, Musial, and Campanella.

One of the guys who fascinated me from a very early age was Carl Furillo. I guess I was attracted to Furillo for a number of reasons although the initial attraction was definitely his name. I recognized the Italian name and the first time I saw a picture of him, I recognized the face as well. Hell, he could have been at any one of my family reunions over the years. He just looked strong, solid, and serious ... and very Italian, or may I be so boastful as to say, Sicilian. When you dig into the story of Carl Furillo you find a man that many would describe as strong, solid, and serious. And he was definitely Sicilian.

Roger Kahn, author of *The Boys of Summer*, the quintessential history of the Dodgers in their heyday, wrote that "Carl Anthony Furillo was pure ballplayer. In his prime he stood 6 feet tall and weighed 190 pounds and there was a fluidity to his frame you seldom see.... He had the look of an indomitable centurion." Sports columnist Maury Allen once described Furillo as a "tough, talented, uncompromising guy who spoke his mind. He was a lunch-pail kind of baseball player, unafraid of a concrete wall, a high and tight fastball, or any attempts at intimidation."

I've known many men like Carl Furillo in my lifetime. So many of the men of my father's generation, "the greatest generation" as they've been called by Tom Brokaw, were like that. The difference with Furillo is that, for a while at least, he was on the center stage with the greatest sports heroes of a beloved era in American history.

My father wasn't a sports fan but my brother Joe was and he was, and is, an avowed Yankee-hater and, therefore, so was I. Naturally then, the team I fell in love with from "the past I never even knew" had to be the legendary Brooklyn Dodgers, "the Boys of Summer." The greatest team that always seemed to fall just short as they spent nearly 20 years battling the mighty Yankee ball club. For me, the Dodgers were the quintessential team of the postwar period, a team that represented the "little guy," the working class neighbors of America's favorite movie suburb and "state of mind"—Brooklyn, New York. They were the team that opened the game up to men of all races by hiring Jackie Robinson in 1946. And, they were a team that employed a number of children of the immigrants who came to America in the early part of the 20th century and made us a world power, "children" like Andy Pafko, Gene Hermanski, George "Shotgun" Shuba, Sandy Koufax, Roy Campanella, and "The Reading Rifle," Carl Furillo.

When I was a kid, my dad and I would go out on Sunday mornings to buy the bread for our afternoon meal and at the bakery he'd pick up a copy of the *New York Daily News*. For years I kept an article that I cut out one Sunday afternoon about Carl Furillo. The article was a "Where is he now?" type of piece that told how he'd become a sheriff's deputy in the Pennsylvania town where he was born. A few years ago, I realized I no longer had the article among my treasured mementos, no doubt a casualty of a basement flood we endured not long after we moved into our current home. However, on a recent trip to the Baseball Hall of Fame in Cooperstown, New York, I found that same article in Carl Furillo's player file. The title reads, "Furillo Now Strong Right Arm of the Law" and it's dated February 23, 1975. The article, by Red Foley, begins "Carl Furillo's right arm, which once dissuaded enemy base runners at Ebbets Field, sliced salami in a Flushing delicatessen and wielded a hammer during the construction of the World Trade Center, is now swinging a nightstick." I was as happy to find that one article in the files of the A. Bartlett Giamatti Research Center in Cooperstown as any of the nuggets of gold I unearthed that day because it had been that article that initiated my curiosity all those years ago to learn more about the man they called "The Reading Rifle."

I always wondered why Furillo was rarely talked or written about in the sports magazines of the 1970s. His lifetime statistics seemed to indicate to me that he was a vastly underrated and under-appreciated ballplayer. I was especially interested in him because he was an outfielder respected for his fielding abilities and his powerful throwing arm. The reasons for Furillo's "anonymity" were complex and many. *The Daily News* article was just the first clue to the Furillo mystery. It wasn't until I actually read Kahn's *The Boys of Summer* years later that I began to understand the saga of Carl Furillo.

In one of the most poignant chapters of a poignant book, Roger Kahn wrote about Furillo in a chapter entitled "The Hardhat That Sued Baseball." In it he talked to Furillo about his playing days and about the controversy that ended his career in 1960 and clouded the years that followed. In 1958 Furillo had reluctantly moved to Los Angeles with the Dodgers and, at the age of 36, hit a solid .290 while driving in 83 runs. In 1959 he played only 25 games in the outfield and served primarily as a pinch hitter—again he finished the year with a .290 average and drove in the winning run in one of the Dodgers' World Series games against the White Sox.

Then, early in the 1960 season, while running out a ground ball in the less-than-even infield of the Dodger Coliseum, Furillo tore a calf muscle. While Furillo was sitting out with the injury, the Dodgers gave him his unconditional release. In a time before players had agents, lawyers, and a union to watch out for their rights, Carl Furillo felt betrayed by the organization to which he had given his all for 15 seasons. His pride was also hurt because Buzzie Bavasi, the Dodgers' general manager, did not tell him to his face but had an underling deliver the blow.

Furillo, who quit school after the eighth grade, pored over his contract in the days following his release and mined the following nugget from it: "Disability directly resulting from injury ... shall not impair the right of the Player to receive his full salary for the period of such disability or for the season in which the injury was sustained." With his pride injured and his livelihood taken from him and his family, Furillo sued the Dodgers for the $21,000 that was still due him on his 1960 contract. He eventually won the court battle but lost the war for his livelihood as he claimed for years that his legal action had blacklisted him in baseball so that no team would hire him. It was a sad and bitter end to what had been an illustrious career.

Carl Furillo was born March 8, 1922, in Stony Creek Mills, Pennsylvania, as the youngest of six children to immigrant Italian parents. He worked since childhood and, like most of the children of the immigrants, gave most, if not all, of what he made to the family pot. His mom died in March of 1940 and soon after he signed a baseball contract with an independent club from Reading, Pennsylvania. The story goes that the Brooklyn Dodgers bought the Reading ball club for anywhere from $1,500 to $5,000 for all the ballplayers, including Furillo, and the team bus. Legend has it that they were really after the bus but got the greatest right-fielder in the history of the franchise in the bargain.

In 1942, Furillo was promoted to the Dodgers top farm team in Montreal, the Royals. He played there for a season under Clyde Sukeforth before he was drafted in November and was assigned to the 77th Infantry division. Furillo's war service would eventually land him in the Pacific theater where he took part in the Battle of Okinawa. He returned to the states in January of 1946 but was unsure if there was still a future for him in baseball. In a 1955 newspaper article by Michael Gaven, Furillo was quoted as saying "I didn't think I had a chance and certainly no major league hopes when I reported to the Dodgers camp for GI's at Sanford in 1946."

In the same article, Furillo went on to say it was the young Branch Rickey, Jr., who convinced his father to give Furillo an extra chance that spring of 1946. Furillo was rusty from his years away from the game but the younger Rickey felt that Furillo had something special. Even as the patience in waiting for Furillo's skill to blossom paid off, Furillo's troubles with the front office also began. "I was promoted to the Dodger squad after they got to Daytona Beach," Furillo told Gaven. "That night the waiters at the hotel where the Montreal club was staying decided to throw me a farewell party. It was in my room. Clay Hopper (Montreal manager) found all the bottles in my room. He told Durocher. I insisted I had only two beers but he accused me of lying. I wasn't but I think my so-called feud with Leo started right there." (Rickey later told Furillo that they had him tailed by a private detective and the report came back that Furillo was nothing more than a "one beer drinker.")

There are myriad clues to Furillo's basic personality in the previous paragraph. Furillo never forgot a guy who treated him fairly—the young Branch Rickey, Jr. He was always more comfortable with the blue-collar types—the waiters at the hotel. He didn't know how to lie—if he had he would have gotten into a lot less trouble for remarks he made to the press over the years. And most significantly, there was no "so-called" feud with Durocher—it was a full-blown vendetta.

When Durocher was manager of the Dodgers he didn't think Furillo was an everyday player. He platooned him with Dick Whitman, a .259 lifetime hitter who played six seasons with the Dodgers and the Phillies. Durocher was also convinced that the right-handed hitting Furillo could not hit right-handed pitching. Furillo proved Durocher to be wrong on all accounts. As a rookie in 117 games in 1946, Furillo batted .284. "The next year I was negotiating my contract and the Dodgers offered me $3,700," Furillo once told columnist Maury Allen. "I told Durocher I couldn't live on that. He said, 'Take it or leave it.' I never forgot that."

The bad blood between Durocher and Furillo really began to boil in 1949. Burt Shotten was now manager of the Dodgers and Furillo was playing every day, hitting at a .300 clip, driving in runs, and having the best year of his career. His old skipper Durocher was now managing the Dodgers' bitter enemies, the New York Giants. The old Dodgers–Giants rivalry of the 1950s made the Yankee–Red Sox games of the 1970s–2010s look like a series of loving family reunions. In a game at the Polo Grounds, a pitcher named Sheldon Jones beaned Furillo in the head. When Jones visited Furillo in the hospital to apologize, he told him that it was Durocher who had ordered him to hit the Dodger star. Furillo had already suspected as much and his desire for revenge began to seethe.

Furillo finally snapped late in the 1953 season. In another game against the Giants, Furillo stepped in against a rookie pitcher named Ruben Gomez. Gomez pitched the ball and hit Furillo in the wrist. As Furillo trotted up the first base line Durocher yelled to him from the visitor's dugout and Furillo made a beeline for Durocher and the Giant bench. Two Giant players stepped out ahead of Durocher to protect their boss. Furillo tossed them both aside and grabbed Durocher in a headlock and was choking him when the full-blown melee blossomed. In the scuffle Furillo and Durocher were knocked to the ground and Furillo ended up with a broken finger. At the time it was reported that someone had stepped on his hand but years later Furillo insisted there were no spike marks on his hand because Durocher had bent his finger back and broken it in the fight. Furillo was forced to sit out the rest of the season and he ended up winning the batting title with a .344 average.

There was another famous Furillo feud with Giant ace Sal Maglie. Maglie, known as "The Barber" because of the close shaves he gave batters with the high and tight fastball, used to regularly dust Furillo off the plate just as he did all the batters he faced. However, Maglie being a Giant and pitching for Durocher, Furillo took umbrage to Maglie's style. Years later Maglie would join the Dodgers and Furillo and Maglie put aside their differences and worked together to help their team win a pennant. A friendship developed between the two old warriors that observers found miraculous. But never with Durocher—Furillo carried that grudge to the grave.

One final Furillo controversy has to do with Jackie Robinson's joining the team in 1947. It was reported at the time that there was a group of Dodgers in spring training who were getting together a petition to let it be known to management that they would not play alongside a black man. Through the years there have been numerous story lines and a variety of player names who supposedly signed a petition. The names that frequently come up are Kirby Higbe, Bobby Bragan, Dixie Walker, Pee Wee Reese, Hugh Casey and Carl Furillo. No physical evidence of any petition has ever been produced although many people and players connected to the 1947 team recalled some aspect of the incident. (Reese would later help speed up Robinson's acceptance to the Brooklyn ball club by his on-the-field show of solidarity for his African American teammate.)

Furillo's recollection was of a group of the southern players in the spring training barracks talking about putting together a petition to keep Robinson off the club. "So I got up—I was only a rookie at the time—and I went over to where they were talking," Furillo recalled, "and one of them asked me what I would do if Robinson was after my job. So like a dumb jerk I came out and I made a remark like 'Well, I'd cut his legs off.' That was stupid for me to even say, but it came out, and from that day on I was pulled on the carpet because I was one that was supposed to be against Robinson. The whole thing was too bad because really, I didn't care who the hell came up. I was only a rookie at the time. I had a lot of friends who were colored in my hometown, I played against colored and I got along with everybody."

Lester Rodney, an iconic sportswriter with the *Daily Worker* who covered Jackie Robinson's story, wrote of Furillo, "He wasn't a bad guy. Originally he was hostile to integration, but he changed. He's the guy that changed before your eyes.... [Furillo] became one of Jackie's best friends on the Dodgers...."

A much more in-depth and fascinating account of the Furillo-Robinson relationship and other aspects of Furillo's life can be found in a fine biography written in 2011 by Ted Reed entitled, *Carl Furillo: Brooklyn Dodgers All-Star.*

During my research at the Baseball Hall of Fame I discovered that the *New York Daily News* article about Furillo in February of 1975 was only one of many "where is he now" type articles done on Furillo over the years. Some articles described Furillo as being bitter and angry at the fact that no one would hire him after his litigious break with the Dodgers. Other articles talked about Furillo's being past any bitterness and grateful for the years he had as a Dodger player. What's interesting is the attitudes seemed to change back and forth over the years from grateful to bitter to grateful again. The picture one draws from the various reports is of a man who felt betrayed, a man who'd been promised the moon but ended up with nothing more than a handful of stardust.

Carl Furillo was a simple man with Old World values and a tireless work ethic. At his funeral, his old teammate Carl Erskine eulogized him saying, "I remember how tough he was, how strong he was, how consistent he was as a player. But he also had great sensitivity and tenderness. Our old manager, Charlie Dressen, when he wanted to compare things, he would say they were 'like dirt and ice cream.' Carl Furillo was like steel and velvet."

♦ 16 ♦

Joe Garagiola
(1946)

Three Hall of Famers (from left), Stan "The Man" Musial, Joe Garagiola, and "Lawdy," aka, Yogi Berra (National Baseball Hall of Fame, Cooperstown, NY).

Joe Garagiola and Larry "Yogi" Berra grew up together on "The Hill," the Italian section of St. Louis, Missouri. Joe was signed to a contract by the hometown Cardinals at the age of 16 while Yogi was rejected as being too small. One scout gave the highly technical argument that Berra just didn't look like a ballplayer. Garagiola went on to have a nine-year career in the big leagues, earned a World Championship ring with the 1946 Cardinals, and finished with a .257 lifetime batting average. Berra went on to an 18-year career with the New York Yankees, 10 championship rings, and a Hall of Fame induction seven years after his official retirement as a player.

It seemed to many that Berra finished far ahead of his pal Joey in the success sweepstakes but consider this: Garagiola went on to have three more highly successful careers as a sportscaster, writer, and television host and in July 2014 was honored by the Baseball Hall of Fame for the second time in his life when he was awarded the Buck O'Neil Lifetime Achievement Award for his extraordinary efforts to enhance baseball's positive impact on society. "Supposedly I made a career out of putting words together, but at this moment, I cannot express what it means to me to receive this honor," Garagiola said in December of 2013 when informed of the award.

A child of Italian immigrants, Joseph Henry Garagiola was born on February 12, 1926, in St. Louis. In a June 1946 article in *The Sporting News*, written by Frederick Lieb, Garagiola is quoted as saying, "When I was 14, the WPA ran a baseball school at Sherman Park. Dee Walsh, the Cardinals scout, saw me there and asked me to come to Sportsman's Park." The Cardinals were impressed enough to invite Garagiola to spend the summer of 1941 with the Cardinals' Springfield team of the Western Association. He was too young to be given a contract but he worked in the clubhouse washing socks and doing odd jobs and was allowed to catch batting practice and work out with the team. By 1942, at the age of 16, he was signed by the club and sent to Springfield as a player.

John Garagiola, a laborer who worked in the brickyards of St. Louis, was somewhat suspicious as to why anyone would be willing to pay good money to his young son to play baseball. It took a little persuading but eventually the young Garagiola and Branch Rickey, the Cardinals' general manager, convinced Papa Garagiola that baseball was an honorable profession. A variety of articles from Garagiola's playing career, however, indicate that neither of his parents ever really understood the fuss and affection that Americans devoted to the game of baseball.

Garagiola wasn't too pleased with his first season in pro ball as he finished the season in Springfield with a .257 average. The Cardinals, on the other hand, thought his showing as a 16-year-old was good enough to earn a promotion to the Columbus club of the American Association for 1943. In Columbus, Garagiola began to come into his own, catching 62 games and compiling a .293 average for the season.

He caught opening day for Columbus in 1944 before Uncle Sam grabbed him and he was drafted into the United States Army and sent to the Pacific. He ended up in the Philippines where he caught for Kirby Higbe and the Manila Dodgers. His seasoned play along with some mammoth home runs that he belted out of Manila

Stadium caught the attention of many of the Major League players and coaches who were stationed there. When he returned to the states after the war his reputation preceded him and he was immediately put into the Cardinal lineup in May of 1946.

It was a magical season for the Redbirds as they fought the Brooklyn Dodgers for the National League pennant. The regular season ended in a tie and the two teams were forced into a one-game playoff to see who would go to the World Series to take on the American League champion Boston Red Sox. Garagiola caught the crucial playoff game and drove in two runs in the Cardinals' 4–2 victory over the Dodgers. The rookie continued his solid play in the World Series, garnering a .316 average while driving in four runs in five games as the Cards defeated the Red Sox to become the champions of baseball. It was quite a whirlwind season for a rookie.

In a 1947 publication called *Sportfolio*, Garagiola is quoted as saying "I thought my biggest thrill came when I caught my first game. Then I thought it was when the fans from the 'Hill' had a 'night' for me at the ballpark. Then the playoffs. Then the Series. I couldn't tell you what I got the biggest kick out of."

Unfortunately, the rest of his career was not as positive an experience as his rookie year. He shared catching duties with Del Rice in 1947 and after getting off to a rocky start in 1948 was sent back down to Columbus. He rejoined the parent club in 1949 but again shared duties with Rice while batting just .261 for the year. In 1950, he suffered a shoulder separation and saw action in only 34 games although he did bat .318 and drive in 20 runs in his limited service. He began the 1951 season with the Cardinals before being traded to the hapless Pirates.

The 1952 Pirates were the worst team in the Major Leagues, managing to win only 42 games, but the stories Garagiola reaped from that dreadful campaign furnished him with a mother lode of comic gems that he used to entertain dinner crowds and as part of his first book, *Baseball Is a Funny Game*, published in 1960. Garagiola remembered the '52 Pirates as "the most courageous team in baseball. We had 154 games scheduled, and showed up for every one. We lost eight of our first nine games and then we had a slump."

The Pirates traded him midway through the 1953 season to the Chicago Cubs along with Ralph Kiner. He hit .276 with the Cubbies but was released in September of 1954 and picked up by the Giants, who were on their way to a pennant and eventually a World Championship. He was excited to get back on a contending team until he learned what the Giants and manager Leo Durocher had in mind when they picked him up. According to Garagiola's account of joining the Giants, "I came bouncing into the locker room about a foot off the ground. Durocher said, 'Kid, I'm going to let you catch today so my regular catcher, Westrum, won't get hurt.'" Garagiola played only five games for the Giants in September of 1954 and was not put on the postseason roster. At the end of the season, he announced his retirement from the game.

Garagiola had been laying the groundwork for his post-playing days from the very beginning of his baseball journey. In the 1947 *Sportfolio* profile it is mentioned that "Garagiola spent much of his off-season time as an unofficial Cardinal goodwill ambassador, appearing at luncheon meetings for civic groups, speaking at banquets and lending his time and name to charitable causes." Once his career was over Cardinal owner August Busch, Jr., hired him to become an official ambassador for the team and the parent company, Anheuser-Busch. His duties eventually led him to the Cardinals' broadcast booth and the beginning of a long and profitable career behind the mike.

He started his broadcast career on KMOX Radio in St. Louis where the legendary Harry Caray mentored him. Garagiola recalls, "I had a lot of help and I needed it. Off my first play-by-play, I wouldn't have hired myself." He led the way for the influx of former players into the broadcast booth. His work as an announcer was both praised and criticized through the years depending on the source but one thing that was never questioned was his passion and love for the game. In a July 1973 article in the *Washington Post*, Lawrence Laurent wrote, "Beneath the jokes about baseball and behind all those funny stories about his boyhood friend, Yogi Berra, is always an unmistakeable [sic] and strong current of reverence for baseball."

Some purists frowned on Garagiola's use of humor in the booth but the same *Washington Post* article quoted Garagiola as saying, "You don't need to worry about the true sports buff. He'll be there. You do need to worry about the fringe-fans. You need them, and you have to prepare shows that will appeal to them."

Ultimately, Garagiola's humor and devotion to the game did appeal to a universal audience. In 1962, he stepped down from his position with the Cardinals to accept a network job with NBC and spent most of the 1960s calling the Game of the Week, All-Star games, and the World Series.

Garagiola's national exposure led to more and more jobs in front of the camera. He was soon making appearances on *The Tonight Show with Jack Paar* and game shows like *What's My Line* and *The Match Game*. His association with NBC also led to his contributing stories to *The Today Show*. By 1968, he was invited to join the show full-time as a co-host with Barbara Walters, Hugh Downs, and Frank McGee. Some predicted he would flop but once again, Garagiola's energy and enthusiasm carried him to success. President Johnson once introduced him to a diplomat saying, "Turn on your TV set tomorrow morning and you'll see this fellow. I watch him every day."

He left *The Today Show* in 1973 but his workload never lessened. He guest hosted for Johnny Carson on *The Tonight Show* and he was the host of a game show called *Sale of the Century* from 1971 to 1974. He began hosting a pre-game show for *Monday Night Baseball* in 1973 called *The Baseball World of Joe Garagiola*, for which he would win the prestigious Peabody Award for excellence in television. By 1976, he was back in the broadcast booth calling the *Baseball Game of the Week* on NBC with Tony Kubek as the color analyst.

In 1983, NBC brought in Vin Scully to announce the Game of the Week and moved Garagiola into the color spot. By late in the '83 season, the *New York Times* wrote, "That the duo of Scully and Garagiola is very good, and often even great, is no longer in dispute."

Garagiola's big thrill came in February 1991 when the Baseball Hall of Fame announced that Garagiola would be inducted into the broadcast wing of the museum as the 1991 winner of the Ford C. Frick Broadcasting Award. "The Hall of Fame!" Garagiola said. "My God, Rickey wouldn't believe it! I couldn't hit my way in here. I talked my way in instead."

By the mid–1990s, Garagiola moved to Phoenix and became an announcer for the expansion Arizona Diamondbacks, whose first general manager just happened to be Joe Garagiola, Jr. He spent 18 years behind the mike for the Diamondbacks before finally calling it quits in 2013 at the age of 87.

Once Garagiola's schedule slowed down to just the one broadcasting job with the Diamondbacks he looked to find more projects to fill his time. In 1994, he helped create NSTEP, the National Spit Tobacco Education Program, to educate baseball players and the American public about the dangers of smokeless or spit tobacco. As a former ballplayer and one-time user of smokeless tobacco, Garagiola was drawn to the cause by witnessing the health issues and even fatalities in former ballplayers and friends.

He was also a founding member of B.A.T., the Baseball Assistance Team, which began in 1986 as an organization to help former Major League players who have fallen on hard times. It has since expanded its scope of coverage to help former major and minor league players, umps, scouts, front office personnel, Negro League players, and women from the Women's Professional Baseball League.

For many years, the big leaguers who played the game between 1947 and 1980 received nothing in pensions or healthcare coverage. Following a 2002 lawsuit by former players, pleas from the MLB Alumni Association, and reams of bad publicity for MLB, Bud Selig announced in 2011 that the Collective Bargaining Agreement would pay $10,000 a year to the affected players ... through 2016.

The Baseball Assistance Team has spent 40 years trying to help those individuals who've suffered to keep up with inflation, rising health costs, and various family tragedies. Garagiola was on the forefront of the crusade to help these forgotten individuals. In 2011, Joe Garagiola was honored with the very first B.A.T. Lifetime Achievement Award for his dedication and hard work in helping his former baseball brothers and sisters.

His list of accomplishments is long but perhaps Garagiola's most personal cause was the St. Peter Indian Mission School on the Gila River Reservation in Bapchule, Arizona. Garagiola first heard about the school in 1993 and soon met with Sister Martha, the school's principal. Garagiola remembered asking her what her first priority for the school was. "I thought she was going to say a computer room or something," Garagiola recalled. But she said, "A basketball court. It would tie the kids together since it would be in the middle of the school ... but most important, kids would come after school to play. They would get attention they weren't getting at home. That impressed me." He was a devoted benefactor forever after.

Through the years, Garagiola obtained buses and sports equipment for the school, uniforms and sneakers for the students, built a baseball field, and created the "Ira Hayes Wall" in honor of one of the Marines who helped raise the flag on Iwo Jima in World War II. Hayes was a Pima Indian. "My goal is to instill self-esteem," Garagiola said. For his dedication to the school and their community, one of the tribe's spiritual leaders dubbed Garagiola, "Awesome Fox."

Garagiola once said, "Every man is entitled to one dream. Mine was to become a major league baseball player and to play in a World Series. That's enough for a man. Then, to have a second career like the one I have is like having a second dream come true." You can't begrudge Garagiola his good fortune because with his success, he made sure that many other people's dreams came true as well.

♦ **17** ♦

Yogi Berra
(1946)

Yogi at his museum in Little Falls, New Jersey (courtesy Scott Pitoniak).

Yogi Berra is one of the great success stories in American history. The son of Italian immigrants started playing baseball in the junkyards of St. Louis using old magazines as shin guards and ended up playing in Yankee Stadium on ten World Championship teams. The press teased him because of his penchant for reading comic books while his roommate, Bobby Brown, read medical books studying to become a doctor. Berra has since written and/or contributed to nearly a dozen books. Yogi Berra was a man who would go to a movie before he'd ever set foot in a museum and now there's a museum all about him. As his immigrant parents might have said, "Only in America."

Larry Berra, or "Lawdy" as his friends and family called him as a kid (his immigrant mother couldn't pronounce Larry so it came out Lawdy), was born in May of 1925 on "The Hill" in St. Louis, Missouri, one of the most famous Italian neighborhoods in America. He and his boyhood pal Joey Garagiola spent their days playing sports—or as much of their day as their fathers would allow. Like most immigrant fathers of the time, Signori Berra and Garagiola couldn't understand the American fascination with games. Bums played games, men worked.

One thing that many of the immigrant parents did understand was education. The better educated you were, the better job you could get. Unfortunately, "Lawdy" had no interest in school. As soon as he was able he begged his father for permission to quit school. His father finally agreed that maybe he'd be better off working than trying to skip school every day. At least this way he could bring some money into the house.

He started off working in a coal packaging plant but he hated it. On nice days, he'd sneak out early to play ball. His employers eventually let him go so he'd be free to play as much as he wanted. His father grew more and more frustrated with his youngest son. Finally a meeting was held with Berra's dad, older brothers, parish priest, and local YMCA coordinator. After much debate, it was agreed to let Larry try to pursue his dream of playing baseball for a living. His parents still didn't understand but they were helpless to convince him of anything different. It went without saying that once he failed to achieve this ridiculous dream, he'd be forced to settle down and find a real job.

He spent two years playing American Legion ball on a club that went to the semifinals of the National American Legion Tournament. The team lost both years but the experience only increased Berra's confidence and exposure. The leader of the American Legion Post contacted a writer on the *St. Louis Globe-Democrat* to tell him about Berra. He wrote a letter stating that "He [Berra] does everything wrong, but it comes out right."

It seems ridiculous now but the truth is that the way Berra "looked" would actually hold him back.

When Berra and his friend Joe Garagiola tried out for the hometown St. Louis Cardinals, it was Garagiola who was given a bonus to sign. The Cards weren't interested in Berra. He did get some interest from Branch Rickey and the Dodgers but they were not offering a bonus and Yogi's pride told him he should get a bonus just like his boyhood teammate, Garagiola. The other St. Louis team, the Browns, also showed some interest in Berra but the problem was that he didn't "look" like a ballplayer. Berra started to think he'd never get the chance to play professional ball.

"Ever since I had been a little kid, I had been used to having the other guys laugh at me because of my looks and poke fun at me because I was so clumsy, but I had always been as good a ballplayer as any of them and better than most of them, so I never minded," said Berra. "Now, for the first time, I didn't even have that. Nobody wanted me as a ballplayer."

In the summer of 1942, his pal Garagiola was off to begin his career as a professional ballplayer. Berra got a job at a shoe factory and made some extra money on the side barnstorming and playing semi-pro ball. The Cardinals defeated the Yankees that year in the World Series and soon after Berra received a visit from a man named Johnny Shulte who identified himself as the bullpen coach for the New York Yankees. He offered him a contract to play on the Yankee farm team in Norfolk, Virginia, for $90 a month. That was great but what about the bonus? The Yankees offered him a $500 bonus to sign. He was overjoyed and happily signed the contract that took him one step closer to achieving his dream.

The Yanks had been tipped off about Berra from a guy named Leo Browne who was something of a bird dog scout in the St. Louis area. Browne was a friend of Johnny Shulte and sent a letter to him about Berra, stating, "All this kid wants is $500 to sign. Whatever you want to give him a month, he'll take it."

Berra wasn't yet 18 so his father had to sign the contract for him. He was initially sent to the Kansas City Blues in the American Association but when the season began he was sent down to the Norfolk Tigers in the Class B Piedmont League. A problem arose when even after Yogi began the season, he or his family hadn't received the $500 bonus check. When he asked the team office about it he was told the bonus was contingent upon him making the Yankee squad. Larry Berra had learned his first big league lesson in contract negotiation and reading fine print. He wouldn't make the same mistake twice. In the years to come, he would prove to be one of the toughest and shrewdest negotiators in the business. He was never arrogant or cocky but Berra always had a healthy sense of his own worth.

The war interrupted the start of Berra's career. He joined the navy and participated in the D-Day invasion of Omaha Beach. Because of the comic persona that grew up around Berra, it seems hard to think of him as a war hero or a husband or a father. He's always seemed more a character rather than a flesh and blood person. What's closer to the truth is that while Berra was certainly a colorful ball player, he was also a man with great strength of character as well.

When he returned to the states, Berra was transferred to a submarine base in Connecticut. They put him on recreation duty but as a boxer, not a baseball player. Again, he didn't look like a baseball player! Eventually, he convinced the manager to let him play and he quickly showed them that while he didn't look like a ballplayer, he could certainly play like one.

Many years later, Berra would tell the story to Dave Kaplan for the book *Ten Rings: My Championship Seasons* about how he was summoned into the Yankee offices in New York near the end of his navy service. He had played against Mel Ott on one of the barnstorming teams and Ott was impressed. So impressed that he called up Larry MacPhail, the new chief of the Yankee ball club, and offered $50,000 for Berra.

As Yogi described it to Kaplan, "MacPhail never saw me but figured if the Giants were offering that kind of money, I must've been worth keeping. He figured he better meet me, so on a weekend liberty I went into the Yankee offices on Fifth Avenue in my navy uniform. MacPhail kind of looked me over, and I think his heart sank. As he said later, 'Here was a funny-looking guy in a sailor suit. He had a homely face, no neck, and the build of a sawed-off weightlifter. My first thought was, Do I turn down $50,000 for this? Never have I seen anyone who looked less like a ballplayer.'"

When he was finally discharged, Berra was sent to play with the Newark Bears. In 77 games with the Bears, Berra hit .314 and knocked out 15 home runs. Many of the coaches in the organization agreed that Berra had the raw talent. The question was whether he could refine it enough to play in the Major Leagues. The one man who believed that Berra had the makings of a big league catcher was someone who knew a little about the subject—his predecessor and future Hall of Fame catcher, Bill Dickey. It would be Dickey who would ultimately be given credit for refining Berra's skills and turning him into a first-rate backstop.

Just like his pal Garagiola, Yogi didn't have to wait long to get into a World Series. In his first full season as a Yankee, 1947, Yogi and company faced the crosstown Brooklyn Dodgers in the fall classic. It was a ritual that would be performed repeatedly over the next two decades. Although he'd ultimately end up being remembered as one of the greatest postseason players in the history of the sport, his first World Series was less than auspicious. He batted only .158 despite hitting his first World Series home run. Even so, the Yankees prevailed over the Dodgers and Berra enjoyed the first championship celebration of what would be many. From 1947 to 1963, Berra participated in 14 World Series with the Yankees and took home ten World Series Championship rings.

Berra's teammate and close friend Phil Rizzuto co-wrote a book with Tom Horton called *The October Twelve*. The title refers to the 12 players that formed the core of the history-making New York Yankee team that from 1949 through 1953 won five World Series in a row—a feat never accomplished before nor equaled since. The "October Twelve," as Rizzuto dubbed them, were Charley Silvera, Bobby Brown, Jerry Coleman, Johnny Mize, Joe Collins, Vic Raschi, Allie Reynolds, Eddie Lopat, Gene Woodling, Hank Bauer, Yogi Berra, and Phil Rizzuto.

Rizzuto, who had played three seasons with the Yanks before Berra came on board full-time in 1947, became one of Berra's closest friends on the team. In fact, the two of them eventually went into business together as owners of a bowling alley in New Jersey. In his book, Rizzuto describes Berra as one of the most secure men he ever knew. "Yogi could be in a room with you for an hour and feel no need to say anything," said Rizzuto. "He is happy with himself. He is sure you are happy with him, and if you are not, it is your problem."

The one place where Berra did a lot of talking was behind the plate. "As our catcher," said Rizzuto, "he was great at talking. I somehow think he thought it was part of his job, like putting on the shin guards. [Ted] Williams hated a blabbermouth catcher, which Yogi was, but he could not hate Yogi. 'Have a good dinner last night?' Yogi would ask. 'The food is all bad here in New York.' [Williams responded] 'If you leave a tip, the food gets better,' Yogi would say and even [Allie] Reynolds might wish the two guys at home plate would shut up and the little one would give him the sign."

While everyone likes to make jokes about Berra, everyone agrees that Berra was no joke between the foul lines. Not only was Berra an integral part of the great Yankee dynasty of the 1940s and 1950s but he was one of the greatest all around players of his era. When he retired as a player after the 1963 season, Berra finished with 358 home runs, the most by a catcher in the history of the game up to that time (Mike Piazza now holds the record with 427). He also won three MVP awards—one in 1951, 1954, and 1955. He still holds, or is tied, for at least a half-dozen different World Series records including those for At Bats and Hits. He was elected to Baseball's Hall of Fame in 1972.

He is remembered as both a fierce competitor and someone who had a great time playing the game. His baseball acumen was so well developed that Casey Stengel, Yankee manager from 1949 through 1960, used to identify him as "Mr. Berra, my assistant manager." Following his playing career, he did become a manager and led the Yankees to the World Series in his first year at the helm, 1964. Berra would become one of only three managers in baseball history to lead teams from both leagues to a pennant when he managed the Mets to the World Series in 1973.

Volumes could be written about Lawrence Peter "Yogi" Berra. In fact, volumes *have* been written about this colorful baseball legend. Ironically, as great a baseball player as Yogi Berra was, he became most famous for his verbal malapropisms over the course of his playing career and beyond. He's been called the most quoted man in sports history. Even though Yogi himself told people that "he didn't say everything he said," there were pearls of wisdom that even he couldn't deny. For example he once said, "Nobody goes there any more, it's too crowded." In his 1998 book, *I Didn't Really Say Everything I Said*, Yogi explained, "I was talking to Stan Musial and Joe Garagiola in 1959 about Ruggeri's Restaurant in my old neighborhood in St. Louis. It was true!"

Most famous is his oft-quoted philosophical insight first uttered by Yogi during the 1973 pennant race when it seemed the Mets were all but out of the race. Yogi just smiled and told reporters, "It ain't over 'til it's over." It may seem funny or silly but in the unpredictable world of sports, no truer words have ever been spoken.

The name "Yogi" was apparently given to him by an old friend from the neighborhood who said that when Berra sat with his legs crossed he reminded him of a yogi from India that he'd seen in a motion picture. Whatever the origins, it's become the most famous nickname in all of sports for one of the most beloved figures in the history of any game.

Yogi Berra remained active in and around the game of baseball for years after his retirement. He even had a museum of his own called The Yogi Berra Museum and Learning Center on the campus of Montclair University in Little Falls, New Jersey. Not too bad for a guy who never finished high school.

His granddaughter, Lindsay Berra, produced a documentary on her grandfather's life and career in 2022 for Netflix entitled, appropriately enough, *It Ain't Over*.

Yogi Berra died on September 25, 2015, at the age of 90. He may have started off as a joke to many but ended up with the last laugh on all those who doubted him. "Yogi" Berra's entire life was a testament to the fact that "it ain't over 'til it's over."

♦ **18** ♦

Vic Raschi
(1946)

Vic Raschi, the "Springfield Rifle."

When I first got out of college I worked as a production assistant and grip (both nice, professional sounding words for grunts and/or gofers) for a local film and video production company that specialized in commercials and industrial films. Quite often, we'd work with the same freelance crew people around town. One of the hardest working and most capable persons I met through this work was a young woman not much older than I was at the time by the name of Mitje Raschi. With the first name Mitje and her fair complexion and dirty blonde hair, I assumed she was of German extraction. We'd made small talk here and there but I never got to know her very well.

One day during a lunch break I must have been talking about one of my million ideas on preserving and celebrating the culture of the past through books or films, and during this particular burst of enthusiasm, my focus must have been baseball. Mitje looked at me very nonchalantly and said, "Yeah, someday I'd like to do something with all of my dad's old World Series films." I looked at her rather quizzically. Then I remember thinking to myself, "Mitje RASCHI." As only a master of the obvious could do, I looked at her and said, "Your father wasn't Vic Raschi?" She smiled and said, "Yes, he was." Here I had worked on and off with this woman for probably three or four years and I never knew she'd been the daughter of a star pitcher of the 1940s and 1950s. Sure he was a New York Yankee, but nobody's perfect!

Sometime around 2006, I began to make periodic visits to Cooperstown for the purpose of doing research in the Baseball Hall of Fame Library. I would spend my days in the A. Bartlett Giamatti Library and Research Center, poring over the files of many of the men about whom I've written in this book: Carl Furillo, Tony Cuccinello, Zeke Bonura, Phil Cavaretta, Babe Pinelli, and Vic Raschi. The Hall of Fame's library is an absolute treasure trove for fans that love the history of the game as I do. While the stories and literature on players like Mickey Mantle, Willie Mays, Babe Ruth, Ted Williams, and Yogi Berra abound, there's far less material to be found in the mainstream media about the great role players of the past like Vic Raschi.

Raschi was born in Springfield, Massachusetts, in March of 1919. His father, Simon, came to America from Northern Italy and became a lumberjack in the woods of Maine. He eventually found his way to Springfield where he worked for the railroad. Young Victor John Raschi was a natural athlete and played all kinds of sports growing up. Raschi considered basketball his strength but Yankee scout Gene McCann spotted young Vic as a sophomore in high school and signed him to a conditional contract. McCann watched Raschi's progress through high school and semi-pro ball.

Upon graduation from high school Raschi wanted to attend Manhattan College, which was a college basketball powerhouse at the time. However, when he went to register at Manhattan he was too late; the class was filled up and they were accepting no more applications. The Yankees told him about William and Mary College, where they periodically sent some of their young ballplayers, and that's where he enrolled to work towards a degree in physical education. The Yankees gave him $150 spending money for the year so he got a job in the cafeteria to supplement his income. It was there that he met his wife Sally.

In 1941 he was signed to a chain contract and sent to the Yankee club in Amsterdam, New York. In 1942 he was sent up to Newark but after only seven weeks he was called into the Army Air Forces. He spent the next three years in the States working for Uncle Sam as a physical training instructor. He was discharged in November of 1945 and went back to Conesus, New York, his wife's hometown. He was told to report to the Binghamton club in March of 1946. Near the end of the '46 season he was called up to Newark, finished their season with them and went back home. As soon as he arrived home, he received a call to join the Yankees. He pitched two games for the big club and won them both.

He trained with the Yankee team during the spring of 1947 but was ultimately sent to the Portland farm club in the Pacific Coast League. Midway through the season, although the Yankee pitching staff had suffered some injury setbacks, the Yanks were winning and Raschi assumed he wouldn't be called back up to the Bombers until at least the next season, 1948.

In an article by legendary sportswriter J.G. Taylor Spink in the August 13, 1947, edition of *The Sporting News*, Raschi tells Spink the story of how he actually did get called up to the big club in July of 1947. "I pitched the second game of a night double-header in San Diego," Raschi said. "The time was 12:20—after midnight. I had taken four straight; I had won eight and lost two for Portland. I was jubilant. But very tired. Turner [his manager] came up to my locker and said, 'Vic, do you suppose you could be ready to work on Sunday. This is Thursday. Not much time to rest. But they will be needing you Sunday.'"

"I wondered who 'they' might be. And I replied that I would be ready to pitch Sunday. 'Well,' said Turner. 'You won't be pitching for us any longer. You have been recalled by the Yankees and Harris [Yankee manager Bucky Harris] wants you to work in Chicago on Sunday. That means you have twenty minutes in which to shower and dress and catch that plane headed for Portland.' I made the plane, then flew to Chicago. I went 48 hours without sleep, dashed into Comiskey Park and worked the second half of a double header."

Naturally, he won. A habit that he would continue for nearly ten years as he became one of the most successful pitchers in Yankee history.

He finished the 1947 season with a 7–2 record but pitched only minimally in the 1947 World Series. In 1948 the Yankees were beat out of the pennant by the Bob Feller/Larry Doby–led Cleveland Indians but Raschi emerged as a force to be reckoned with, compiling a 19–8 record and a 3.84 earned run average.

Despite the Yankees' not making the postseason in 1948, Raschi nevertheless earned a special distinction in that summer's All-Star game. In fact, in 1970 Raschi described the game to journalist Dennis Lustig by saying, "The highlight of my career was the All-Star Game in 1948. I knocked in the winning run with a single and was the winning pitcher."

Raschi was a fierce competitor whose focus was always on winning. At 6'1" and 200 lbs., and seemingly always sporting a two-day growth of beard, Raschi went out of his way to be an intimidating figure on the mound. According to writer David Halberstam in his superb book about the Yankee–Red Sox pennant race of 1949 entitled *Summer of '49*, Allie Reynolds, Raschi's pitching mate on the Yankees, once observed, "Vic pitched angry." Prior to the game Raschi would sit silently on the bench scowling and building his anger towards whatever team he was facing that day. He'd get particularly indignant if anyone tried to talk to him on the mound. It was common for him to yell at Yogi Berra to get back to home plate if/when Berra ever tried to come out to the mound to calm his pitcher down or relay a message from manager Casey Stengel.

When Raschi first came up with the Yankees he was good but did not yet possess the great concentration and determination that would define his career. Yankee pitching coach Jim Turner saw the potential in Vic Raschi and developed it to the fullest extent. He taught Raschi to be more of a cerebral pitcher. He taught him the necessary breaking pitches to set up the young hurler's fastball.

It was also Turner who taught Raschi to view the hitter as the enemy. Turner once told Raschi, "Vic—those hitters are your enemy. If they get their way you're out of baseball," he would say. "I've seen pitchers with talent who might have made the major leagues but they didn't hate the hitters enough." Raschi always credited Turner as a great teacher and pitching coach.

Raschi would quickly become the anchor of a pitching staff that would make history, along with the whole Yankee squad, as they won five World Series titles in a row from 1949 to 1953. In that five-year period the Yanks won 487 regular season games with the trio of Raschi, Eddie Lopat, and Allie Reynolds winning 255 of those games. In the World Series the trio's dominance was even greater, winning 15 of the 20 World Series games the Yankees won in that historic streak.

Raschi was always known as a "big game pitcher." His competitiveness was one of those intangibles that teammates and managers could always count on to help a ball club when the pressure was on. Evidence of that is the game at the end of the 1949 season against the Red Sox to decide which team would go to the World Series. It was Vic Raschi who got the call.

The 1949 pennant race between the Bosox and the Bombers was such an epic contest that David Halberstam wrote an entire book about it, the aforementioned *Summer of '49*. His descriptions of that final regular season game of 1949 present Raschi as a man on a mission with no plans for failure. "At last Raschi went out to the mound, and started to pitch. Within minutes he was pleased. Everything was working that day; he had speed, placement, and his little curve," Halberstam wrote. "And he was pleased to be pitching against Ellis Kinder. Kinder was tough, too.... Kinder would almost surely pitch well and make the game close. Raschi wanted that; he wanted a close game where the pressure was on the pitcher."

Raschi and Kinder battled for seven and a half innings to a scoreless tie. In the bottom of the eighth Red Sox manager Joe McCarthy, playing the percentages, pulled Kinder from the game with left-handers Berra and Tommy Heinrich leading off the bottom half of the inning. The Yankees ended up scoring five runs off the Red Sox relievers. In the top of the ninth, Raschi gave up three runs, two on a fly ball that the injured Joe DiMaggio couldn't reach. After the play, DiMaggio took himself out of the game.

With two outs, a man on first and Bosox catcher Birdie Tebbetts coming to the plate, Halberstam wrote, "Tommy Heinrich was playing first, and he walked over to Raschi to give him a small pep talk, to remind him that he needed only one more out. 'Give me the Goddamn ball and get the hell out of here!' Raschi snarled. Heinrich turned, and grinned to himself. We've got it, it's a lock, he thought, there is no way Birdie Tebbetts is going to get a hit off this man right now."

And of course, Birdie didn't. The Yankees won the pennant and went on to win the first of their five championships in a row.

Raschi's World Series record was 5–3 with a 2.24 ERA. As good as those numbers are, they're a bit misleading. In the 1949 series he was 1–1. The game he lost was a 1–0 defeat at the hands of Dodger pitcher Preacher Roe. Raschi pitched eight innings giving up just one run in the loss. In Game Five he was winning 10–2 going into the seventh. He let up a bit, allowing the Dodgers to break through with four runs in the bottom of the inning. Regardless, the Yanks and Raschi won the game and the series. Even so, the four runs served to inflate his World Series ERA.

The ERA was a statistic that plagued Raschi at other times during his career. Yankee GM George Weiss often used Raschi's ERA numbers against him during contract negotiations. What Weiss failed to realize was that Raschi was not the type of pitcher to concern himself with individual stats. He didn't worry about his ERA. He just believed that as long as his team gave him some support, he'd be able to do whatever was necessary to win. Weiss's parsimonious nature caused a great deal of animosity between him and many Yankee ballplayers. However, when Weiss dealt Raschi to the Cardinals after the 1953 season without first informing the pitcher, Raschi never forgave him.

One thing that few people knew, particularly his opponents, is that Raschi played much of his career in pain. He had broken his leg at age nine and it left him with a slight limp. During the 1950 season he suffered an injury to his right knee in a home plate collision with Cleveland catcher Jim Hegan. He had an operation on it in 1951 but then re-injured it in a fall that winter. In a 1987 article for *William & Mary*, Raschi's alumni magazine, Mickey Mantle is quoted as having called Raschi "a battler, always pushing himself to the limit of his abilities ... playing much of his career on damaged knees."

Raschi pitched in 30 less-than-memorable games in the National League as a member of the St. Louis Cardinals. However, he did do one thing while with the Cardinals that made history. He gave up the first Major League home run to a rookie named Henry Aaron.

Raschi was always very proud of another distinction. For 13 years, Raschi held the record for the most RBIs in a single game by a pitcher with seven. Tony Cloninger of the Braves broke the record in July of 1966 but Raschi still holds the record for pitchers in the American League.

Only one other Yankee pitcher, Spud Chandler, had a better lifetime winning percentage as a Yankee than Vic Raschi. Chandler's winning percentage was .717 and Raschi's was .706. However, Chandler won three World Series rings while Raschi retired with six.

Vic Raschi left baseball after the 1955 season. Although the war had interrupted his studies, he did graduate from William and Mary in 1949. He and his wife Sally had three children, including Mitje, and for the last 20 years of his life he owned and operated a liquor store in the small town of Groveland on Conesus Lake in upstate New York. Upon his sudden death in 1988 at the age of 69, he was remembered by his fellow townspeople as "the most down-to-earth person you could imagine ... a considerate, generous person."

His baseball records show him to be the most successful pitcher on the most successful team in baseball history. What the records don't show is that in addition to the rings, the awards, and the accolades, Vic Raschi also had the heart and soul of a champion.

◆ 19 ◆

Sam Mele
(1947)

Sam Mele was a steady ball player who found more fame as a manager, leading the Twins to their first pennant in 1965.

"I like the way he swings that bat … he's a great hitter, make no mistake about that. I love to watch him hit." Ted Williams made that statement in 1946 about a young rookie that was coming up with the Boston Red Sox named Sam Mele. The young outfielder hit .302 in his rookie year with the Red Sox in 1947. He never hit .300 in a season again but he lasted 10 years in the Major Leagues as a player and was considered an excellent defensive outfielder. He also had one of the best baseball minds in the game which is why at the age of just 39 he became the manager of the Minnesota Twins in 1961.

Sam Mele is not a name that's well remembered among baseball fans today but from the late 1940s right through the 1990s, Mele was a solid baseball man. He knew the game and he knew it well. In fact, he literally grew up with the game. Mele's two uncles, Tony and Al Cuccinello, both played in the Major Leagues during the 1930s. Al Cuccinello played just one year with the New York Giants in 1935 but Tony Cuccinello was a 15-year veteran (1930–45) with the Dodgers, Braves, and White Sox. Tony also spent another 20 years as a Major League coach. The Cuccinellos were his mother's brothers so baseball, you could say, was in his blood.

Sabath Anthony Mele was born on January 21, 1922, in Astoria, Queens. Some records list his birth date as 1923 but, as Mele told SABR (Society for American Baseball Research) writer Bill Nowlin in 2006, "[My uncles] told me 'cheat a year on your age because you'll last a year longer in the big leagues.' So I did."

Mele's parents Anna and Antonio were immigrants from Avellino, Italy. They met and married in America and raised a family of seven children. Mele remembers playing stickball on the dirt road in front of his home with a broomstick and a rubber ball. Mele told Nowlin, "If you could hit on a dirt road, you could hit in the damn Major Leagues, the way the ball bounced. Up and down, all directions."

He never played any organized league ball until his freshman year at Bryant High School. Unfortunately, the school dropped the baseball program following his freshman year and so he began to play in community leagues. His uncles continued to teach and inspire their young nephew. Baseball talk was all around him in his home and through the Cuccinellos he got to meet baseball Hall-of-Famers like Al Lopez (Uncle Tony's good friend and teammate) and Babe Ruth. "It was amazing," Mele recalled. "When I went away to play ball, I knew more than the damn managers that I played for because of those guys."

Sam Mele may have grown up with baseball but the truth is, he was a much bigger basketball star in his youth than he was a baseball player. He received a basketball scholarship to NYU and in 1948, sportswriter Ed Rumill wrote of Mele, "Had Sam stayed with the court game he would by now be wearing the uniform of a pro team.…"

At NYU, Mele was a standout in both basketball and baseball. He broke his leg sliding into a base in 1940 and still came back in 1941 and hit .405 for the NYU Violets. When he hit .369 in 1942, he began to get serious attention from a number of scouts. The Cubs, Braves, Tigers, Dodgers, and Senators were all interested in him.

His NYU coach, Bill McCarthy, promoted football games at Fenway Park during the off-season and knew people in the Red Sox organization. McCarthy drove Mele up to Boston on occasion and Mele was allowed to work out with the Red Sox. There he took batting practice and received batting tips from the greatest hitter of them all, Ted Williams. Following one of the batting practice sessions, Mele remembered, "I walked around and this guy called me over and it was Ted Williams. He explained to me about batting, and from that day on, whenever I'd see him ... he took a great liking to me for some reason."

In 1942, the Cubs and Senators made offers but for very little money. Mele's uncle, Al Cuccinello, was acting as his representative and the Red Sox scout, Neil Mahoney, told them not to sign with another team until they checked with the Red Sox first. Eventually, Mahoney brought Mele and Al Cuccinello to New York to meet with Red Sox owner Tom Yawkey. The Sox offered him $5000—$2500 up front and $2500 when he returned from the service. Sam Mele signed with the Red Sox that day.

The war was on and Mele had signed up for the Marines knowing he was going to be drafted. He did his training at Yale and while there, played on the service team under former big leaguer Red Rolfe. In a matter of months, they sent Mele to California to play with the Marine team. He eventually traveled to Hawaii and other bases in the Pacific and played against other Major Leaguers such as Phil Rizzuto, Barney McCoskey, and Joe DiMaggio.

Mele was honorably discharged in 1946 and reported to the Red Sox training camp that spring in Florida. He was initially sent to AAA Louisville but struggled, hitting just .226 after 15 games. The Red Sox moved him to A-level Scranton in the Eastern League where he proceeded to hit .342, leading the league in batting, triples and total bases while being named league MVP.

He might have returned to Louisville in 1947 but gave such a strong showing during spring training that the Red Sox decided to bring him north with the team. Despite winning the American League pennant in 1946, the Red Sox had tried five different players in right field. In 1947, the position was won by Mele and the Red Sox couldn't have been more thrilled as he hit .302, drove in 73 runs and belted 12 homers.

Red Sox manager Joe Cronin wisely made Dom DiMaggio the young rookie's roommate on the road so the veteran outfielder could pass on his knowledge of the game to his young charge. In a 1948 interview, Mele told Ed Rumill, "Dom was wonderful to me. What a swell break for a rookie to room with a guy like him. He told me how to play the hitters, what to look for against certain types of pitching and all that. A million things. He even told me the mistakes he made as a kid, so that I could profit by them."

As for DiMaggio, he was equally effusive in his praise of Mele. "Sam will be a great ball player because he wants to be," DiMaggio told Rumill. "He has that intense love for the game that is a must with all great ball players. He thinks about it, studies it, and is always trying to learn. He'll sit and listen just as long as you'll talk to him."

"Ted Williams, Joe Cronin and some of the others were swell, too," Mele told Rumill. "Ted emphasized the importance of studying the pitchers—the sort of stuff they throw and what that stuff does. He used to say, 'Study your pitchers, too, Sam, because you never know when they might be pitching against you.'" However, when it came to the art of fielding, Williams didn't even attempt to help the young outfielder. Mele would run out to left with Williams after hitting practice and Williams would tell him, "Go on over with Dom. He can teach you a lot more about this racket (fielding) than I can."

Unfortunately for Mele, Cronin moved to the Red Sox front office in 1948 as general manager. The new field manager was ex–Yankee skipper Joe McCarthy. McCarthy quickly made Mele change his wide open stance at the plate to a more closed stance and it adversely affected Mele's batting. His .233 average for 1948 was 65 points lower than his rookie year. Mele also lost a ball in the sun on opening day and Mele felt McCarthy held it against him. Whatever the reason, Mele only got into 66 games in 1948. He began the '49 season hitting an awful .196 before he was traded to the Senators. In 78 games with the Senators, he hit .242 and drove in 25 runs.

In his two full seasons with the Washington Senators in 1950 and 1951, Mele batted .274 both seasons and drove in an average of 90 runs. He also led the American League with 36 doubles in 1951. He began the 1952 season hitting .429 before he was traded to the White Sox. He finished the year with a .259 average.

The year 1952 was also when Mele was pictured on a baseball card with a tattoo on his right arm. Most baseball card collectors agree that this was the first known instance of a player depicted with a tattoo on a trading card.

He spent the first half of 1954 with the Orioles before being picked up off waivers by the Red Sox in July. As a role player with the Bosox, he hit .318 in 42 games. He made two more stops in the big leagues with Cincinnati in 1955 and Cleveland in 1956 and then spent two more years in the minors before he officially ended his playing career following the 1958 season. Mele was known as one of the best outfielders in the game during his 10-year career. Unfortunately, the annual Gold Glove Awards for fielding weren't initiated until the year after Mele retired in 1957.

He spent 1959 and 1960 as a coach with the Senators and made the move with the team to Minnesota in 1961. He was named manager after the Twins let Cookie Lavagetto go during the 1961 season. It was a tough situation as Mele and Lavagetto were good friends. "I hated to see Cookie go," Sam said. "But, in this business a friend often replaces a friend, so I took over."

Mele finished the 1961 season as the Twins' manager with a less than stellar 47–54 record. When the Twins started slow in 1962, it seemed as if Mele would be an early casualty of the season. However, the team got hot and finished with 91 wins, just five games behind the pennant winning Yankees. It was the first time the Twins/Senators finished with 90 or more wins since 1933. In September of 1962, Mele's uncle and Chicago White Sox coach, Tony Cuccinello, told John Carmichael of the *Chicago Daily News*, "He [Mele] sort of grew on people. The Twins players couldn't quite get close to him at first, or felt they couldn't, but now they're crazy about him."

By 1962, Mele's uncle Tony Cuccinello was the bench coach for his old pal Al Lopez, who was the manager of the White Sox. Cuccinello told the *Chicago Daily News* that Sam would often call the Chicago clubhouse after the game for advice. "He's done that every so often ... since he became manager," said Tony. "Asks advice. Always asked questions. Always wanted to learn."

Mele's inquiring mind certainly paid off. He won 91 games again in 1963 but this time the Twins finished third behind Uncle Tony's White Sox and the American League Champion New York Yankees. The Twins suffered an off year in 1964, dipping just under .500, and, according to a July 1965 article by Charley Feeney, "[Twins owner] Griffith indicated Mele's days were numbered."

Figuring he had nothing to lose going into the '65 season, Mele shook things up. He ordered coach Billy Martin to work with the players to develop a more aggressive base running game. He also implemented a plan for more hit-and-run play. Mele also became a firmer disciplinarian with his team. When Zoilo Versalles loafed in a spring training game, he was fined $300 by his manager. According to Max Nichols in an October 1965 edition of *The Sporting News*, "Versalles has not loafed since. He played all but one game until the champagne flowed."

The champagne did indeed flow as the Twins won their first American League pennant in 1965. They faced the National League champ, the Los Angeles Dodgers, in a tight, seven game World Series.

The Twins won the first two games at home. The Dodgers won the next three games in a row in Los Angeles. The Twins came back with a 5–1 victory in Game Six before losing a Seventh Game nail-biter, 2–0, at the hands of Dodger ace Sandy Koufax.

Nevertheless, it had been an incredible season for the Twins and Sam Mele. The skipper had juggled players all year long as stars like Harmon Killebrew, Tony Oliva, and Camilo Pascual suffered through injuries. In the end, Mele deservedly won the Manager of the Year honors.

All sports, however, are "what have you done for me lately" businesses. The Twins finished 2nd in 1966 with 89 victories and Sam Mele was fired 50 games into the 1967 season with a 25–25 record.

SABR writer Bill Nowlin reports that Mele and Red Sox owner Tom Yawkey had remained friends since Mele's days at Fenway, and Yawkey hired Mele soon after his departure from the Twins. Sam Mele worked in the Red Sox organization for another 25 years as a minor league instructor, spring training instructor, roving scout, etc.

Mele was instrumental in the Red Sox signing Jim Rice. He went to South Carolina to check on a report from scout Mace Brown. There was another scout from the Tigers there to look at Rice. When Rice didn't show up after the first three innings, the Tigers scout left disgusted, saying, "He don't want to play." "Mace Brown and

I talked to Rice after the game," Mele told Nowlin. "[Rice] had worked at a variety store. His replacement didn't show up, so he stayed on to help the owner. We called the owner; he said, 'That's exactly true.' Houston was after Rice, too, but when they took a pitcher, the Red Sox pounced and signed up Jim Rice."

Mele worked with Rice in spring training and the instructional league level. "You know how, as an instructor, you've got to get the kid and say, 'Let's go, we've got extra work to do?' He used to grab me, every day," said Mele. "Every day. I didn't get him; he got me. And we became great, great friends."

Mele drifted away from the game in the 2000s. He died on May 17, 2017, at his home in Quincy, Massachusetts, at the age of 95. His is not a name young people know today but for those of us who love and cherish the history of the game, he will always be remembered as "a great baseball man."

♦ 20 ♦

Roy Campanella
(1948)

That "little boy grin" of Roy Campanella's was there throughout his career (National Baseball Hall of Fame, Cooperstown, NY).

I became a baseball fan in the early 1970s. At the time, a natural extension of baseball fandom was collecting baseball cards, which I began doing with a passion in 1972. These were the last days of baseball card collecting done for the pure joy of it. We collected the cards so we could have a little piece of our heroes, some kind of memento that strengthened our identification with those players to whom we felt a special connection. And, of course, the rock hard bubble gum.

My collecting quickly turned into obsession. I think a pack of cards at the time cost about 15 or 20 cents. I can still remember the guy at the corner store where I used to get most of my cards. When I'd put a pack on the counter he'd growl, "Twenty cents for the cards and don't forget the penny for Rocky." At the time Nelson Rockefeller was the governor of New York State and there was a one-cent sales tax on a 20-cent pack of cards.

There were days when I might only have 17 or 18 cents, which meant, of course, that I didn't have enough to buy a pack. That would drive me crazy—to be so close but still not have enough to get a new pack. I'd try to dig up those few extra cents wherever I could. I'd do odd jobs, I'd look around the house or outside for spare change on the ground, but my ace in the hole became my brother Bob's penny jar. Bob is 12 years older than I am and in his room he always had a jar on his dresser where he'd put his pennies so, whenever I was two or three pennies short, I'd help myself to a discreet loan from the ever-present, tempting stash of ignored riches.

I'd sit for hours on the floor of our family room or my bedroom and count my cards. I'd put them in order of teams or else I'd make special piles of my favorite players. I'd study the statistics that filled the backs of the cards. Before long I was a walking/talking encyclopedia of baseball trivia.

A primary goal was to collect all the players on my favorite teams. I remember trying to get every card of the 1972 Pittsburgh Pirates. Of course, you'd always try to collect the best players as well; in 1972 that meant Hank Aaron, Brooks Robinson, Roberto Clemente, Willie Mays, Tom Seaver, Juan Marichal, etc. And then there was another group—the Italian American ballplayers. It's fascinating for me to think back to those years now and realize that even at that young age I had a very conscious realization that I was an "Italian American" and that I was very proud of the distinction. I can remember making a special pile of the cards with guys like Rico Petrocelli, Jim Fregosi, Ray Fosse, Joe Torre, Phil Gagliano, and Tony Conigliaro.

Early on in my baseball years my oldest brother Joe had taught me that the New York Yankees were the bad guys. Despite the legendary stories I'd heard about the great DiMaggio from my parents' generation, I could never bring myself to root for the Yankees. The Yankees always seemed to win and that offended my sense of fairness. I was born a contrarian; I almost always root for the underdog, anytime, anywhere, no matter what the situation.

In addition to my card collecting mania, I also read every book and magazine I could get my hands on having to do with baseball. Despite the fact that they ceased to exist seven years before I was even born, I loved the Brooklyn Dodgers. There was so much for me to relate to and/or admire about the Brooklyn team. They were underdogs, of a sort. After all, in the ten-year period from 1947 to 1956 they were in the World Series six times—not exactly underdog statistics. However, they won the series only once. In every other instance they lost ... to the Yankees!

Another reason for me to love the Brooklyn Dodgers was they had been the team to break the color barrier by recruiting Jackie Robinson—few events in the history of baseball were as important as that one decision by Branch Rickey and the Dodgers. The fact that Brooklyn had been the team to come forward and reverse nearly half a century of discrimination appealed to my aforementioned sense of fairness and/or justice.

And then there were the Italian Americans—the Dodgers of the 1940s and 1950s had guys like Dolph Camilli, Al Gionfriddo, Cookie Lavagetto, Ralph Branca, Carl Furillo, and Roy Campanella. Now while some might be anxious to point out that the Yankees of that same time period also had quite a few Italian Americans on their team, it didn't matter. They were still the Yankees.

My favorite Italian American Brooklyn Dodger was Roy "Campy" Campanella. Later on I'd come to love Furillo almost as much but Campanella was certainly on the Mt. Rushmore of my first baseball heroes along with Roberto Clemente, Willie Mays, and Brooks Robinson.

As I said, the fact that the Brooklyn Dodgers had broken the color line in baseball with Jackie Robinson was significant in my admiration for the team. The fact that Campanella was an individual who had dealt with being the child of a mixed marriage during his youth in the 1920s and 1930s only endeared him to me even more. In Campanella's memoir *It's Good to Be Alive*, he explains the roots of his journey: "My father's name is John Campanella. He is white. My mother's maiden name was Ida Mercer. She is Negro. My father is Italian. His mother and father both came from Sicily."

I think I read Campanella's book for the first time when I was about ten years old. My initial interest came from the fact that Campanella was one of the greatest baseball players in history whose career was cut short by a tragic car accident in January of 1958 that left him a quadriplegic. Part of me felt sorry for him because of his accident. However, at the same time, I was amazed by his positive attitude and the courage he showed in facing the setbacks in his life.

In addition, I also remember feeling very proud of his father when I read Campy's book. What a special person his father must have been to disregard the opinions of society and marry a black woman in the 1910s. It was amazing to me. I felt so proud as a Sicilian American that this guy had not looked at the color of his future wife's skin but instead at the content of her character and had fallen in love. I remember thinking how incredible both of Campanella's parents must have been and, as a confirmation of that fact, he speaks of them with nothing but love and admiration in his memoir.

In truth, although he was still an active player when he was permanently injured in the car accident, he was near the end of his career. Segregation had cut into his career before it even got started. He played ten years of professional baseball in the Negro Leagues and in Mexico before the Dodgers recruited him as the second African American ballplayer to be signed to a Major League club. He was almost the first, but in his initial talks with Branch Rickey, Campanella thought he was hinting about playing for a new black team to be owned and run by the Dodgers so the young catcher balked at Rickey's overtures. As a kid, it used to upset me to think that Campanella was supposed to be the first African American player, not Jackie Robinson.

Campanella finished his Major League career with 242 home runs over ten seasons. In 2024, Major League Baseball finally acknowledged the talent of the Negro Leagues and incorporated the statistics accumulated by players who played in the Negro Leagues from 1920 to 1948 into the official Major League records. It's an important acknowledgment and a move forward but, sadly, it's still an incomplete picture because only a fraction of the records remain from the Negro League seasons. In the case of Campanella, it did push his lifetime RBI total over 1,000. Nevertheless, it seems likely that had he been allowed to play all his years in the Major Leagues, he would have hit 350–400 home runs. As it was, he won three MVP awards in his ten year Major League career, led the league in 1953 with 142 RBIs, and is still the Major League leader, more than 65 years after playing his final game, in throwing out baserunners who attempted to steal against him. You read that correctly—no catcher in the *entire* history of the game has thrown out a higher percentage of runners attempting to steal bases than Campy did.

When I started collecting baseball cards in 1972 I also began collecting "old" cards—cards from the 1960s and before. By the mid–1970s my friend Mariano Pierleoni, who had started me on my collecting hobby, had discovered a few guys around the country who were beginning to sell old cards. It was a novel idea back then and we were excited to no end at the possibilities this new pipeline to "collectible cards" offered. I remember poring over the lists he received in the mail of cards I could only dream of owning: Aarons, Musials, Williams, Robinsons, and dozens more.

On one of those lists I spotted a 1953 Topps Roy Campanella. The price was $3.25. I had trouble enough getting the 21¢ for the new packs let alone $3.25 for one old card! I remember asking my dad for the money to buy the card. He looked at me as if to say, "What are you, nuts?" My father had almost no interest in sports. My desire to spend over three dollars on a single card was, to him, complete lunacy.

Nevertheless, I somehow managed to eventually get the money from him in exchange for some odd jobs around the house. I remember when I received the card in the mail it was as if the postman had just delivered the Hope Diamond to my door. The card was in mint condition and I meant to keep it that way. I cut out a couple of pieces of plastic from an old book report cover and stapled them around the edges, careful not to get too close to the card, and set it apart from the rest of my cards. It was the prize of my burgeoning collection.

Years later, in the spring of 1980, it was announced that there would be an

Old-Timers' Sports Reunion Dinner held in Rochester, New York, in September. I wanted to go but didn't think there was much of a chance. My dad had died a few years prior to this and my brothers were busy with their own families. However, as the summer wore on our local newspaper started printing the names of the different personalities who were expected to attend. Once I saw Campanella's name, it was a done deal. I knew that I had to be there.

I don't remember exactly how it went but on September 13, 1980, my buddy Joe and I were dropped off at the Mapledale Party House. Here was this room full of men in their 50s and 60s looking to revisit their childhoods while Joe and I were there to meet with men who were nothing short of mythological heroes to us.

Naturally, I still have the program from the dinner. On the cover are autographs of Bob Feller, Mel Allen, Johnny Antonelli, Enos Slaughter, Vic Raschi, Sal Maglie, Johnny Mize, Lefty Gomez, Red Ruffing, Gabe Paul, and Tommy Holmes—six are Hall of Famers and arguments could be made for two more, Raschi and Maglie. It was just amazing. Looking at the program now I realize there were guys in attendance whom I should have sought out but didn't know enough to do so—guys like Dante Lavelli, Al Cervi, and Jocko Conlan.

The reason I didn't have the time or the chance to seek out more legends was because I was primarily interested in just one—Roy Campanella. While the other participants mingled all around the ballroom prior to the formal dinner, Campanella was wheeled to his place on the dais where he sat in his wheelchair while people went up and talked to him.

I waited for a few minutes while a few other people spoke to him and I tried to muster my courage to go up and say something to him. I wanted to tell him how much I admired him. I wanted to tell him that I despised the Yankees and I wished the Brooklyn Dodgers had won more than just the one championship in 1955. I wanted to say something memorable. Instead, I went up and asked him for his autograph. He smiled and said "Sorry, I can't but you can have one of these cards." He had pre-printed postcards with a picture of him in his Dodger uniform and a copy of his autograph across the front. On the back of the card were his lifetime statistics.

As a quadriplegic, Campanella was, of course, unable to sign his autograph; or at least to do it with enough ease and speed to accommodate hundreds of fans at a public event. I knew as much, if not more, about Campanella than almost anyone in that room. I should have known he couldn't sign autographs but I panicked and as soon as I asked him about it I felt awful. He smiled that famous Campy smile and tried to put me at my ease.

I think I eventually recovered enough to ask him about the final game of the 1955 series and Johnny Podres' impressive outing. Having failed at the autograph I asked him if I could get a picture of him. I was thrilled when he said, "Sure, come on up here and stand next to me." I handed my camera to my friend Joe and jumped up on the dais. Joe snapped our picture and I thanked Campanella and took my leave.

Later that night when we were leaving the dinner, I dropped the camera in the parking lot. The film latch popped open exposing the film. It was ruined. I was beyond heartbroken. I went home with mixed feelings over a night that had started with huge expectations and finished with less than stellar results.

The next morning when I came down to breakfast I pulled the sports section out of the *Rochester Democrat & Chronicle* as I did every morning. I was curious to see if the paper would mention anything about the reunion. There on the front page of the Sports section, bottom right, of the paper, was a picture of Roy Campanella ... and standing next to him was Yours Truly with the dopiest grin in the world on my face. Apparently, the newspaper's photographer had taken a picture of Campanella just as my friend was taking the ill-fated picture of us. Rarely have I ever been so thrilled, relieved, proud, and very, very grateful.

A few years later I sold almost my entire baseball card collection to help pay for college. It was a nice gesture of responsibility on my part at the time, but in retrospect it was a really dumb financial move. Had I held on to the cards for ten or 20 more years I could have easily sold them for three or four times as much as I did. Better yet, if I'd kept them that long, I probably would have held on to them to pass them down to my sons who are now baseball fans.

As years went by, I learned more about Campanella and specifically about his sometime strained relationship with Jackie Robinson. The older I've grown the more my appreciation has grown for Robinson and the more obvious it is that Robinson was indeed the proper choice to be the man to break baseball's color barrier. Robinson was often impatient with Campanella's willingness to wait for change and progress to come slowly and incrementally. Robinson became a civil rights activist in a way that Campanella never could have been.

While politically, I might have been more in line with Robinson's way of thinking, I still admired Campanella. He was a role model not only to the millions of kids who loved the game of baseball but to all the people who've dealt with life-changing injuries and health issues in the years since Campanella was first confined to his wheelchair. President Eisenhower once described Campanella as "an example of what man can do if he refuses to quit."

Roy Campanella was elected to Baseball's Hall of Fame in 1969 by the Baseball Writers along with Stan Musial. Waite Hoyt, and Stan Covoleski were also inducted that year by the Veterans Committee. Campanella continued to work with Dodger catchers at spring training for years after his retirement. The great catcher died in 1993 at 71 years of age.

When I sold all my cards prior to college I kept just a few. One of the cards I kept was my prized 1953 Roy Campanella. When I look at that card today I'm reminded of Campanella's most famous quote in which he said, "You have to have a lot of little boy in you to play baseball for a living." On that '53 card, Campy's little boy grin is still as bright and inspiring as ever.

♦ 21 ♦

Johnny Antonelli
(1948)

Even into his eighties, Johnny Antonelli was always itching to pitch (courtesy Scott Pitoniak).

Growing up in Rochester, New York, it seems that I've always known the name of Johnny Antonelli. He is, without exaggeration, a local legend. I first remember seeing Johnny's name when I was a kid going to Silver Stadium, the ballpark that was home to our minor league Rochester Red Wing baseball team. Antonelli Tires were always a sponsor of the team and so you'd invariably see the name on signs in and around the park and in the yearly programs sold at the stadium. I don't really know how many years it was before I ever realized Antonelli was more than just a successful local merchant who sold tires, let alone a Major League pitcher and star for the World Champion 1954 New York Giants.

As familiar as the Antonelli name has always been, the details of his life and career had always been little more than bullet points found on the back of a bubble gum card. In 2012, Antonelli filled in the blanks with a memoir of his glory days, entitled *Johnny Antonelli: A Baseball Memoir*, written with the help of a very talented writer named Scott Pitoniak. The book is a simple, unadorned story from an unpretentious man who would never fit into the mold of our modern definition of "professional athlete." The book paints the picture of an individual confident in his abilities but short on the arrogance so prevalent in today's sports world. A man who more than 50 years after he left the game of baseball was proud of his accomplishments, grateful for the opportunities that baseball gave him but not in the least bit defined solely by his storied past.

John August Antonelli was born on April 12, 1930, in Rochester, New York, to August and Josephine Messore Antonelli. His father was an immigrant from the Abruzzi region of Italy and his mother was the child of Italian immigrants.

Antonelli remembered his dad as a self-assured, independent-minded person; qualities that would eventually serve the young Antonelli very well in his pursuit of a Major League career. In a time when so many Italian immigrants saw sports as frivolous, what drew Gus Antonelli to the game of baseball?

"To be honest with you, I don't know how my dad became interested in baseball," Antonelli writes in *Johnny Antonelli: A Baseball Memoir*, "But I think he was like a lot of immigrants at the time. Baseball truly was our national pastime back then and if you wanted to assimilate into American society, there was no faster way to do that than by learning about and following baseball. Plus, I think my dad looked at the box scores in the newspaper and was intrigued to find Italian names like Lazzeri, Crosetti, DiMaggio, and Berra."

Johnny Antonelli never played organized ball until he was a freshman at Jefferson High School in Rochester, New York. Antonelli remembered, "One day during infield practice, I was wheeling around making throws from first base to home when the varsity coach, Charlie O'Brien, noticed there was a lot of movement on the balls I threw. He asked me if I ever pitched, and I told him, 'No. I'm a first baseman because I like playing every day.' He said, 'Well, I notice your throws have a nice tail on them, so I'm going to have Pat Arioli work with you a little bit as a pitcher.' I grudgingly gave it a try, but deep down in my heart, I wanted to stay at first base.... I wanted to be out there all the time, every game. Looking back, I'm happy Coach noticed I had a 'live arm' because as much as I liked hitting and playing first base, I doubt I would have made it as far as I did if I didn't switch to my natural position."

Antonelli insisted he learned more about baseball from Charlie O'Brien than from all the Hall of Fame players and managers he associated with during his 12-year Major League career.

As Johnny's legend grew locally during his years at Jefferson High, so did the scrapbooks his mother put together featuring articles about his victories, shutouts, and no-hitters. Scrapbooks that his father would eventually bring with him to all the various Major League spring training camps trying to generate interest in his young son. In a June 1955 cover article for *SPORT* magazine, Gus Antonelli told writer Al Hirschberg about his early networking efforts at the Florida camps on behalf of his son. "They thought I was crazy—just another father with more pride than common sense," Gus told Hirschberg. "Johnny was just a kid then—a sophomore in high school. I couldn't convince anyone at the time that he had it, but they all came flocking around later."

At 15, Antonelli impressed Cardinal scouts at a tryout camp at Red Wing Stadium. That performance earned him an invitation to the Hearst National Championship Game in the Polo Grounds where one of the Cubs scouts called him "the best pitching discovery since Bob Feller." Shortly before his high school graduation in June 1948, in what Antonelli recalled as "a calculated risk," his father set up an exhibition game at Red Wing Stadium where Antonelli would face off against a team of semi-pro players. The scouts were invited to come and watch. Antonelli was scheduled to pitch three innings. He mowed down the first nine batters and figured he was done for the night but the scouts wanted to see more. He ended up staying in the whole game and pitching a no-hitter. The calculated risk had paid off and the scouts literally lined up outside the Antonelli home to negotiate with Pop Antonelli and make their offers for the future diamond star. In the end, Gus Antonelli signed with owner Lou Perini of the Boston Braves for $52,000, one of the biggest bonuses ever paid for an untested rookie. It was a dream come true for Antonelli but he had no idea at the time that his "Bonus Baby" distinction would also be the beginning of a Major League nightmare.

Looking back on it, Antonelli remembered the excitement that spread through his neighborhood the night he signed his contract with the Braves. There was a celebration at his house before he, his dad, and his older brother Tony flew to Boston with Lou Perini on the owner's private plane. It was a heady experience for an 18-year-old just a few days out of high school. Braves manager Billy Southworth was initially enthusiastic until he was told that Antonelli had been signed to a "bonus baby contract" which meant that the Braves were required to keep him on the Major League roster for two years or else be forced to put him on waivers and possibly lose him to another club. For a team in the midst of a pennant race, this was not exactly the kind of news Southworth wanted to hear. His exact quote was, "I'll just have to find room for him somewhere." Antonelli recalled, "The last thing in the world I wanted to be was excess baggage, but that's what I became."

To say Southworth used Antonelli sparingly during the 1948 pennant race would be an understatement. The rookie pitcher got into exactly four games and pitched a total of four innings, spending most of the late summer and fall pitching batting practice. Southworth also kept him off the World Series roster versus the Indians. Many of the veterans on the team resented his bonus baby status and the contract he'd been given.

The next two years weren't much better for Antonelli. He pitched 96 innings in 1949 and only 57 innings in 1950 with a 5–10 win-loss total and two shutouts. He did, however, make history on June 12, 1949, along with catcher Del Crandall, when they became the youngest battery (pitcher and catcher) ever to win a Major League game. They were both 19 years old.

Antonelli spent 1951 and 1952 in the military. The general on the post where Antonelli was stationed wanted the best baseball team possible representing the district of Washington, D.C., and recruited the young Braves rookie to pitch for him. Antonelli remembered playing against guys like Whitey Ford, Willie Mays, and Bobby Brown. His pitching record during his military service was 42–2 with 44 complete games. "I matured a lot physically and emotionally during my two years in the service," Antonelli wrote. "Looking back, I tell people that I got my minor league experience pitching in the army."

On his return to the Braves in 1953, Antonelli felt like a new man and, in a sense, he'd returned to a new team, the Milwaukee Braves. The franchise moved to Milwaukee after the 1952 season. He had regained his confidence and was ready to contribute to the Braves pennant hopes. Billy Southworth was gone and Charlie Grimm was manager by the time Antonelli returned. He won nine of his first 12 decisions but midway through the season he came down with pneumonia that left him in a weakened condition and, combined with some problems on the index finger of his left hand, he never regained his early season success. He finished the campaign with a 12–12 record although he was fifth best in the National League with a 3.18 earned run average.

The year 1954 would change Johnny Antonelli's life once again. On February 1, 1954, Antonelli was part of a trade that sent Don Liddle, Ebba St. Claire, Billy Klaus, and $50,000 to the New York Giants for Bobby Thomson and backup catcher Sam Calderone. The Braves felt they were a home run–hitting outfielder away from another pennant and although the Milwaukee general manager claimed he tried to hold onto Antonelli, Giants owner Horace Stoneham made it clear that there would be no deal for Thompson without Antonelli.

On the one hand, Johnny Antonelli was disappointed because he wanted to prove to Braves owner Lou Perini that he was worth the money he'd paid for him. On the other hand, Antonelli was excited about the opportunity to play for the tenacious Leo Durocher. There were those who felt Durocher was difficult to get along with but there was no doubting the baseball acumen of "Leo the Lip."

Both the 1954 *SPORT* article and Antonelli's memoir recall the pitcher's first appearance as a Giant in an intrasquad game in Phoenix. He looked terrible. When he came out of the game he asked pitching coach Frank Shellenback, "What's the matter with me?"

"'You're over-striding,' the coach replied. 'You too tired to go to the bullpen and work on it now?'

"'Let's go,' said Johnny.

"'He was all right after a few minutes,' Shellenback explained, 'but you know what Leo and I liked most about him? The fact that he was willing to go right to work on top of a five-inning session in that dry Arizona heat. The kid knew something was wrong, and he couldn't wait to correct it.'"

Antonelli went on to say in the *SPORT* article that "Shelly never let me forget that he thought I was a great pitcher. Pretty soon he had me thinking the same way." That, combined with the fact that Durocher told Antonelli that he was going to be his number one starter, did wonders to boost his confidence.

Despite the confidence of his coaches, Antonelli still had a problem. Bobby Thomson was a folk hero in New York due to his pennant-winning "shot heard round the world" that defeated the Dodgers in 1951. To Giant fans, Antonelli was just another young bonus baby who had yet to prove his worth and the fans were not receptive to his arrival. He quickly won them over as he won five of his first seven decisions in 1954, two of them against his old team, the Braves. He would finish the year leading the league in winning percentage (.750), ERA (2.30) and shutouts (6) while compiling a 21–7 record. There wasn't yet a Cy Young Award but *The Sporting News,* which at the time was considered the bible of baseball, voted him Pitcher of the Year. The Giants reached the World Series against the Cleveland Indians and Antonelli picked up both a win and a save in the series. In fact, he would go on to become one of only two pitchers in the history of the game to record both a victory and a save in both the World Series and the All-Star games (the other is Hall-of-Famer Bruce Sutter).

In *Johnny Antonelli: A Baseball Memoir*, the pitcher recalled what it felt like to deliver the final pitch of the 1954 World Series. "So many thoughts raced through my mind at that moment," he writes, "I thought of my dad and mom, and the people I grew up with in Rochester. I thought about the struggles I had endured with the Braves, the times when I questioned if I had what it took to be a big league pitcher and wondered if I would ever get a true opportunity to prove myself. It was mind boggling to me that I had finally reached the top of my profession at age twenty-four."

Antonelli returned to Rochester and a hero's welcome. He spent a long winter on the "Rubber Chicken Circuit" as the honored guest at a number of dinners around the country. He took a job with the Genesee Brewing Company in Rochester during the off-season and not long after that invested in his first store selling Firestone Tires. He eventually grew that business into 28 stores employing nearly three hundred people.

Johnny Antonelli (left) with author/columnist Scott Pitoniak (courtesy Scott Pitoniak)

He would continue to pitch well through the rest of the decade with the exception of one off year in 1957. He won 20 games again in 1956 and 19 games in 1959 but he was never as comfortable pitching in the cold, windy surroundings of San Francisco as he had been in the pitcher-friendly Polo Grounds. In 1961 he was traded to the Indians and then finished the season with his old team, the Braves, before retiring at the end of the season at the youthful age of 32. He had grown weary of the travel and his heart just wasn't in it anymore. Antonelli wanted to go home to his young family, spend time with his children, and build up his new business.

Johnny Antonelli Tires became such a successful and iconic Rochester institution that kids like myself who were born in the 1960s and 1970s had to be taught and told that Antonelli had ever been someone more than an important local businessman.

What stands out most in Antonelli's memoir is his pride in his entire life, not just his baseball life. For Antonelli, his family was as important as his baseball career, which was as important as his business career, which was as important as his community service. For a former pitcher who always believed he hit 17 big league home runs instead of the official 15 credited to him, I'd say he's still wrong. I think he hit 18 because the perspective he had on his life sure sounds like a home run to me.

Antonelli died at the age of 89 in 2020. At the time of his passing, his friend and co-writer Scott Pitoniak wrote that "John was so much more than a five-time National League All Star, World Series hero and immensely successful entrepreneur. He was a decent, big-hearted man with a wonderful sense of humor and self. When I think of John, the first word I think of is 'class.'"

♦ 22 ♦

Joe Altobelli
(1955)

Our hometown Rochester Red Wing skipper in the 1970s and 1983 World Champion manager, Joe Altobelli.

In today's world of multi-million dollar salaries being paid to players and managers alike, what would you say if, for $500, I offered you a clutch hitting, agile fielding first baseman with a strong work ethic and a sincere interest in becoming an active member of the community? And what if I further suggested that this player would someday make a great coach and manager, could evaluate talent and even be a visionary fundraiser for the future expansion of your operation? Well, you'd either run for your checkbook or be taken away in a straitjacket for passing up such a deal. Luckily for fans of minor and Major League baseball, and particularly the fans of Rochester, New York, George Sisler, Jr., the son of Baseball Hall-of-Famer George Sr., made such a deal in 1963 to the everlasting benefit of the Rochester, New York, community.

In 1963 George Sisler, Jr., was the general manager of the Rochester Red Wings, a successful and storied franchise in the Triple A level International League. In need of a first baseman, Sisler Jr. asked his friend Buzzie Bavasi of the Los Angeles Dodgers to loan him a veteran minor leaguer named Joe Altobelli who had played for the Dodgers' Omaha ball club in 1962. Bavasi complied and Altobelli played about a hundred games for the Wings in 1963 but wasn't in top form due to some nagging injuries. Nevertheless, he felt immediately comfortable with the ball club and the fans. In the book *Silver Seasons: The Story of the Rochester Red Wings*, authors Jim Mandelaro and Scott Pitoniak note that "he [Altobelli] had been one of the International League's top players for years, and his heritage made him a big draw in Rochester's large Italian-American community."

Altobelli told me in an interview in February of 2010 that "With a week or so left [in the season] George Sisler came in and asked me how I liked playing for Rochester. I told him I liked it fine [but] I wished I could have done more for you and the ball club." Sisler then asked him if he like to play for Rochester again the following season. Altobelli told him he'd be very happy to stay in Rochester so Sisler went up to his office, called Buzzie Bavasi, and purchased Joe Altobelli's contract for $500. At the time, no one could have known that it would be the most rewarding acquisition in Rochester's long baseball history.

Rochester would become Joe Altobelli's home forever after but the journey there and back was a long one that began on the streets of Detroit, Michigan, during the challenging years of the Great Depression.

Joe Altobelli was born on May 26, 1932, in Detroit and grew up in a working class immigrant neighborhood. While most young Italian American boys of the day were worshiping the hitting style of Joltin' Joe DiMaggio, Altobelli was loyal to his hometown team and their own slugging hero, Hank Greenberg. Altobelli said, "In the Italian household the kitchen was the most important room in the house. When I was growing up, we had an 8 × 10 photo of Hank Greenberg hanging on our kitchen wall."

His dad began bringing him to Tiger games when he was only five years old. Altobelli got to see some of the greatest baseball players of the day: Greenberg,

Charlie Gehringer, Rudy York, Pinky Higgins, Bobo Newsom, Schoolboy Rowe, and a host of others. With examples like that, who wouldn't want to follow in their footsteps? Nevertheless, despite his appreciation for the game, Altobelli says that, like most Italian American fathers of the day, his dad wasn't crazy about him looking to baseball for his livelihood.

Altobelli also had older brothers who were all good baseball players and they taught him much of what he knew about the game as a youth. They were all substantially older than Altobelli though and served their country in World War II. Any possible chances they might have had for professional careers were deterred by war injuries and lost time.

In high school, Altobelli excelled in baseball, football, and basketball. In fact, he was offered college football scholarships to four different schools including the powerhouse University of Michigan. However, at 6 feet tall, 180 pounds, he took a look at the size of the players who played Division I college football and decided baseball was the direction in which to go.

Following his high school graduation in 1950, he was working out with the Tigers whenever they were in town. In those days, there was no Amateur Draft so scouts could sign whoever they wished to sign and it was a highly competitive business. Altobelli remembered the afternoon he was supposed to meet his dad at the Tigers' office after his father got out of work to discuss a contract. Prior to meeting his dad, a scout from the Cleveland Indians, who had shown interest in the young ballplayer, showed up at his front door begging him to come to Cleveland and meet with the Indians' management. Altobelli felt sorry for the guy and left that day for Cleveland with the scout. Naturally, his father was furious when he found out what had happened.

Altobelli chuckled when he recalled the experience: "I thought I was doing the guy a favor. Cleveland knew my father was mad because I'd called him from their offices and he said, 'You're never going to sign with Cleveland.' Of course in those days, just as it is today, my dad had to sign because I was under twenty-one. The only Italian they had in the Cleveland organization was working in the Accounting Department so they sent him home to talk to my dad—he wasn't even a scout! So that's how I signed with Cleveland ... they knew their business."

He spent eight seasons with the Cleveland organization from 1951 to 1958, playing parts of two seasons with the big club, 1955 and 1957. He had some power, and was a fine fielding first baseman, but never sustained a position in the majors. He would later play part of the 1961 season for the Minnesota Twins but that was his last taste of the Major Leagues ... as a player.

One benefit of his time with Cleveland was the opportunity to establish a friendship with his boyhood idol Hank Greenberg. The retired Tiger Hall of Fame first baseman became GM of the Cleveland ball club while Altobelli was with the Indians and he got to know Greenberg very well. Many years later when Altobelli was managing the 1984 American League All-Star team, his honorary captain was Hank Greenberg.

Following his stint with the Twins in 1961 he was picked up by the Dodgers and sent to Omaha in the American Association for the '62 season. He eventually landed in Rochester in 1963 and played for the Red Wings for the better part of three seasons.

When Bavasi sold Altobelli, he sold him to the Red Wings and not to the Baltimore Orioles, which was the parent club of the Wings in 1963. Therefore, in 1966, when the Orioles wanted Altobelli to manage their rookie club in Bluefield, West Virginia (the Baby Birds), he had to make a decision whether to leave the security of Rochester and begin a whole new journey towards a career as a manager. In fact, he had been made a player/coach with the Red Wings in 1964 and there were many in baseball who believed he showed great promise as a future coach and/or manager. What made his decision even tougher was that Morrie Silver, president of Rochester Community Baseball, knowing that Altobelli's playing days were winding down to an end, had told Altobelli that he could always have a job with the Red Wings in whatever capacity he wished.

Ultimately, Altobelli had to think about his future. At 34 his playing days were done but he had a tremendous amount of energy and knowledge to apply and he wanted to take on the challenge of managing. In his characteristically humble way, Altobelli told me, "I thought I'd give managing a try and it worked out well for me."

He managed the Bluefield team for two years. In 1968 he spent a year with the Stockton, California, club and then managed at Dallas–Fort Worth of the Texas League during the 1969 and 1970 campaigns. In 1971, the Orioles reassigned Cal Ripken, Sr., to Dallas–Fort Worth and promoted Joe Altobelli to be manager of the Rochester Red Wings. In *Silver Seasons*, Altobelli is quoted as saying "When I learned I was going to Rochester, I was excited. I'd waited five years to manage in the place where I lived. But I said to myself, 'Boy-oh-boy, Joe, you'd better win. You're from there. You're going to have to live there not only during the summer but the winter as well.'"

Altobelli and his wife Pat had liked Rochester so much that they had built a house there in 1965. When he switched to managing and started to travel all around the country, his family remained in Rochester year round. Now Dad was on his way home.

The 1971 season started sluggishly with Altobelli's club losing their first five games on the road. It was a tradition in Rochester that the club held a welcome home dinner for the team every spring before the home opener. Altobelli told me, "I was embarrassed to go to that dinner when we returned home [from the first road trip]. I know our record after 67 games was 33–34, one game under .500. But we ended the season 32 games over .500." It ended up being a dream team and a storybook season. Joe Altobelli cemented his legend with the fans of Rochester in 1971 with a Governor's Cup Championship and a Junior League World Series title. Over 50 years later that '71 team is still considered the best in Red Wing history.

I've lived in Rochester all my life and began attending Red Wing games in 1972 when I was eight years old. In fact, my first game in May of 1972 was the exhibition game against our parent club, the Baltimore Orioles. Two of the Orioles who were introduced at the start of that game were heroes of that 1971 championship team: Bob Grich and Don Baylor. I vividly remember Grich and Baylor being introduced and receiving a thunderous ovation from the appreciative Rochester fans as they welcomed home their new Major Leaguers. The year 1971 had been Altobelli's first as manager of the Red Wings and many of his players believed his calm, steady influence contributed much to that '71 odyssey.

In his autobiography entitled *Nothing but the Truth: A Baseball Life*, Don Baylor pays tribute to his former minor league skipper, saying "Alto [Altobelli's nickname] taught me the importance of good work habits. He was a tireless worker himself, serving as manager, batting-practice pitcher, third base coach, and, when you got right down to it, a babysitter. He taught us to respect the game. He was a friend and a teacher." That's quite a tribute from a former American League MVP and Major League manager.

Joe Altobelli would manage a total of six years for the Rochester Red Wings. He was named IL Manager of the Year three times in those six seasons. After the 1976 season, he announced to the fans of Rochester that he would not return in 1977. Instead, he was heading to the Majors to manage the San Francisco Giants. I remember that we were at once saddened by our loss and thrilled that "our friend" was going to get a shot in the big leagues.

He led the Giants to a fourth place finish and 75 wins in his rookie season as a manager in 1977. In 1978 the team improved to 89 wins and moved up to third place. It was the most wins the Giants had managed since 1967. Unfortunately, the following season the Giants fired Altobelli with 22 games left in the 1979 season and the club struggling in fourth place.

In 1980 he returned to the International League as manager of the Columbus Clippers, the farm team of the New York Yankees. He promptly won another Governor's Cup title and was promoted to the Yankees' coaching staff for the 1981 and 1982 seasons.

In 1983 he received a call from Hank Peters, the GM in Baltimore. Earl Weaver, the longtime Oriole skipper, had retired and Peters offered Altobelli the job of managing the Baltimore Orioles. After six years, Altobelli would rejoin the Baltimore organization and about a half dozen players he'd coached at Rochester. Altobelli recalled his two years coaching with the Yankees as an opportunity "to see the American League real well from my dugout and third base positions and it kind of helped me when I got the job with Baltimore in 1983."

Altobelli, as always, proved to be a quick study. In his first year with the Orioles they captured the American League East title with 98 wins. They lost the first game of the American League Playoffs to the White Sox before winning three in a row to clinch the pennant and then lost the first game of the World Series to the Phillies before winning four in a row to become World Champions. Altobelli remembers

Three old friends meet at the 2003 Rochester Press-Radio Club Dinner. From left, Johnny Antonelli, Joe Torre, and Joe Altobelli (Ken Pamatat/Rochester Press-Radio Club).

that the team took three buses to Philadelphia for that fifth game and on the victorious ride home people lined the streets, stopped their cars, and cheered the new champions as the caravan of buses made its way back to Baltimore. It was a sweet night that Altobelli would savor. Less than two years later the impatient Orioles would fire Altobelli and rehire Earl Weaver. As of 2024, the Orioles haven't been to another World Series since Altobelli's championship season.

Following his stint with the Orioles he coached for a few more years, most notably with the Chicago Cubs from 1988 to 1991 working for manager Don Zimmer. "I liked Don," Altobelli said, "He wasn't afraid to take a chance any time … he was a gambling type of manager. He kept his ball club very alert." Of course, Altobelli was a bit of a gambler himself which he displayed in Game Four of the '83 World Series when he sent up four pinch-hitters in a row as his team was losing 3–2. A risky move that paid big dividends as the team rallied to win the game 5–4. In describing his own managing style Altobelli said, "I [always] went by gut feeling."

He returned home to Rochester in the early 1990s and took a front office job with the Red Wings. It's been said that he was never truly comfortable in the executive position but, if nothing else, his last move proved to be invaluable to the franchise. He hired Red Wing GM Dan Mason, who has been with the club since 1995 and has proven to be one of the very best general managers in all of minor league baseball. Mason has always praised Altobelli saying, "Joe was the best teacher I've ever had. I've never been around a man who could get the most out of his people like Joe did and I've always tried to emulate his management style."

Altobelli took on one more job with the Red Wings in 1998 when he became the color commentator of the local radio broadcasts of games. "He had an endless array of tales but also was so engaging when telling them. I'm so happy that our fans had the opportunity to hear many of those stories because of his time on our radio broadcasts," Mason said.

When he retired in 2008, Altobelli continued to be a fixture around the ballpark talking to fans, friends, and media alike. He suffered a stroke in 2017 that prevented all but one more visit to the stadium when one of his former players, Rich Dauer, was inducted in to the Red Wing Hall of Fame. "Alto" died in March of 2021 at the age of 88.

The Red Wings have enjoyed a long and storied history as a member of the International League. The names that either began, or in some cases ended, their careers in Rochester are legendary: Harry Walker, Stan Musial, Rip Collins, Bob Gibson, Luke Easter, Boog Powell, Earl Weaver, Jim Palmer, Don Baylor, Eddie Murray, Cal Ripken, Mike Mussina, and the list goes on and on. Nevertheless, any fan in Rochester will tell you that our town's title of Mr. Baseball does not belong to any one of those famous personalities but instead to an adopted son of our city, Joe Altobelli.

Dan Mason once said of his mentor, "Rochester is blessed to have a living legend like Joe as an active member of our community." As a grateful member of that community, I wholeheartedly agreed.

♦ 23 ♦

Rocky Colavito
(1955)

"Don't Knock the Rock." One of Cleveland's most beloved heroes of the diamond, Rocky Colavito.

"Don't Knock the Rock." It was the battle cry of one of the most passionate fan clubs in the history of Major League Baseball, the devoted followers of one Rocco Domenico Colavito, better known simply as Rocky Colavito. He was one of the most fearsome sluggers of the 1950s and 1960s. He appeared headed for a Hall of Fame career when his journey to Cooperstown was derailed by one of the most infamous trades in baseball history. Although he had many productive years after being traded from the Indians to the Tigers in 1960, the media tended to define his career forever after by that trade and "the curse" it was believed to have leveled on the Indians franchise.

Rocky Colavito was a magical name during my childhood even though I never saw him play. He retired after the 1968 season when I was just four years old. I don't remember watching my first baseball games until the 1971 World Series and yet, I knew who Colavito was from the first moment I showed any interest in the game.

There were two brothers, Kevin and Dean Ussia, who lived across the street from me when I was a kid. We did everything together from the time we were toddlers until we were teenagers. We rode bikes, watched TV, listened to music, and played every sport under the sun together, including baseball. Frank Ussia, their dad, was like a second father to me. Frank loved baseball and not only took us to the local minor league baseball games but coached our little league teams as well.

To demonstrate just how much I love and respect Frank Ussia: he's one of only two guys I never gave a hard time to for being a Yankees fan. He and my friend Joe Tempesta both grew up in the Bronx so I gave them a pass. I mean you can't fault a guy for rooting for their neighborhood team, right?

Frank used to tell us stories of his youth playing ball on the streets of New York. There were two mythic figures that came from the same neighborhood as Frank Ussia: Bobby Darin and Rocky Colavito. His allegiance to both of these men and their importance to our popular culture became our allegiance.

While we could listen to Darin's music and quite naturally become fans of the great singer, Colavito was something else again. We were never able to see him play; when we were kids there were no videotapes, no DVDs, and no YouTube or MLB Network to provide us with video footage of Colavito's career on the diamond. All we had were the stories from Frank and from assorted baseball books. For that reason, Colavito was one of those guys who always seemed larger than life to me, a mythical figure.

Rocco Domenico Colavito was born on August 10, 1933. His parents, Rocco and Angela, were immigrants from the Bari region of Italy. His mother died when he was just nine years old. The Crotona Park section of New York's Bronx was a tough neighborhood and many kids ended up on the path to crime and imprisonment. However, according to a 1959 *Saturday Evening Post* article written by Edward Linn, "Rocky's family ... always exerted a far stronger influence upon him than his associates did. He was the youngest of five children of a closely knit, religious household in which the father, in the patriarchal Italian manner, was firmly in control."

In the same article, Colavito's oldest brother, Dominic, was quoted as saying that Rocky had been considered "something of a sissy ... [because] he did most of the shopping for us and, when he had to, he could cook us up a pretty good meal." I just hope that no teammates or opponents who read that 1959 article tried to call Colavito a sissy. He was called "The Rock" for a reason, and it wasn't just a play on the words of his given name.

The Linn article goes on to say that Colavito was never bothered much by the neighborhood tough guys. He was such a good-natured kid that everyone seemed to like him and watch out for him. He did spend a lot of time in the local pool halls and became quite proficient at the game, but baseball was always his sport. He acquired a reputation as the kid who was going to be a big league ball player. According to Linn, when Colavito was as young as five years old, his brothers would take bets that he could throw a ball farther than any nine or 10-year-old around. They never lost a bet.

The young Colavito had natural power, one of the strongest arms in the game, and a tremendous work ethic and enthusiasm for his sport. His greatest weakness was his lack of speed. Due to Colavito's flat feet, there wasn't much room for improvement in that regard.

At the time of Colavito's signing the Cleveland GM was Hank Greenberg, the former Hall of Fame first baseman for the Tigers and Pirates. Greenberg became a great booster of, and ally to, Colavito within the organization. Greenberg saw a lot of his youthful self in Colavito and marveled at his abilities, particularly his strong throwing arm. "I wish I could say his personality reminded me of myself too," Greenberg told the *Saturday Evening Post* in 1959. "He had such a sunny disposition. He still does."

The Indians started Rocky off in D level ball in the Florida State League in 1951 when he was just 17 years old. He showed his power right away by belting 23 home runs in 140 games. He was moved up to B ball in 1952 but the most important stop of Colavito's career may have come in 1953 when he was promoted to the Reading team in the A level Eastern League. It was there that he met Carmen Parotte, whom he wed in 1954. The couple have enjoyed a long and happy union and raised three children: Rocky Jr., Marisa and Steven.

The years 1954 and 1955 were spent in Triple A ball with the Indianapolis team of the American Association. He had two magnificent years hitting a total of 68 home runs and compiling 220 RBIs over the two seasons. Colavito was certain he'd make the Indians club after such a stellar performance in Indianapolis. He started 1956 on the Cleveland roster but after two months was told that manager Al Lopez had decided to send him to San Diego in the minor leagues. Colavito was upset and threatened to quit. Hank Greenberg settled him down and promised that he'd be back soon. In just 35 games in San Diego, Colavito batted .368, hit 12 home runs and drove in 32 runs. He was recalled to the Indians where he finished second in the

Rookie of the Year voting for 1956, hitting 21 home runs in just 101 games. He never saw the minor leagues again.

Colavito enjoyed four spectacular seasons with the Cleveland Indians from 1956 to 1959. He was an idol to the bobby soxers and a hero to the little leaguers of Cleveland. Unfortunately, he never had an amicable relationship with the mercurial Frank "Trader" Lane who had taken over the general manager duties from Hank Greenberg in 1957. Most general managers of the time were famously cheap and would look for any reason to maintain or lower a player's salary from year to year. Colavito never had a bad year from 1956 to 1959, but Lane remained steadfast to his frugal nature. In a 2007 article with the *Boston Globe*, Colavito said Lane promised him a raise and then refused to honor his promise. Their relationship never recovered. Lane would make comments to the press making it clear that he was not as impressed with Colavito's skills as the rest of Cleveland was.

As early as 1958, Lane began to talk about trading Colavito. Hal Lebovitz of the *Cleveland News* wrote a column responding to the trade rumors with the headline "Don't Knock the Rock." It immediately became a battle cry of Colavito's teammates and fans. Ultimately, it made no difference to the egocentric Lane. After two superstar years in 1958 and 1959 when Colavito hit 40-plus home runs and drove in more than 100 runs in each season, he was traded to the Tigers right before the start of the 1960 season.

The Cleveland fans were enraged. Lane traded the 1959 home run champion straight up for Harvey Kuenn, the 1959 batting champion. But Colavito meant far more than numbers to the Cleveland faithful. He was one of them. To add insult to injury, when asked for a comment after the deal, Lane told reporters, "What's all the fuss about? All I did was trade hamburger for steak."

In 1994, author Terry Pluto wrote a book titled *The Curse of Rocky Colavito*. The author's contention was that the Cleveland Indians organization was forever cursed by the infamous deal that sent Rocky to Detroit. Somehow over the years, the belief sprang up that it was Colavito who put the curse on the organization. Colavito has dismissed all the talk about a curse as baloney. "I never put the evil eye on them," Colavito said in the 2007 *Globe* article. "It's not like in the old country in Italy where one of those old grandmothers drops oil into the water and if it doesn't spread, the curse is on. No.... I never put a curse on the Indians."

Reading through the newspaper clippings of Colavito's career, there emerges the image of two Colavitos: the nice guy who routinely stood outside the stadium until he fulfilled every autograph request from the kids waiting outside the locker room door, and the guy who, by 1964 following a trade to the Athletics, had been labeled by some in the press as "a problem player." It would seem that Colavito's great sin, if any, might have been a certain naïveté in dealing with press and management. Colavito, by all accounts, was an honest, forthright, and trusting man. He took you at your word. However, if you lied or misrepresented yourself, or worse yet Colavito, there could be trouble.

"I was always amiable unless somebody took potshots at me," said Colavito in the 2007 *Boston Globe* article. For example, there was a particular Detroit sportswriter who had a stormy relationship with the Tigers' slugger. "He had a column for me—'runs not batted in'—only when we were on the road 'cause he was afraid I would strangle him."

The most unfortunate result of all the press about Colavito and the curse is that it served to overshadow the truly impressive career that Colavito put together from 1956 to 1968. His power at the plate was never in question. The American League slugger hit 20 or more home runs for 11 consecutive seasons. On six occasions from 1958 to 1965, Colavito drove in 100 or more runs. He appeared in nine All-Star Games and hit three home runs. In fact, Colavito accounted for five of the A.L.'s nine runs in the 1962 All-Star Game in Chicago's Wrigley Field with a three-run homer, a sacrifice fly to drive in another run, and a run scored.

In the midst of a deep 3-for-28 slump in June of 1959, Colavito broke out of it by hitting four consecutive home runs in one game against the Baltimore Orioles. He is one of only 16 MLB players to have ever hit four home runs in one game. Amazingly, he came very close to being the only man to achieve the feat twice, as he told *Sports Collector's Digest* in August of 1998. It happened in Detroit while he was playing for the Tigers in 1962. Colavito hit three in a row and, according to writer Ross Forman, "what could have been number four went foul into the upper deck by about 15 feet. If it was fair, it would have been a home run anywhere in the park."

"I already had that other four-home-run game, so I wanted this one even more," Colavito told Forman.

Unfortunately, as previously noted, Colavito lacked any speed to go along with his power. "I ran a little below average, but I always dreamed of having incredible speed," Colavito told *Sports Collector's Digest*. "I always said, 'Just let me run incredibly well one time, just to see what it feels like.' I hit so many balls that, if I had just a drop more speed, I would have been safe. I can't tell you how many balls I was thrown out by half-a-step."

In my research on Colavito, I was amazed to discover what a great fielder he had been. In an article by Joe Trimble and Joe Lane, his old nemesis Frank Lane complained that despite his strong arm, Colavito didn't throw out too many base runners. The writers pointed out that the answer to Colavito's low numbers in throwing out base runners may have been provided by Casey Stengel who said of Colavito, "He sure does keep you from taking that extra base. Not many men dare run on him."

He deserved to win the Gold Glove in 1965 when he played in every game (162), compiling 1,428 innings in the outfield without committing a single error. He also threw out nine runners. Even with those gaudy numbers, he was overlooked as one of the three best outfielders in the American League, although not one of the three players chosen had better numbers than Colavito.

Colavito's lifetime statistics are equal to many players who are in the Baseball Hall of Fame but he has yet to be asked to join the Cooperstown elite. With typical

Colavito frankness, he told the *Boston Globe* that "I told my wife and son, 'If I die and they want to put me in, tell them to stick it 'cause it ain't gonna do me any good when I'm dead.'" That one statement endeared The Rock to me more than any other because he's absolutely right. The HOF has a habit of refusing people until after they're dead. If you're going to honor a guy, do it while he's still here to appreciate it. His numbers and legacy don't get any better after he's gone.

When asked in 1998 how he wanted to be remembered, Colavito said, "I mean this from the bottom of my heart: I want to be remembered as a decent human being, much more than anything else I've done. I want people to say, 'He was a good guy, a decent guy, a good human being.' I prefer that over anything baseball-related that they would say."

As far as this writer is concerned, I have but one thing to say: "Don't Knock the Rock." He was my kind of ballplayer.

♦ 24 ♦

Frank Malzone
(1955)

From 1957 to 1964, Frank Malzone was a reliable presence at the plate and the hot corner for the Bosox.

Frank Malzone is arguably one of the most beloved players in the history of the Boston Red Sox. Shy and unassuming, the quiet Malzone was a Fenway favorite for more than ten years at the hot corner. While his offensive numbers were solid but never spectacular, he was generally regarded as one of the finest fielding third basemen in all of baseball during the 1950s and 1960s. The struggles and obstacles he overcame to reach success in the big leagues are nothing short of inspirational.

Malzone was born on February 28, 1930, and grew up in the Clason Point section of the Bronx, New York. His father was an immigrant from Salerno, Italy, and his mother was born in America. He was the third of four children and as a kid he tagged along with brother Tony and sister Mary when they played ball with the neighborhood kids. As captain of the neighborhood team, Mary put her little brother Frank in right field when he was just seven years old. By the time he was 17, Frank Malzone helped lead Samuel Gompers High to the 1947 city championship. He had the desire to play Major League baseball but little hope of achieving his dream. He was undersized and received little attention from the big league scouts.

Having studied to be an electrician in his vocational high school, Malzone was ready to look for work in his chosen trade when a bird dog scout named Cy Phillips interceded. Phillips, who ran a sporting goods store in the Bronx, was a friend of George "Specs" Torporcer who in the late 1940s was the farm director for the Boston Red Sox. Phillips called Torporcer and suggested the Red Sox take a look at Malzone.

The Red Sox offered Malzone a $150 per month contract to sign and play in their farm system. Older brother Tony wanted his parents to hold out for a better deal but Malzone's dad, who worked as a laborer in the city water department, overruled him. The elder Malzone signed the contract one month before his youngest son turned 18.

Ironically, Malzone never heard from Phillips again until about ten years later when he called Malzone about getting tickets to a ballgame. Torporcer and Charlie Niebergall, the chief scout who signed Malzone, both left the Red Sox organization the year after Malzone signed on. Prior to his departure, Torporcer made it clear that although he was willing to give Malzone a chance in the farm system, he didn't think he was Major League material. Malzone was initially sent to Milford in the Class D Eastern Shore League where he batted a very respectable .304 and earned a promotion to Oneonta in the Class C Canadian-American League.

Oneonta would prove to be the greatest promotion of Malzone's life for reasons beyond the diamond. It was there that he met Amy Gennarino, a baseball fan and student at a local teachers college. They literally met in the local ice cream parlor on Main Street. Their courtship lasted two years before they were married in August of 1951 when Malzone's manager gave him two days off to tie the knot.

Prior to his nuptials, Malzone tore up his ankle while playing for Scranton in 1950. His leg was in a cast for three months and it was uncertain whether he would ever be able to play again. Fortunately, he suffered no permanent damage and worked hard to get back on the field for the '51 season. After a full season with Scranton in

1951, he was drafted into the Army. He went through basic training in Hawaii and was waiting to be sent to Korea when his orders changed and he was placed on one of the Army baseball teams. In a 1990 interview with *Sports Collectors Digest*, Malzone said, "So it worked out fine and I had a fine two years. Actually, I learned a lot about playing another position. I played shortstop in the service."

Upon his return to the states he was assigned to Louisville in the American Association, just one step away from the majors. His first season back he hit .270 with 11 home runs and 63 runs batted in. He played another full season with Louisville in 1955 but this time he batted .310 and took home the honors as the league's Most Valuable Player. At the end of the season he was called up to the parent Red Sox and started in both games of a doubleheader. He came through with six straight singles in his Major League debut. He played six games with the Bosox at the end of the 1955 season hitting .350 and handling 17 chances in the field without an error. He was on top of the world. Unbeknownst to Malzone, his world was about to come crumbling down around him.

Malzone and his wife had started their family in 1954 with the birth of a daughter, Suzanne. Their first son, James, was born in 1955. Four days after Christmas of 1955, Suzanne died suddenly. Both parents were understandably distraught. According to an April 12, 1958, article in the *Saturday Evening Post*, "Frank was inconsolable. Day after day he sat in one corner of the living room and stared wordlessly into space."

The article goes on to describe the two horrible months before the start of spring training. No one could get through to Malzone. His wife, his parents, his siblings all tried to get him to concentrate on something other than his grief but to no avail. He started the 1956 season with the Red Sox and did horribly. He just couldn't focus on the game. He was hitting .165 after 27 games when the Red Sox were forced to send him back to the minor leagues.

It took him nearly two weeks before he reported to his new assignment with the San Francisco Seals of the Pacific Coast League. Once in uniform for the Seals, Malzone's troubles persisted. He couldn't hit, he was making errors in the field, and the fans on the West Coast were wondering how and why Malzone had ever been named MVP of the American Association.

Amy Malzone, not knowing what else to do and desperate to help her husband and her family, turned to the parish priest for advice. The priest asked her if the couple had talked about their daughter Suzanne since she'd died and Amy said they had not. He encouraged her to force the subject with Frank in an attempt to "talk it out." It was wise advice from a clergyman in 1956. After all, this was years before people routinely talked about the importance of sharing and expressing their innermost feelings, especially Italian men.

According to the 1958 *Saturday Evening Post* article, "That night Amy brought up the subject of Suzanne when Frank came home from a twilight-night doubleheader. 'It was like opening a door that had been closed for months,' she [said].

'Everything that Frankie had been holding in came spilling out. We talked most of the night—not just about Suzanne, but about Jimmy and baseball and the future. And the next day, when Frankie smiled after kissing the baby and me good-by, I knew everything was going to be all right.'"

The emotional weight that had been lifted off Malzone's shoulders began to show results on the field. Manager Joe Gordon sent increasingly positive reports on Malzone back to the Red Sox on a monthly basis. Finally, on September 9, 1956, Gordon wrote this report to the Red Sox: "Malzone homered with bases full first inning. If this boy lays off bad-breaking ball because he's overanxious, he can hit any one. Is definitely worth another shot, and I think he can make it." Many years later Malzone remembered, "I finished strong in San Francisco. Joe Gordon was the manager at the time and he was a good man to play for. He kind of stayed with me, for which I was glad and everything worked out fine."

Malzone did indeed return to the Red Sox in 1957 and won the starting third baseman job. His first full season of Major League play exceeded everyone's expectations as he hit .292, drove in 103 runs, and was spectacular in the field. In fact, defensively, he led the league in putouts, assists, and double plays. Malzone remembers, "In '57 I set a Major League record in fielding for leading every category, even in errors. (Laughs) I had the highest fielding percentage so that means I got to a lot more balls than other guys did. It was a strange state, 'cause usually the guy with the highest percentage doesn't have the most errors, also. I think it was the first time in history an infielder did it."

Nevertheless, his fabulous season actually led to controversy. The Boston sportswriters wanted Malzone to be chosen as Rookie of the Year. The New York writers argued for Tony Kubek, reasoning that Malzone could not be considered a rookie because he played 27 Major League games in 1956 with 103 at bats. The Boston writers looked to the American League office for a ruling on what constitutes a "rookie." In the end, it was determined that since the writers give the award, the writers should determine the definition of a rookie. Kubek won the award. The 1958 article in the *Saturday Evening Post* also states, "Malzone was later named the Sophomore of the Year, a title he didn't know existed."

Following the controversy over the 1957 Rookie of the Year award, the Baseball Writers of America did establish formal guidelines as to what constitutes a rookie. In fact, while those guidelines have continued to evolve over the years, it's interesting to note that by today's standards, Frank Malzone would have been considered a rookie in 1957.

When manager Mike Higgins was asked for his appraisal of the young Malzone, he was effusive with his praise. "We're not only happy with Malzone, we're practically hysterical about him," he was quoted as saying. "I couldn't carry his glove. Neither could anyone else I can remember. He's the best third baseman I've ever seen."

Higgins was not alone in his assessment. In fact, Frank Malzone has the distinction of being the very first Gold Glove winner at third base in baseball history. The award was first presented in 1957 to the outstanding fielders at a given position in the Major Leagues. The following season, 1958, they began to give Gold Gloves for the best fielders at their positions in each separate league. Malzone would go on to win two more in 1958 and 1959 before a young upstart from the Baltimore Orioles named Brooks Robinson broke onto the scene. Amazingly, Robinson would go on to win the next 16 Gold Gloves in a row at third base from 1960 through 1975. However, in the 1990 interview with *Sports Collectors Digest*, Malzone admitted, "I always kid Brooks Robinson about the first Gold Glove. I say, 'You might have more than I have, but I've got one you'll never get!' It says 'Major League' on it, it doesn't say 'American League.'"

The slick fielding third baseman followed up his successful "sophomore year" in the Major Leagues with another great year with the glove and at the plate in 1958. He not only took home the first Gold Glove as the best third baseman in the American League but he knocked out 15 home runs for the second year in a row. He only drove in 87 runs compared to the 103 in 1957 but he raised his average to .295 and led the league in games played with 155.

For nearly a decade, Frank Malzone was a model of consistency and endurance for the Boston Red Sox. From 1957 to 1964, Malzone won three Gold Glove Awards, played in eight All-Star games and played in more than 150 games every year except for 1964 when he appeared in 148 games. In those eight years, he hit .280 and drove in 670 runs. The only thing Malzone didn't do was play in a World Series. The Red Sox released him at the end of the 1965 season. He signed with the California Angels and played one more season before retiring in 1966. The Red Sox finally made it back to the World Series in 1967. The lack of postseason play would be his only expressed regret in an otherwise gratifying career.

Malzone looked back at his first Gold Glove and his All-Star appearances as highlights of his long career in the game. He remembered with fondness traveling to St. Louis for his first All-Star game in 1957 with Red Sox legend Ted Williams. In his second, the 1959 All-Star game, Malzone hit a home run off Don Drysdale to tie the score in a game the American League eventually won 5–3.

Following his retirement in 1966, he returned to the Red Sox in 1967 as an advance scout, a position he held for over a quarter of a century before stepping down due to the extensive travel. During that time, he also served as an instructor during spring training camps, working with future Red Sox stars such as Rico Petrocelli and Jim Rice. As late as 2011, Malzone was still on the Red Sox payroll as a consultant, which amounts to a 60-year relationship with the same organization.

As a sign of the esteem in which fans and management held Malzone, he was selected in 1995 as one of the inaugural members of the Red Sox Hall of Fame. Malzone died four days after Christmas 2015 at the age of 85.

The strength and consistency of a Frank Malzone is hard to find these days in professional baseball. For a decade, he was the "iron man" of the Red Sox lineup and for those fans that remember with fondness his stellar play at the hot corner, he will remain an all-time Red Sox hero.

♦ 25 ♦

Jim Gentile
(1957)

Jim Gentile was anything but gentle against opposing pitchers.

He pronounces it Gen-TEEL. Italians pronounce it Gen-TEEL-ay. Either way, the irony is evident when you look at the image of the hulking behemoth who graces his old baseball cards. You can be sure that opposing pitchers thought of Jim Gentile as anything but gentle. In his prime, the 6'4", 215 pound first baseman with bulging triceps and a cyclone swing connected for 162 home runs during the five seasons from 1960 through 1964. For that five-year period, Gentile was one of the premier sluggers in the Major Leagues. Prior to and after those five years, it was a struggle.

Jim Gentile was yet another of the great number of Italian American baseball stars of the mid–20th century born in San Francisco, California. He started playing CYO baseball as a kid and eventually played in the San Francisco Park League. He attempted to try out for his high school varsity team as a sophomore and was turned away without a tryout because of his age. The coach told him to play JV. Gentile remembered the incident in a November 1960 article in *SPORT* magazine, "That got me real mad," Jim said. "I had been playing against college guys in the park league and here was this coach telling me that I couldn't even try out for the high school team. A couple of weeks later, I transferred to Sacred Heart High School."

He wasn't able to play that year anyway because the transfer made him ineligible. But it left a hint of things to come for Gentile. All too often in the ensuing years, he would let his temper influence his actions on and off the field.

He played well for Sacred Heart in his first year on the field as a junior and became the star of the team in his senior year, leading them to a city championship. He hit over .400 and compiled an 11–1 pitching record, striking out 17 batters in the high school all-star contest.

His performance, and no doubt his physical presence, caught the attention of the Yankee, Red Sox, and Dodger organizations. After discussing the various offers with his family, Gentile signed with the Brooklyn Dodgers. Following high school graduation, he was sent south to Santa Barbara, the Dodgers' class C farm team. His performance was far from spectacular. In 39 games he hit only .167 but three of his 16 hits were home runs. He also learned that pitching professionally was a little different from pitching in high school.

Despite the poor showing at the end of the 1952 season, he was sent up to the Dodgers' class A team in Pueblo for the 1953 season and started to make good on the promise he'd displayed to the Dodgers in high school. He played in 156 games, hitting a respectable .270 and belted out 34 home runs while driving in 102 runs. "The only trouble was," Gentile related to Larry Klein in the 1960 *SPORT* article, "I missed the ball a lot. In fact, I set a Western league record that year by striking out 135 times."

He was done as a pitcher and began to focus on his first base skills. The next three years he played A-ball in Pueblo and AA-ball in Mobile and Fort Worth. He hit well on all levels, keeping his batting average above .290 while averaging 34 home runs a season. His fielding was improving and he was gaining confidence. There was just one small problem and that was Gil Hodges.

Gil Hodges was a stellar first baseman who led all Major Leaguers in RBIs during the decade of the 1950s. It was impossible for the Dodgers to replace such a proven entity with a raw, young kid. Even so, in the fall of 1956, Gentile was invited on a trip to Japan with the Dodgers. During the exhibition games, Hodges played left field while Gentile played first base. Gentile caught fire, hitting .417 while smashing out eight home runs and 19 RBIs in just 17 games.

In spring training of 1957 Hodges played a lot of third base while Gentile took the role at first base. Gentile had a solid spring hitting .300 but was still cut from the Major League squad on the last day. Dodger GM Buzzie Bavasi told Gentile they were sending him to Montreal, the Dodgers' Triple A ball club, because he was too young to sit on the bench. It was a bitter disappointment for Gentile. He was angry and he let his emotions hurt his performance. "I just lost the desire to make good," Gentile said. "I argued with umpires, kicked lockers, smashed light bulbs and didn't care what happened. Then, Tommy Holmes, the old Braves star, took over as the Montreal manager and really straightened me out. 'Just knock off all this foolishness,' Tommy told me. 'You're too hotheaded and you're acting like a baby. Don't throw your career away. Be sensible. You've had four good years in the minors and you're sure to get your chance soon.'"

While Gentile would indeed get his chance, it would never be with the Dodgers. Even though he finished the season in Montreal with 15 home runs in the last five weeks, the Dodgers moved to Los Angeles in 1958 and all of a sudden they were looking for right-handed power to take advantage of the short left field porch in the LA Coliseum. Gentile was sent to Spokane where his frustration again lit his now famous temper. He missed a cut off and the manager bawled him out and sent him to the clubhouse. On his way in, he smashed the water cooler with his fist and required eight stitches to sew up his hand. Gentile would spend two more frustrating years in the Dodger farm system before getting his chance at the Major Leagues.

In October of 1959 Gentile received a call informing him that he'd been sold to the Baltimore Orioles for two minor-leaguers and cash. However, it was a conditional deal so if the Orioles didn't like what they saw, they could send him back to St. Paul in the American Association.

He headed to spring training of 1960 knowing he had to impress the Orioles to make the big club. Unfortunately, while playing winter ball in Panama, he'd developed a heel spur and needed to have some minor surgery to fix it. He showed up to camp with his foot in a cast. Once he made it on to the field, things only got worse. His play was anything but impressive. He muffed ground balls, made throwing errors, and did not hit a single home run throughout the entire spring training season.

No one was more surprised than Gentile when Paul Richards, the Oriole manager, announced that Jim Gentile would start at first base on Opening Day for the Birds. Richards conceded that "Jim looked pretty bad down south, but we wouldn't have bought him if we didn't think he could help us." Richards went on to say, "You all know that if he doesn't make good in 30 days, we can send him back to St. Paul and cancel the sale. But I can assure you that Jim is going to get a fair chance to show us he can do the job."

Richards's words were like music to Gentile's ears. All he'd been hoping for was a chance to prove himself on the Major League level and he wasn't going to waste it. "Just wait and see," Gentile said. "When the bell rings, I'll be a better ballplayer."

True to his word, Gentile came out hitting. He drove in four runs in the first two games of the season. He had such an incredible start that by the All-Star break he was leading the American League in hitting with a .328 average. He slumped a bit after the break but finished the year with a very respectable .292 average. He also hit 21 home runs and drove in 98 runs. Not too bad for a guy who'd languished in the minors for eight years.

As for his post–All-Star break slump, Gentile told sportswriter Larry Klein, "As far as averages go, I honestly believe in the old saying that 'water seeks its own level.' I was never much better than a .280 hitter in the high minors, so I don't really expect to go much over that in the majors." Gentile's wife Carole admonished him, saying, "Stop that kind of talk. You're such a pessimist. You're always downgrading yourself, expecting the worst to happen."

It was the severe self-criticism, quick temper, and impatience that many felt had held Jim back in his pursuit of that chance in the majors. He never blamed anyone else for his mistakes but sometimes he was unable to forgive himself and to look at his play objectively.

Manager Richards was a patient skipper and a good influence on the volatile Gentile. Richards was amply rewarded for his belief in his young first baseman. After "Diamond Jim's" initial 1960 success, he followed up with an even better 1961 campaign, destroying any thoughts whatsoever of a sophomore jinx. In fact, 1961 would be Jim Gentile's "career year" as he hit 46 home runs, drove in an astounding 141 RBIs and hit over .300 for what would be the only time in his Major League career.

Unfortunately, Gentile's 1961 accomplishments were somewhat overshadowed by the historic offensive numbers put up that year by Mickey Mantle, Harmon Killebrew, and Roger Maris. He did, however, find ways to stand out from the crowd. For example, he became the first player in baseball history to hit grand slams in consecutive innings. He also tied Ernie Banks's record for the most grand slam home runs in a season with five. That record would stand for 26 years before Don Mattingly broke it in 1987.

The rest of the league began to take notice of "Diamond Jim" Gentile, a nickname given to him years before by a Dodgers clubhouse man. "Gentile turned out to be one helluva ballplayer," said White Sox manager Al Lopez. "I'd classify him as one of the five best all-around ballplayers in the American League," Lopez said in early 1962.

Hall of Famer Hank Greenberg said at that time, "Gentile is a better fielder than Gehrig right now." Gentile's teammate, future Hall of Famer Brooks Robinson said,

"I don't know of anyone I'd rather throw to—he has a great stretch." Unfortunately, it was all too good to last. In the end, Gentile was never able to overcome his debilitating temper.

After his breakout performance in 1961, Gentile's batting average plummeted 51 points in 1962 to .251 while hitting 13 fewer home runs than the year before. In fact, Gentile would never hit above .251 again. The following year was even worse as he hit .248 with 24 home runs.

In a *Chicago Daily News* article by Milton Gross in the spring of 1963, Gentile admitted he was confused and frustrated by the way his play had dropped off. He also knew there was only one person to blame. "There's only one guy can help me and that's myself," said Gentile. "I'm my own worst enemy. I think myself into trouble. I talk to myself to stop it, but I just can't." According to Gross, it was suggested to Gentile that he get hypnotized or psychoanalyzed but Gentile balked at the idea. "I'd be afraid to," Gentile said. "I'd be afraid of what they'd find out. I know what's wrong with me. If I could only figure out how to handle it."

Reading all the old clippings now, it's a sad story. Gentile never did "figure himself out"—at least not in time to save his baseball career. After the disappointing '63 season, Gentile was traded to the Kansas City Athletics. He hit 28 home runs but struck out 122 times in his one full year in Kansas City. He spent part of 1965 with KC before being traded to the Houston Astros and then was traded again by the Astros to the Cleveland Indians in 1966. That was the end of the line for Gentile in the majors. He spent two more years with San Diego of the Pacific Coast League before hanging up his spikes for good after the 1968 season. At 34 years old, he was done.

He tried to get jobs in baseball as a coach after his playing days were over but he had no luck. His reputation as a hothead preceded him. It's tough to get a job that requires patience and calm when you've spent almost 20 years in baseball smashing helmets, busting bats, and demolishing water coolers.

He moved to Oklahoma and eventually retired as the manager of a department store. Then after being out of the game for more than 30 years, he got a job managing the Fort Worth (TX) Cats of the All American Association. As a 67-year-old rookie manager, he was philosophical about his past. "I was temperamental," he said. "I guess I was an angry kid after having all those years in the minors. After I had that great year (1961), Gus Triandos said to me, 'You had the kind of year guys would die for, and you weren't happy one day.' You know what? He was right."

In a *Baltimore Sun* article by John Eisenberg, he described Gentile as a man who now "looks back at his life and career with wry humor. He's just a big puppy now, kind and funny and able to poke fun at the way he was."

Jim Gentile hit 245 minor league home runs and 179 Major League home runs for a total of 424 round-trippers in 20 seasons of professional baseball. It's an impressive slugging legacy. One hopes he enjoyed at least some of those trots around the bases.

♦ 26 ♦

Joe Torre
(1960)

Joe Torre had strong enough credentials as a player to make the Hall of Fame but entered as a manager.

Joe Torre entered baseball's Hall of Fame as one of three managers in the Class of 2014 but he easily could have entered the hallowed hall as a player as well. Torre, who broke in as a rookie in 1960 with the old Milwaukee Braves, spent 18 years in the big leagues winning the 1971 MVP Award and finishing with a solid .297 lifetime batting average, 2,342 hits, and 1,185 runs batted in. I would have much preferred to have Torre go in as a player because then he would have had to go in as a member of the Braves or the Cardinals. As it is, he entered the Hall of Fame as a manager of the team that he led to four World Championships, the New York Yankees.

As a fan, you can either love or hate the New York Yankees. That may be why one of my favorite lines in Torre's 1997 autobiography, *Chasing the Dream: My Lifelong Journey to the World Series*, written with Tom Verducci, is when Torre says, "I never had liked the Yankees—everybody in my family grew up fans of the Giants and the National League." So how, then, does a nice National League boy like Joe Torre end up becoming synonymous with the most famous American League franchise in baseball history? *La forza del destino!*

Joseph Paul Torre was born on July 18, 1940, in Madison Park Hospital in Brooklyn. The youngest of five children, Torre had two older brothers, Rocco and Frank, and two older sisters, Josephine (who joined the convent and became Sister Marguerite) and Rae. His mother was born Margaret Rofrano in Italy and came to America as a young girl. His father was born in America.

Torre's dad was a New York City police officer. He was also an abusive husband. Torre remembers coming home from school and checking to see if his father had gone to work yet by looking for his car. "If I saw the black Studebaker out front," wrote Torre in *Chasing the Dream*, "there was no way I was going home. I'd go to a friend's house or stay outside and play." He can remember his dad raising the back of his hand to his mother and then nothing—his memory blacks out. He blocked out as many of the bad memories as possible. In speaking of his father, he writes, "Although he never physically hurt me, he verbally abused me often."

But, according to Torre, that was only part of the story. "Don't get me wrong—our home was filled with plenty of love too. In fact, I was smothered with attention and affection because I was so much younger than my siblings," remembers Torre. "I think the nervousness that pervaded our house made us cling to one another a little more tightly. Of course, my mother was especially protective of me in that environment because I was the youngest. This much I knew for sure: I was loved very much, but my father frightened me."

His strongest male role models came in his older brothers Rocco and Frank. Rocco became a beat policeman and a solid family man and Frank a professional ballplayer with the Milwaukee Braves. Joe had an easy, secure relationship with his oldest brother Rocco. He was more emotionally accessible than Frank. In his autobiography, Torre writes, "It was a very comfortable feeling to be around Rocco and to be at his happy home."

His brother Frank was a different story. Frank Torre was Joe Torre's idol. He was also his harshest critic. Joe Torre was overweight in his teens and Frank would tease him mercilessly, calling him a fat slob and telling him he was too fat to be a ballplayer. At the same time, Joe says he always knew Frank's bark was worse than his bite. Frank was also very generous with his family and even paid for his younger brother to go through private school. When Frank Torre's Milwaukee Braves won the 1957 World Series over the New York Yankees, his 17-year-old brother Joe was right there in the locker room seeing his future dreams unfold in front of him. Like his big brother, he, too, dreamed of one day being a World Champion.

In *Chasing the Dream*, Joe Torre said, "I'm forever grateful that Frank is a little rough around the edges. He was exactly what I needed, especially when our father left. I was this shy, overweight kid with terrible self-confidence who was being coddled by his mother and sisters. Frank was the kick in the butt I needed to amount to anything in life. It was Frank who toughened me up, Frank who turned me into a catcher.... Frank who was everything I wanted to be. He was a ballplayer. I may not have had a father in my life then, but I sure as hell had a hero."

His lack of confidence prevented him from trying out for the high school baseball team but he did try out for the Cadets, which was a local sandlot team that Frank had helped lead to a national tournament victory in 1949. Joe played so well for the Cadets that he finally worked up the courage to try out for his St. Francis Prep team during his junior year. He made the team without a problem. He played two years for both St. Francis Prep and the Cadets, primarily at first and third base and then finished his senior year at St. Francis with a .500 average. Even with his standout success at St. Francis Prep, not a single scout was interested in him. The Yanks, Dodgers, Red Sox, and even the Braves were all less than flattering in their assessment of Torre—he was too big and too slow for the big leagues.

Following graduation, Joe got a job as a page on the American Stock Exchange and although he was asked to play with the Brooklyn Royals in a better division than the Cadets, he chose to stay with the teammates he knew. Frank interceded with the coach of the Cadets and asked him to move Joe to the catcher's position. Joe Torre says Frank wanted to toughen him up but logically, no one ever hurried to play catcher. It was a tough, thankless position so if you were a good catcher, it was easier to move ahead. Frank knew that. After one season with the Cadets, the Braves scouts did a complete turnaround on Joe Torre and recommended that management sign him for a five-figure bonus. When the GM asked the scout what had changed he was told, "He's [Torre] catching now and he looks great there."

For a first baseman or third baseman, he was slow. For a catcher, he was just fine. Ironically, in the second half of his big league career, he would almost exclusively play either first or third base.

Torre moved up the minor league ladder quickly. He was always a solid hitter. In his first year in the Braves system they sent him to Eau Claire, Wisconsin, in the Class C League where he proceeded to win the Northern League batting title with a .344 average. When the season ended he was told to report to the parent Braves. On

26 ♦ Joe Torre (1960)

September 25, 1960, pinch-hitting for Warren Spahn, Joe Torre got his first Major League hit off Pirates pitcher Harvey Haddix in his first big league at-bat. He was 20 years old. Less than two years earlier, he'd been told by half a dozen clubs that he wasn't Major League material.

Joe Torre went on to have a very successful 18-year Major League career. He spent nine years in the Braves organization, moving to Atlanta with the team in 1966. It was with the Braves that he had the opportunity to play alongside the heroes he'd idolized as a kid, the men who'd eaten at his dinner table in Brooklyn but who he'd been too shy to even talk to when they visited—Eddie Matthews, Hank Aaron, Del Crandall, Lew Burdette, and Warren Spahn. Unfortunately, he didn't get to share the experience with his brother Frank. Just a few months before Joe had been called up to the Braves, Frank Torre had been sent down to the minor leagues. Torre remembers, "My only regret was that Frank wasn't there with the Braves when I broke in. We played against each other later, in 1962 and 1963 when Frank was with Philadelphia, but we never played on the same team, except in spring training. Frank had had more to do with getting me to the big leagues than anybody else, so I would have loved to share the experience with him."

In 1969, Joe Torre was traded to the St. Louis Cardinals where he made lifelong friends like Tim McCarver and Bob Gibson and won the National League MVP Award in 1971 while leading the league in hits (230), RBIs (137), and batting average (.363). In 1975 he was traded to the Mets. By 1977 he was 36 years old and not playing every day. His mother had recently died and he was increasingly unhappy as a part-time player. Torre was growing restless when he was asked in May if he was interested in managing the team. He accepted the offer and on May 31, 1977, he took over from Joe Frazier as manager of the New York Mets.

In recalling his first days as a big league manager, Torre remembered, "My energy and my outlook were completely rejuvenated by becoming a manager. The best job in baseball is playing every day. The next best job in baseball is managing—it easily beats playing part time. I wasn't nervous at all about managing, even though I had never done it before (although Gibson used to accuse me of doing it all the time with the Cardinals). My excitement was equal to being called up to the big leagues for the first time."

Torre won his first game as the Mets manager and went on to win his first 11 out of 16 games. Then, just two weeks after his hiring, the Mets pulled off what has since become known as the Midnight Massacre, trading Tom Seaver to the Reds and Dave Kingman to the Padres just before the June 15 trading deadline. The team finished in sixth place with a 64–98 record. Eventually, Torre realized that "If the Mets had been more committed to winning, they would have hired a more experienced manager."

Following his tenure with the Mets, he was hired to manage his former team, the Atlanta Braves, owned by communications mogul Ted Turner. His first year at the helm, the Braves won the division but lost three straight games to the National League East Division-winning Cardinals. He managed the Braves for two more seasons before they parted ways. He never got along well with Turner, who reneged on an attendance clause in Torre's contract. In the 1997 autobiography, Torre recalled, "Steinbrenner gets a lot of notoriety for aggravating his managers, but George isn't nearly as meddlesome as Ted was in those days."

With the phone not ringing, Torre turned to broadcasting and went to work for Gene Autry and the California Angels for five years as a color commentator. Then in July of 1990 he received a phone call from his old friend Dal Maxvill of the Cardinals. Longtime Cardinal skipper Whitey Herzog was stepping down and Torre was offered the job of Cardinals manager, which he happily accepted.

He lasted just about the same amount of time with the Cardinals as he did with the Mets. The management of the Cardinals had difficulty with Torre's frankness and when he was fired by the Cards during the 1995 season, he was certain that was the end of the line—his dream of making it to a World Series would never come true. In his own words, "Who would want a fifty-five-year-old manager who had been fired three times, had never been to the World Series, and had a lifetime record of more losses (1,003) than wins (894)? Nobody, I figured."

A few months later, Torre interviewed for the New York Yankee general manager's job that went to Bob Watson. Soon after, a Steinbrenner advisor who was a friend of Torre's asked if he'd be interested in managing the team because Buck Showalter was leaving. Torre said, "Absolutely." When Joe phoned his brother Frank to tell him the news, Frank said, "You don't need this crap anymore." Joe replied, "But Frank, it's a good opportunity to get to a World Series."

The rest, as they say, is history. Torre's Yankee experience was quite different from his previous managing jobs. Steinbrenner, for all his faults, always wanted to win so he invested the time, money, and personnel in doing everything possible to field a winning club. Torre worked fabulously with his coaches, knew when to be patient and when to be tough and finally, after 4,200 games, longer than any other player or manager has ever had to wait, he made it to his first World Series game on October 20, 1996. The opponents were the Braves, the team with whom Torre had begun his career. The Braves pummeled the Yankees, winning the first two games of the series by a combined score of 16–1. Seizing the drama of the moment, Torre led his Bronx Bombers back to win four games in a row and become World Champions. Joe Torre would go on to lead the Yanks to three more championships during his 12 years at the helm. He had fulfilled his dream and then some.

It took a while for his personal life to match the success of his professional career. He endured two failed marriages before finding true love with his third wife Ali, whom he married in 1987. Together they had a daughter, Andrea Rae, as well as founding the Joe Torre Safe at Home Foundation, inspired by his childhood experiences with domestic violence. The foundation helps fund a dozen domestic violence resource centers in the greater New York City area. He also has three children from his first two marriages: a son, Michael, and two daughters, Lauren and Cristina.

The last three years in New York, the Yankees failed to advance beyond the first round of playoffs. When the Yankee brass wanted to make a cut to Torre's salary, he elected to move on. In 2008, Torre returned to the National League as manager of the Los Angeles Dodgers. He would spend three years at the helm, leading the Dodgers to the postseason twice but never making it into the World Series. He resigned after the 2010 season and went to work in the front offices of MLB. Since 2020, he has been a Special Assistant to the Commissioner of Baseball.

Torre is the only man to have recorded 2,000 hits as an MLB player and 2,000 victories as an MLB manager. In addition to his place in the Baseball Hall of Fame, he is also a member of the Cardinals Hall of Fame and the Braves Hall of Fame, and has had his number retired by the Yankees.

Joe Torre has spent more than 60 years in professional baseball. He is a devoted family man and a grateful father and grandfather. He was a talented catcher, a respected manager and, by all accounts, a loyal and valued friend. Not too bad for a shy, chubby kid from Brooklyn who had a dream and kept relentlessly chasing it until happiness finally caught him.

♦ 27 ♦

Ron Santo
(1960)

Both on the field and in the broadcast booth, the fans of Chicago loved Ron Santo.

A warhorse on the field despite a career-long battle with diabetes, Ron Santo won the admiration of fans and players alike on the road to induction into the Hall of Fame.

Growing up in Western New York in the early 1970s, Santo was little more than a picture on a baseball card to me. I knew he was a good ballplayer but I never even thought about the possibility that he might be Italian like Rico Petrocelli, another third baseman of the era whom I admired. I suppose it was Santo's reddish brown hair and ruddy complexion that fooled me. I knew he was a solid hitter and a tough competitor, but that was about it.

Years later, I heard some of his work as an announcer for his beloved Cubs and I had to chuckle because his style reminded me of Phil Rizzuto when he was broadcasting for the Yankees back in the 1970s and 1980s. There was never a doubt who Santo was rooting for—it was a style that was at once unprofessional and at the same time totally engaging. I hated it when Rizzuto had done it, but that was because I've spent my entire life loathing the Yankees. I have no such distaste for the Cubs so I found Santo's histrionics in the booth distracting but somewhat charming.

Not having been a Cubs fan or a native Chicagoan, I knew nothing of Santo's lifelong struggle with diabetes until talk of his Baseball Hall of Fame votes began to draw national attention. However, I didn't need to be a lifelong Cubs fan to feel Santo deserved induction into the Hall of Fame long before he finally got in. In fact, I was angered that the call didn't come until after Santo had died. Now, after reading Santo's autobiography *For Love of Ivy*, written with Randy Minkoff, and *Ron Santo: A Perfect 10*, by Pat Hughes (Santo's old broadcasting partner) and Rich Wolfe, it's inconceivable to me that it took 32 years for Santo to be given his rightful place alongside baseball's greatest in Cooperstown.

Santo was everything that Major League Baseball could possibly want in a player—he was tough, reliable, loyal, hardworking, fan-friendly, and inspirational. Most fans and opponents had no idea just how inspirational he was until he'd been playing in the majors for more than 10 years, because no one but management and his closest teammates knew he was a diabetic. He wanted to be recognized as a good ball player without limitations, not as a good ball player with diabetes.

Ronald Edward Santo was born in Seattle in February of 1940. He grew up in an ethnic neighborhood called "Garlic Gulch." His childhood was far from ideal. He described his birth father as "a wonderful Italian man when he was sober, but, sadly, he had a drinking problem that made him vicious." Despite young Ron's attempts to intervene and protect his Swedish mother, his father would beat his wife. The couple separated when Ron was six and divorced a year later. His father would pick up Ron and his sister every two or three weeks for a short while until eventually he stopped showing up completely. Ron didn't see his father again until he started being scouted by the Major League clubs as a star high school athlete.

Fortunately for Santo, his mother was tough but loving. She worked hard to put him through parochial school, where he remembered "Sports saved [him]." He starred in football, basketball, and baseball, but it was baseball that found a special place in his heart.

He was chosen to play in the Hearst All-Star game at the Polo Grounds in New York in 1958. It was a premier game for high school baseball players and was heavily scouted. He was catching at the time and although he made a couple of errors in the field, he also knocked out a couple of hits. After the game, scouts from the Yankees and Indians both talked to him about working out with their team for a few days. Instead, he went straight home to discuss the situation with his stepfather, John Constantino, whom he loved and trusted.

Upon his return, he learned that his family had been inundated with calls from all 16 teams. The Reds had made the most generous offer of $80,000 to sign. The last club Santo heard from was the Cubs, which surprised him because a Cubs scout named Dave Kosher had scouted him through high school. It turned out Kosher was somewhat embarrassed to approach him because the Cubs weren't willing to even come close to matching his best offer. The head scout for the Cubs, a man named Hard Rock Johnson, told Santo, "We're offering $20,000. There's no way you're ever going to be a third baseman in the Major Leagues, son. Maybe you can make it as a catcher. But that's about it."

There was something magical about Chicago for Santo. He'd grown up watching the Game of the Week on TV and was a fan of Ernie Banks, and he figured he'd have a better chance getting to the Major Leagues faster with a club like the Cubs than the veteran-laden Reds. "I just didn't want to get lost in the maze of the minor league system, where some clubs had 20 teams in their organizations from Class D up to the majors," Santo remembered in *For Love of Ivy*.

Unfortunately, it wasn't just as easy as signing the contract and heading into professional baseball for Santo. Prior to leaving for his first minor league camp in 1959, he went to the doctor for a routine annual physical. The doctor was distressed to find sugar in his urine and sent him to the hospital for further tests, where his blood sugar registered over 400. Ron Santo, the strapping, solid high school sports star who was heading into professional sports, was a diabetic.

"It was unbelievable," Santo recalled. "I woke up that morning a happy, healthy teenager, and suddenly I had a disease I had never heard of. And no one could tell me whether I could play baseball again."

Just as all his dreams had begun to come true, they all seemed to be falling apart. He headed to the library to learn as much as he could about this mysterious disease and was distressed to find out that the life expectancy of a juvenile diabetic at that time was 25 years. He was terrified and confused. He was just about to begin his career with the Cubs. As he remembered it, his quandary was: "Should I keep my secret and give myself a chance to let them judge me without prejudice? Or should I tell them up front, and risk having them look only at the disease instead of looking at the player?"

He attended a two-week clinic in Seattle for diabetics to learn more about the disease, the symptoms, and the treatments. He was told that he would, eventually, have to go on insulin. He recalled being in denial at the time but his doctors assured him whether he went a year or two without needing it, eventually he would require daily insulin shots. In the meantime, Santo headed to his first spring training with a heavy secret and a burning desire to prove he could be a big-league ball player.

He was picked up in Arizona by Gene Lawing, the director of player personnel, whose first words to the young Santo were, "Kid, I got to tell you, you aren't going to make it to the Major Leagues." Elvin Tappe, a veteran catcher and coach at the camp, also showed little interest and confidence in Santo. Despite the fact that he'd played third base for most of his high school career, the Cubs had signed Santo as a catcher. The one person who was impressed by Santo was hitting instructor and Hall-of-Famer Rogers Hornsby. At the end of the three-week rookie camp, Hornsby had singled out only Billy Williams and Santo as potential Major League hitters.

He was assigned to Class AA San Antonio in 1959. He began the season poorly and was hitting .169 when his manager Grady Hatton informed him he was going to be sent down to Class B ball. Santo pleaded with Hatton to give him just one more week to prove himself. Hatton relented and Santo went on a tear. He remained with San Antonio, finishing his first season of professional ball with a .327 batting average, 11 home runs and 87 runs batted in.

Santo had a great spring training in 1960 and was originally told by the Cubs that he would be their third baseman for the season. At the last minute, they made a trade with the Dodgers for Don Zimmer with the explanation that they felt Santo was still too young to be a daily starter in the big leagues. Santo was crushed and nearly quit, but his wife and GM John Holland convinced him to take a Major League contract to play for AAA Houston with the assurance he would be with the Cubs in short order. By Sunday, June 26, 1960, he joined the Chicago Cubs in Pittsburgh for a double-header against the Pirates. In his Major League debut, Santo went 3-for-7 with five runs batted in. He finished the year with the Cubs hitting .251, driving in 44 runs, and belting nine home runs. He finished fourth in the balloting for Rookie of the Year. He was 20 years old.

The year 1961 saw his first full season in the majors and he excelled. He smashed out 23 home runs and drove in 83 runs with a .284 batting average and a .362 on-base percentage. By the end of the season, however, he began to feel some pain in his right leg. He was also losing weight and urinating frequently. He knew he was in trouble. He still had not told anyone in the Cubs organization, so he contacted his son's pediatrician and shared his secret with him. The doctor examined him and immediately left the room and came back with a bottle of insulin and told Santo that if he didn't start taking it immediately, he would lose his leg.

He spent that winter before spring training of 1962 educating himself not only on the use of insulin, but on his own body and the symptoms he would encounter when his blood sugar was low. He pushed his body to dangerous limits to see how far he could go and what the results of waiting too long to address the problem would be. He scared himself enough to know that the predictions of the Seattle doctors had finally come true—he would be on insulin for the rest of his life. Regardless, he was still going to play baseball and, for the time being, keep his disease a secret.

As it turned out, 1962 was an adjustment period for Santo and it was reflected in his statistics. His batting average fell to .227 and although he only hit 17 home runs, he still managed to drive in 83 runs. He also played in all 162 games, which in and of itself was an amazing feat considering the circumstances, which were unknown to all but his family. Once he'd learned how to manage his blood sugar levels, he bounced back with a stellar season in 1963, lifting his batting average 70 points to .297 and once again playing in all 162 games. The 1963 season also marked his first year as an All-Star. The following year, 1964, Santo hit .313 and led the league in triples, bases on balls, and on-base percentage. He finished eighth in MVP voting and won his first of five Gold Glove awards at third base.

From 1961 to 1971, Santo played in 1,749 games, averaging 26 home runs while driving in 80 or more runs every season. He was also named captain of the Chicago Cubs. There was something special about Santo that endeared him to both fans and teammates alike. Santo didn't just play for the Chicago Cubs, he *was* the Chicago Cubs.

As the '60s wore on, management and teammates learned of Santo's daily struggle with diabetes. It only served to increase their appreciation and admiration for him. He never complained, never asked for special treatment. He went out on the field, day in and day out, and gave the game, and his team, everything he had.

Santo—like his Hall of Fame teammates Banks, Williams and Jenkins—never made it into a World Series. The closest they ever came was the magical 1969 season in which they led the National League Eastern Division for most of the summer before giving way in September to the "Miracle Mets." It was a heartbreaking disappointment but Santo always chose to remember the greatness of the team and the camaraderie of its members.

The Cubs, looking to rebuild in the early 1970s after Banks retired in 1971, wanted to trade Santo away to the California Angels. By that time, Santo had put down roots in Chicago and didn't want to leave, and so, as unthinkable as it seemed at the time, he was traded to the crosstown Chicago White Sox. He spent one unhappy year in a White Sox uniform before retiring at the end of the 1974 season.

He was involved in a variety of successful business ventures throughout his lifetime but baseball finally lured him back in 1990 when he joined the Cubs broadcast team as the WGN radio color commentator working with partner Pat Hughes. He became as beloved for his colorful exuberance in the booth to a new generation of Cubs fans as he had been on the field to their parents.

When Santo finally went public with his diabetes in 1971, he immediately took advantage of the opportunity to become a spokesperson for JDRF, the Juvenile Diabetes Research Foundation, and used his fame to help raise awareness and money to further research in finding a cure. Prior to his death in 2010, it was estimated that

Santo had raised well over $65 million for JDRF. That work continues today through sales of a wonderful documentary film entitled *This Old Cub*, an entertaining and inspirational documentary directed by Santo's son Jeff, as well as the annual JDRF Ron Santo Walk to Cure Diabetes.

Santo liked to say that he was given a gift to play baseball. That may be true, but it's what he did with his gift along with the obstacles that were thrown in front of him that was truly special. He inspired by example through hard work, being grateful for the good in his life, and choosing not to dwell on the negative, and always using whatever he had to try to help others. Ron Santo was truly someone special.

♦ 28 ♦

Jim Fregosi
(1961)

Fregosi was the "face of the franchise" for the first 11 years of the Angels' history, 1961–1971.

A baseball lifer, he excelled as a player, manager, executive and scout, inspiring all who knew or played him with his grit, will to win and knowledge of the game.

Jim Fregosi is not a member of Baseball's exclusive Hall of Fame and probably never will be. However, when he died on Valentine's Day of 2014 at the age of 71, he was generally considered to be one of the most knowledgeable, colorful, and respected individuals ever involved in the game. He spent all 53 years of his adult life in Major League baseball as a player, manager, executive, and scout.

He was the very first star for the epically indecisive American League franchise that plays in Anaheim, California. When Fregosi began with the team in their first year of existence in the majors, they were the Los Angeles Angels. By the time he was traded 11 years later, they were the California Angels. In the years since, they've been the Anaheim Angels, the Los Angeles Angels of Anaheim, and they have now returned to their original moniker, the Los Angeles Angels. While they can't make up their minds about what they'd like to be called, one thing is certain—Angels fans, scholars, and scribes all recognize that, as a player and manager, Fregosi helped bring respect to the franchise in their nascent years.

Fregosi spent 18 years as a Major League player, the first 11 years of them with the Angels. In a span of eight years from 1963 to 1970, he was named to six All-Star teams, garnered MVP votes all eight seasons, won a Gold Glove at shortstop and, as of the end of the 2024 season, still holds the Angel team record for 70 lifetime triples. He is also the only Angel to hit for the cycle more than once. Fregosi did it twice: once in 1964 and again in 1968.

James Louis Fregosi was born on April 4, 1942, in Italian America's baseball capital of San Francisco, California. He was the youngest of three children born to a couple who owned a grocery store and young Jim started playing baseball for the Fregosi Market Nine, the youth team sponsored by his dad's store. He went on to win 11 varsity letters for baseball, football, basketball, and track. One of his high school teammates remembered Jim playing baseball and running track at the same time. Between innings he'd run to the track while getting out of his baseball uniform, make his leap in the broad jump competition and then run back to the baseball game while putting his uniform back on.

Fregosi had scholarship offers to play college football but chose to sign with the Boston Red Sox for a reported $20,000 bonus in 1960. He played one year of D ball for the Red Sox before getting picked by the Los Angeles Angels in the 1960 expansion draft. He jumped all the way to the AAA level when he was assigned to Dallas–Fort Worth in 1961. He played in 11 games with the Angels at the end of the 1961 season but began 1962 back in Dallas. Midway through the '62 season he was called back up to the Angels and never looked back. In 58 games with the Angels in 1962, the 20-year-old Fregosi finished with a .291 average.

Fregosi considered it a lucky break to have been chosen by the expansion Angels. In a 1989 interview with the *Los Angeles Times*, Fregosi said, "I probably would not have had an opportunity to get to the Major Leagues as quickly as I did with the

Angels." In that same interview, he recalled the strong relationships he forged and maintained with Angel fans and management. "They knew I was a good player. And I say good player because I was not a great player. But I took a great deal of pride playing hard and playing tough. Those things mean a lot to me," Fregosi said.

Fregosi's attitude and style of play also meant a lot to the men he played with and against. Whether he was having an all-star season or not, he was respected throughout the league. When Fregosi took over the manager's job in Philadelphia in 1991, a former teammate told sportswriter Ron Rapoport of the *Los Angeles Times*, "I don't like him. He doesn't like me either ... but I'd rather have him on the field with me than anyone else I can think of. He hates to lose."

When Fregosi was called up to the Angels midway through the 1962 season he struggled for the first few weeks before he finally began to hit the ball. In fact, the entire Angels team, in just their second year in the league, was hovering near first place until the end of the season. The Yankees ended up winning the division but the Angels finished the season 10 games over .500 for a respectable third-place finish. "I feel that Fregosi, with his great speed and line-drive type hitting, could easily become one of the most exciting players in the league," general manager Fred Haney said following the '62 campaign. "He certainly adds a great deal of speed to our lineup. Of course, Jim has a lot to learn, but he has shown us that he is willing and desirous to improve himself. This means a lot in baseball."

As strong-willed and opinionated as Fregosi could be, he was known as a serious student of the game who was always willing to learn.

The year 1963 was Fregosi's first full year in the Major Leagues at the tender age of 21 and he showed that he could play with the best. He hit a solid .287 while smashing 12 triples and scoring 83 runs. Many of the baseball writers, however, considered 1964 to be Fregosi's breakout year as he racked up 18 home runs, 72 RBIs, and 86 runs. He also drastically reduced his strikeouts and increased his walks while making his first All-Star team.

By the end of the decade, he was the unquestionable face of the franchise and recognized team leader. The 1970 California Angels Scorebook reported that a 1969 poll among fans named Fregosi the "Greatest Angel Ever." A 1971 article in *All Sports* magazine said of Fregosi, "That he's the heart and soul of the Angels, the standard against which others are measured, is proven virtually each time another player, manager, or club executive is interviewed." When Fregosi was out of the lineup to have surgery on his foot during the '71 season, his manager, Lefty Phillips, said, "He was going to be the key to this club, both in ability and leadership. We're just not the same club without him."

Proving that baseball is every bit as much a business as it is a game, after missing over 50 games and batting a disappointing .233 during an injury-plagued 1971 season, Fregosi was traded to the New York Mets for Frank Estrada, Don Rose, Leroy Stanton, and a young pitcher named Nolan Ryan. For years after that, Fregosi was remembered primarily as being on the wrong end of one of the worst trades in baseball history. In truth, it wasn't such a bad deal at the time. Fregosi was a proven team leader who was thought of as one of the very best shortstops in all of Major League baseball. Ryan was a 24-year-old pitcher who had a losing record after playing four full seasons with the Mets. He was a fireball pitcher with questionable control. Tom Verducci of *Sports Illustrated* said following Fregosi's death, "There was a reason the Mets traded Nolan Ryan to get him [Fregosi]—he was that good."

As it turned out, Fregosi never was the same player again once he left California. He was with the Mets for one mediocre campaign in 1972 before being sold to the Texas Rangers during the 1973 All-Star break. He came to the Rangers as a utility player and a seasoned veteran who could help give a young Rangers team the benefit of his years of baseball experience. He rarely played shortstop as he was switched to the less demanding corners of the infield at third and first base.

By the end of the '72 season, Fregosi was looking ahead to what he wanted to do after his playing days were over. In the off-season between 1969 and 1970, Fregosi had managed in the Puerto Rican League and led his team to a championship. At the time, Fregosi said, "It was an experience that I think every player should have. The responsibility involved really makes a difference in attitude. I know now how it must feel for Major League managers to try to direct all facets of the game."

Fregosi enjoyed managing. Following the 1972 season, his old manager Bill Rigney advised him to stay in the game as long as possible and soak up as much knowledge as he could if he wanted to become a Major League manager. When the Rangers sent him a 1973 contract with a pay cut, he promptly signed it and mailed it in to the front office.

"I knew my value," Fregosi told baseball writer Tracy Ringolsby. "Baseball had been my whole life. I wanted to stay in it. I knew I could learn a lot by sitting on the bench and watching. I could concentrate more on things than I did when I was playing every day. I could get a better overall picture of situations." Fregosi remained an active player for a little more than five years. On May 31, 1978, as Fregosi was in Cincinnati playing for the Pirates, he received a call from Buzzie Bavasi offering him the job as manager of the California Angels. The next day, Fregosi was sitting in the Angels dugout as the new skipper. He was just 36 years old with one off-season of managerial experience.

When Fregosi arrived in Anaheim he immediately created a more relaxed atmosphere in the Angel clubhouse. "The less rules you have, the less they [the players] have to break and the less problems you have," Fregosi explained. "I'm not saying there won't be discipline, I'm saying I will not have any rules."

His inexperience and laissez-faire approach didn't seem to be an issue as the team finished the '78 season with a 62–54 record. In fact, the entire team blossomed under Fregosi, winning the first division title in franchise history in 1979, Fregosi's first full year at the helm. They lost to the Orioles in the playoffs in four games but the expectations for 1980 were high.

Unfortunately, the Angels let future Hall of Famer Nolan Ryan get away to free agency in the off-season when he signed with the Houston Astros. Once the 1980 season began, the Angels were almost immediately beset by injuries. The team proceeded to endure a steady decline from the previous year's successful campaign, ending the 1980 season 30 games under .500 with a 65–95 record.

According to a *Los Angeles Times* article, following the 1980 season, the Angels appointed Gene Mauch "director of player personnel, a phantom position that seemed to undermine Fregosi's confidence and will." Fregosi withdrew from the front office and the media as he waited for the ax to fall. He was fired at the end of May 1981 and replaced by Mauch.

Fregosi was angry and hurt. He criticized the front office for creating an environment that diluted his authority. Four years later he expressed a new perspective, calling his initial remarks "foolish." "My feelings were hurt," Fregosi said. "My Italian blood was flowing. I was being beat from all sides, but I can see now that's part of the game. The important thing is how you handle the outside influences, not what they are."

When Fregosi lost the Angels job, he regrouped and went to Louisville where he spent three and a half years managing the Louisville Redbirds of the American Association. Under his management, the team earned two first place finishes and an American Association Championship. Midway through the 1986 season he was hired by the White Sox and returned for a second chance at managing in the big leagues. At the time of his hiring, VP of baseball operations and former player Ken Harrelson said of Fregosi, "We were never that close [as players] but you couldn't help admiring the way he played. He was a hard-nosed guy who gave 100 percent. He might go only one for four, but that one hit would beat you. He was a money player and I look for him to be the same way as a manager."

He never did lead the White Sox above a fifth place finish. He was relieved of his position in Chicago after the 1988 season. In 1991, he was hired by the Philadelphia Phillies and spent almost six full seasons as their manager. In 1993, he led a rowdy bunch of diverse Philly players from a worst-to-first pennant race only to be defeated in the World Series in six games by the Toronto Blue Jays and Joe Carter, who ended the series with a dramatic home run.

In remembering Fregosi, Mitch Williams, the Phillies closer from 1991 to 1993 known as "Wild Thing," said, "I thought the word that best described him was trust. He trusted everybody that coached for him, that played for him ... he put that trust in you. In '93 we shouldn't have won anything but he made us believe we were a whole lot better than we were."

Ironically, Fregosi went on to one last manager's job with the Toronto Blue Jays in 1999 and 2000. He was let go after two winning seasons and shortly thereafter began the final chapter of his life in baseball: 13-plus years as a special assistant to the GM of the Atlanta Braves.

Prior to his stint with the Blue Jays, Fregosi spent some time as a special assistant to Brian Sabean, GM of the Giants. When Fregosi died in February 2014, Sabean said, "The passing of Jim Fregosi leaves a hole in the unique fabric of our great game. He was a great friend and mentor to so many no matter what hat he wore. His bigger-than-life personality will be sorely missed. He was a one-of-a kind baseball lifer."

Fregosi was known around the league for his scouting abilities and his gift as a master storyteller, sharing the secrets of a lifetime of baseball experience with anyone who was willing to listen. Fregosi once said, "Baseball has been my whole life and I haven't regretted my decision to enter it. It is bigger than any individual player and what you get out of it you owe back." Jim Fregosi gave as much to the game as any player who ever put on a uniform.

♦ 29 ♦

Dave Giusti
(1962)

Meeting your heroes: the author with Dave Giusti at PNC Park, 2014.

29 ♦ Dave Giusti (1962)

In 1971, my hometown Rochester Red Wings were the last stop in the minor leagues before a ball player made it to "the show" as a Baltimore Oriole. As a result, Rochester was an Oriole town. Therefore, in October '71, it seemed that everyone around me was rooting for Baltimore to defeat the Pittsburgh Pirates in the 1971 World Series. It just so happens that those are the very first baseball games I have any memory of watching. I was just seven years old. Everyone I knew was rooting for the Orioles: my family, my friends, and my neighbors. Therefore, I felt drawn to the team in black and gold that no one else seemed to be rooting for and so I backed the Pirates.

When all was said and done, the Pirates upset the Orioles in seven games to win the World Series behind an MVP performance by "The Great One," Roberto Clemente, and superb pitching from a Pirates pitching staff that included Steve Blass, Nelson Briles, Bruce Kison, and Dave Giusti. While Giusti garnered only one save during that postseason, he appeared in seven of the ten games in which the Pirates played, pitching ten and two-thirds scoreless innings while surrendering only four hits. It was a masterful performance.

Those of us who are baseball fans tend to remain fans throughout our entire lives but it's the names and the memories of those first childhood heroes and games that remain absolutely sacred to us. The entire baseball world celebrates and reveres Babe Ruth, Jackie Robinson, and Ted Williams as well they should, but for me, names like Clemente, Stargell, Cash, Blass, Sanguillen, Oliver, and Giusti will always be just as magical.

Years back, I had the opportunity to interview and spend some time with the relief ace of that 1971 team, Dave Giusti. It sounds clichéd but it's always a dream come true to be able to meet your childhood heroes but it's extra special to discover they're as unpretentious and kind as you hoped they'd be. I found Giusti to be engaging and easy to talk to with a keen knowledge of the game, a wonderful sense of humor, and a delightfully mischievous laugh.

Retired now, Giusti still lives just a few miles outside the city that played host to his greatest professional accomplishments. He and his wife Virginia have been married for more than 60 years and they have two grown daughters and four granddaughters of whom he is exceedingly proud. The few times we spoke, he apologized for some issues he had in remembering names or not being able to say something just the way he wanted to, explaining that he had had a stroke in 2011. Honestly, I didn't notice any problems until he mentioned it. His difficulties seemed no more labored to me than any of the typical challenges we all face in remembering names or dates as Old Man Time starts to accompany us on our travels.

David John Giusti, Jr., was born in November of 1939 in Seneca Falls, New York, to David and Mary (nee Pannucci) Giusti. He has a younger brother, Frank, who also played professional baseball in the minor leagues for the Yankee and Astro organizations. Even his dad played semi-pro baseball but Giusti says it was his Uncle John Pannucci, just five years his senior, who was the real influence on him when it came to baseball. "The love of the game came from my Uncle John, who's still alive and lives in Seneca Falls," says Giusti. Pannucci played on Syracuse University football with Jim Brown and was captain of the Syracuse baseball team. He alerted the Syracuse coach about his talented nephew and helped Giusti get a scholarship to SU. Dave went on to compile a 17–3 record in three years at SU and even lettered one year in basketball although he said he played basketball just to keep in shape for baseball.

A standout pitcher at Syracuse, Giusti also played third base and outfield. In fact, he was such a solid hitter that both the Reds and the Cubs were interested in him as a potential third baseman. Ultimately, he signed for a bonus of over $30,000 with the expansion Houston Colt .45s. He shrewdly chose Houston, anticipating less competition to make the big league roster than if he'd signed with a more established team. His calculations proved correct. In 1962 at the age of 22, with just a little over 130 innings of minor league action, he started his first game for the Houston Colt .45s and lost. In fact, he lost his first three starts with the club. As a sign of things to come, he actually posted his first victory in a nine inning, three-hit relief appearance against the Chicago Cubs in May of 1962.

He spent all of the 1963 season in the Pacific Coast League with Oklahoma City where he went 13–11 as a starter with a solid 2.72 ERA. The highlight of the year, however, came after the season ended, when on October 26 Giusti married his college sweetheart Virginia Frykman.

He spent most of 1964 in Oklahoma City before finishing the season with the big club. By 1965, his years in the minors were finished. He made the Houston team out of spring training and never looked back.

In his first full season in the majors, Giusti was used as both a spot starter and a middle reliever. He finished the year with an 8–7 record and 131 innings pitched. By 1966, he was in the rotation as a starter and from 1966 to 1968 he logged over 200 innings pitched each year. Unfortunately, Houston was a young expansion team and Giusti usually got very little run support from his teammates. What he did get was years of invaluable experience facing some of the toughest hitters in the history of the National League.

When asked who hit him hardest during his years on the mound, Giusti did not hesitate with an answer. "The guy that gave me the most trouble was Billy Williams," remembered Giusti. "It's not like he beat me a lot of games, it's just that he never had a bad swing off of me. I couldn't get him out. And then there was Ron Santo one year had five home runs against me ... but never beat me in a ballgame."

Ironically, through the course of his career, Giusti had his greatest success against the Chicago Cubs. Of his lifetime 100 victories, Giusti told me that 25 of them came against the Cubs. "When I was in Houston, we loved to go into Wrigley Field and then with the Pirates ... with all those guys who could hit, I mean we loved that too," Giusti said.

Right from his earliest days out of Syracuse University, Giusti began working on an array of different pitches. In many of the earliest articles about the promising rookie, he gave credit to his SU coach, Ted Kleinhans, for teaching him the palm ball that he would use so effectively for the rest of his career. Former MLB pitcher and coach Billy Muffett called Giusti's palm ball "the best change-up in the league." In a 1965 newspaper article, Muffett told writer Neal Russo, "He can throw the palm ball over the plate just about any time he wants to. He's not afraid to throw it no matter what the situation is. He never tips off the pitch."

In a *Houston Post* article dated March 30, 1962, Giusti was asked about his rookie season in the minor leagues. "I guess the main thing I learned last year," said Giusti, "is that you got to have a change of speeds. I relied mostly on a fastball in college. You can't win with just a fastball in pro ball, in any class. I don't care where you are. I've been using a palm ball since college, and I use a curve and a straight change."

The *Post* article, written by Mickey Herskowitz, goes on to say, "Giusti discusses the art of flinging a baseball with the same detached, scholarly air he saves for his science classes back in upstate New York. In fact, one of the few criticisms of him as a pitcher is that maybe he does too much thinking."

The criticism about Giusti being "too much of a thinker" was something that came up in many of the articles and profiles about the pitcher during the 1960s. I was both amused and puzzled by it and asked Giusti what it was all about. "Well, you know what," Giusti said, "some of the coaches thought that and it was probably true. The real [issue] was that I was giving the hitters too much credit and not enough credit to myself and my abilities."

It's also possible that some in management and the media approached Giusti with wariness because of his advanced education. He'd earned his master's degree in 1967 and taught high school science in the off-season. That wasn't a very common occurrence in the world of sports during that era. Ultimately, his intelligence and education may have been one of the factors that led to his earning the trust and respect of his teammates which, in turn, resulted in their choosing him to be their player representative for the Major League Baseball Players Association. He served as a player rep during his time with both the Astros and the Pirates.

At the end of the 1968 season, Giusti was traded to the St. Louis Cardinals. His '69 season, however, proved to be a disappointment. He injured his back during warm-ups in May and never fully recovered. He finished with a 3–7 record and a 3.61 ERA. That substandard year may have been a blessing in disguise for Dave Giusti.

On October 21, 1969, the Cardinals traded Giusti to the Pittsburgh Pirates. Pirate GM Joe Brown was hesitant to pick up Giusti due to the 1969 back injury but, assured by doctors and Cardinal management that he was healthy, he made the deal. "I did something I never did before," Brown told reporters. "I talked to another player before making the trade. I talked to Roberto Clemente about Giusti and Roberto thought that Giusti could definitely help the club if he is physically sound. He said he has a good palm ball, a real good change and is a fine competitor." Giusti confirmed to me that Clemente had been instrumental in getting Giusti to

Extra added attraction: Dave Giusti, Christina Briles (daughter of Pirate pitcher Nelson Briles), and author meet at a Pirates game, 2014.

Pittsburgh. "I used to get him out," remembered Giusti, "not regularly, but enough to where I was noticed by him."

Giusti's move to Pittsburgh gave new life to his career. He'd hoped and intended to be a starter for the Bucs but fate had other plans for his future. In an August 29, 1970, article by Charley Feeney in *The Sporting News*, the headline declares "Late Rescue Stints Earn Giusti Bucs' Leader Tag." Following a horrible spring training where, in his own words, "I couldn't get anybody out," Giusti was moved to the bullpen. In *The Sporting News* article, Manager Danny Murtaugh said, "It wasn't until the men I had counted on as my late-inning relievers didn't do the job that I began to think of Giusti. I used him in late April and he did the job and he has been doing the job ever since."

In fact, Murtaugh came to regard Giusti as the leader of the pitching staff, a rare compliment for a relief pitcher. "Giusti," said Murtaugh, "has lifted our club where we need it most. It seemed when Giusti began to do the job, the other relievers responded. He has been a fellow who shows he is a leader. He does it in so many little ways. He is kidding around one minute, serious the next. He keeps everybody loose.... He doesn't believe his job begins in the late innings. He believes his job begins when he gets to the clubhouse every day. His dedication is something that is natural with him."

Giusti's first year with the Pirates was also the first year the team made the postseason in a decade. They lost in the playoffs to the Reds but would return to the postseason in 1971 when they would lose to no one. Following a decade of professional baseball, Dave Giusti was a World Champion.

In retirement, he became active in the Pirates Alumni Association. Former Pirate pitcher Nelson Briles started the group in 1992 and Giusti was one of the first teammates he brought on board to help him organize the undertaking. At the time, Giusti was working in Corporate Sales for American Express and he was happy to participate in bringing his old teammates together. Sadly, Briles died in 2005 after suffering a heart attack at one of the Pirates Alumni golf tournaments but the Pirates Alumni Association is one of the strongest such groups in all of baseball. Giusti is justifiably proud of the thousands of dollars they raise every year for various Pirates charities.

In addition to staying close to old teammates through the alumni group, there were always fellow Pirates he'd see around the new ballpark like Manny Sanguillen and his old roommate, Steve Blass. In fact, Blass and his wife Karen have been neighbors of Dave and Ginny Giusti for over 50 years. They have supported one another during the good times and the bad. Following the 1972 season, Steve Blass had a well-publicized control problem that eventually ended his pitching career. All of a sudden, as if out of nowhere, he could not throw a strike. The malady, which has since struck other ballplayers, became known as "Steve Blass Disease." In his 2012 book, *Pirate for Life*, Blass recalls pitcher Dave Giusti, the ballplayer, being "as mentally tough when a ballgame was on the line as anybody I have ever been around." He describes Dave Giusti, his friend, by saying, "Dave was with me every night on the road, and I will never forget his support and friendship."

Giusti helped clear the path for all those relief pitchers known today as "Closers." In the current marketplace, a pitcher of his caliber would make millions. Giusti told me he made a good salary for the time in which he played and he saved his money. He has no regrets. He's always felt fortunate to have played with the Stargells, Clementes, Sanguillens and Blasses of the world. He wouldn't trade that experience for anything.

For over three quarters of a century, Dave Giusti has been an athlete, a scholar, a friend, a philanthropist, a competitor, a champion, and a devoted family man. He's got all the bases covered.

♦ **30** ♦

Rico Petrocelli
(1963)

A picture that adorned the wall of my childhood bedroom, a hero of the hot corner, Rico Petrocelli.

30 ♦ Rico Petrocelli (1963)

Not too long after my meeting with Dave Giusti, I was able to set up a phone interview with former Red Sox shortstop and third baseman Rico Petrocelli. He was as kind and cooperative as could be and it was a pleasure to talk with him. When your job is to write articles about people, a cooperative interview subject is a tremendous asset in crafting a good story. However, when the person you're interviewing is someone whose picture you had hanging on your wall as you were growing up, it adds a little pressure and anxiety to the exercise. It took only a few minutes for Petrocelli to ease my tensions and make me once again feel very good about the people I chose to admire as a kid.

Baseball has always been my sport and while Roberto Clemente was my first baseball hero he was certainly not the only player I looked up to during my impressionable years. The positions I played were primarily outfield and third base so I idolized Brooks Robinson because, well, he was Brooks Robinson! But Rico Petrocelli was the other third baseman I always admired and, quite honestly, I think my initial attraction to him was due to the fact that his name was Rico Petrocelli. I mean, c'mon, you don't get too many names that are cooler than Rico Petrocelli. Even at eight years old I was proud of my Italian American heritage. I didn't really know why but, nevertheless, I was always happy whenever I could find another Italian in the sports pages for whom I could root. In this case, it was merely by chance that the guy with the awesome name also happened to be an outstanding player.

Americo Peter Petrocelli was born in Brooklyn, New York, in 1943 to Attilio and Louise Petrocelli, immigrant parents from the Abbruzzi region of Italy. The youngest of seven children, his father was 50 years old and his mother was 40 years old when he was born. Petrocelli told me that his parents were more like grandparents to him while his brothers and sisters filled the parental role.

His family moved to different sections of the borough during his childhood but always remained in Brooklyn. He was an accomplished athlete in football, basketball, and baseball but it was the national pastime that eventually won his heart. He was, however, offered numerous college basketball scholarships upon graduation. He knew that with his size he'd have little chance to play in the NBA so with the guidance of his brothers and parents, he signed a professional contract with the Boston Red Sox when he was 18 years old.

Like so many immigrant parents of the time, Petrocelli's dad wanted him to go out and get a real job. As Petrocelli told it, "my pop never really understood that [someone] could get paid to play ball." Thanks to the intervention of his brothers and interest from a number of Major League teams, including the Yankees and the Mets, Petrocelli signed with the Red Sox for a $65,000 bonus. Needless to say, his father was duly impressed.

He originally wanted to be a Yankee because the Yankees of DiMaggio, Rizzuto, and Berra were the only thing Rico Petrocelli's dad knew about Major League Baseball, but Petrocelli told me that he was thankful he signed with the Red Sox. "It was a great ballpark for me," said Petrocelli, "and the city [NYC] was only 200 miles away … and they [Boston] had the big Italian section there, the North End. It was terrific."

The Yankees may have been his childhood team but when Petrocelli broke into the big leagues, both the Yankees and the Red Sox were struggling in the basement of the American League. The difference was that the Red Sox were putting all their money on the youth movement. "The Red Sox were rushing the kids up," Petrocelli remembered, "because I guess they were losing money and there was talk about selling the franchise … but then '67 came about and changed things."

Petrocelli's first two seasons with the Bosox were often difficult and frustrating. He did not have a good relationship with the Boston manager Billy Herman. According to Petrocelli, Herman wanted to start the veterans ahead of the rookies. The front office, however, was committed to playing the rookies.

Petrocelli's troubles came to a head with Herman during a 1966 midseason game. Petrocelli was struggling at the plate and not playing regularly. At one stretch he had been out of the lineup for a while. He was frustrated and approached the manager and asked, "Billy, am I going to play again?" Petrocelli says that Herman turned to him and barked, "Go down and sit on the bench and be quiet!" Petrocelli was dumbfounded and pursued it further when Herman said, "I don't know if you're going to play again." Petrocelli was so angry he went back to the clubhouse, got his stuff and went home.

At the time, he was making $6,000 a year. The Red Sox fined him $2,000 and eventually lessened it to $1,000. Naturally, he regretted his actions but ultimately, he and Herman just couldn't see eye to eye. When Billy Herman was fired near the end of the 1966 season after two horrendous campaigns, he blamed Petrocelli. The Red Sox replaced Herman with the sarcastic and volatile Dick Williams. As difficult as Williams could be, he was 20 years younger than Herman and had coached many of the current crop of young Red Sox players at Toronto, the Red Sox Triple A farm team. Williams's results with the younger Red Sox were immediate and monumental.

In Boston it was called "The Impossible Dream." The Red Sox had not enjoyed a winning season since 1958 and they finished 9th out of 10 teams in both 1965 and 1966. In 1967, they turned the ship around with a starting lineup whose average age was 24 years old. The veteran on the field most days was 27-year-old Carl Yastrzemski. At 24, Rico Petrocelli was the starting shortstop for a pennant-bound team.

"No one in their right minds expected us to win it," remembered Petrocelli. "We were hoping to improve. Dick Williams came in with a kind of National League style, hit and run, bunts … good defense, hit the cut off, fundamentals. Right from spring training that's what he talked and that's what he demanded. Little by little we got better and better as a team, fundamentally. You look back and … that whole year just brought interest back to baseball in Boston. That was the big thing. People would come up to [us] in a store or restaurant and want to shake hands, thanking us for bringing excitement back to Boston baseball. It was just great ... it was exciting."

Bob Ryan, sportswriter and columnist for *The Boston Globe,* went even further in 2006 when he said, "Everything the Red Sox are today, all the sellouts, stems from 1967. That team can never be honored enough; 1967 is the great dividing line in Red Sox history."

The Bosox lost that 1967 World Series in seven games to the Cardinals and Bob Gibson, who won three games and took home the trophy for series MVP. It doesn't matter now, the Red Sox have broken their curse with World Series victories in 2004, 2007, 2013, and 2018 but the "Cinderella Sox" are still remembered with affection in Beantown. In fact, Rico Petrocelli, along with journalist Chaz Scoggins, wrote a book in 2007 entitled *Rico Petrocelli's Tales from the Impossible Dream Red Sox,* fondly recalling that glorious season.

For Petrocelli, it certainly wasn't his greatest year at the plate or in the field but he did make the All-Star team for the first time in his career while slugging 17 home runs and driving in 66 runs. His production fell off in 1968 but the breakout year of his career was just around the corner.

In 1969 Rico Petrocelli hit 40 home runs, breaking the single season record of 39 for most home runs in a year by a shortstop previously held by Vern Stephens. He also tied Phil Rizzuto for the record of fewest errors in a season at shortstop with only 14 mistakes in 749 chances handled. In addition, he drove in 97 RBIs and scored 92 more runs in a career year for the 26-year-old.

Petrocelli enjoyed two more stellar campaigns at the plate in 1970 and 1971, pounding out 29 and 28 home runs respectively. He set a career high with 103 RBIs in 1970 and scored 82 runs both seasons. However, in 1971, he went from being a slugging shortstop to a power-hitting third baseman after the Red Sox acquired future Hall of Fame shortstop Luis Aparicio in a trade with the Chicago White Sox.

The move to third base was one that Petrocelli made without too much difficulty although you wouldn't have known that by his comments. In 1971, his first season as a full-time third baseman, Petrocelli led all American League third sackers in fielding percentage. Even so, Petrocelli told journalist Larry Claflin, "Fielding averages mean nothing. They are not a reflection of a fielder. When you watch the way Brooks Robinson plays third base, you know who is the best."

The comparison, of course, wasn't in any way fair. Brooks had always been a third baseman and Petrocelli moved to the position in mid-career. Not only that, comparing yourself to Brooks Robinson is like a sculptor comparing herself to Michelangelo and deciding she's no good because she didn't create the statue of David. The Red Sox and the Boston media identified Petrocelli as a worrier early in his career and the reputation stuck for years. In fact, many of the headlines in his early career read like an outline for a soap opera.

In a 1972 article for *Super Sports, Boston Globe* reporter Ray Fitzgerald outlined the lowlights: "Rico Petrocelli jumped his minor league team in 1964. In 1966, he went home in the middle of a ball game. He announced in 1968 he was going to quit baseball and become a carpenter. Add the incidents together and Rico Petrocelli is a troublemaker. That's the Petrocelli of the headlines. The real Petrocelli is another person altogether—a shy, sincere, introspective human being, a friendly decent family man who sometimes still can't believe he's a major league star drawing big money."

When Petrocelli signed with the Sox in 1961 he was 18. He'd never been away from home or family. He found an understanding and patient teacher in his first manager, Eddie Popowski, who managed Petrocelli in 1962 at Winston-Salem and again in 1963 at Reading. Following his first two years under the tutelage of Popowski, Petrocelli quickly learned that most coaches aren't there to babysit and connect to you as a father figure. It was a tough adjustment for Petrocelli to make. He was a perfectionist and demanded the best from himself. When he didn't meet his own high expectations, he'd become moody, volatile, and disheartened. In the 1972 article for *Super Sports*, Ray Fitzgerald opined, "Popowski became Red Sox coach in 1967 and a big part of his job was to be Petrocelli's confessor, to keep him from brooding."

More likely was that Popowski was brought in to help all the younger players. He had managed many of them in the minors and was known to be a more soft-spoken and patient teacher than manager Dick Williams. Petrocelli remembers, "They brought him up to the big leagues … and that was great because it was somebody we all really knew and Dick Williams was tough. Dick Williams would not get close to a player but Eddie Popowski would come up to you and talk, talk baseball, encourage you and all that stuff so, that was a good mix."

Near the end of the challenging 1960s, Rico Petrocelli had another weight on his shoulders. His wife Elsie was diagnosed with uterine cancer in 1969. The couple had an infant and three other sons under the age of four at the time. It was a difficult time, especially with Rico being on the road half the season. Elsie had a partial hysterectomy and the Petrocellis were told that if she went five years without a recurrence that she'd probably be cancer-free. Petrocelli spent the next five years carrying that burden. In 1974, as the five-year anniversary was approaching, the Petrocellis got down on their knees to pray for God's help. Elsie was declared cancer-free. The experience changed them and put Rico Petrocelli on the road to a much deeper relationship with God.

Through all the controversy during Petrocelli's early years with the club, the legendarily tough Boston sports media was usually supportive of Rico Petrocelli. His teammates also respected his contributions to the team.

When he was passed over for Gold Glove in 1969, teammate Jim Lonborg was aghast. In a 1970 article by Phil Elderkin, Lonborg was quoted saying, "For Mark Belanger to get the Golden Glove Award at shortstop last year was a huge mistake. Belanger was good all right, but Petrocelli set records." Second baseman Mike Andrews once said, "Rico has the ability to inspire. He just played with a whole lot of intensity." And his coach Eddie Popowski once commented on Petrocelli's ability as a clutch hitter, saying, "He's the one I'd want up there with the winning run on second."

The Red Sox reached the World Series one more time in Petrocelli's career, in 1975. Once again they lost in seven games, this time to the Cincinnati Reds. Nevertheless, it's considered by many baseball historians to be the greatest and most exciting World Series ever played. Unlike his 1967 experience, Petrocelli was a veteran in 1975 and showed it by batting .308 in the series. He retired the following year at 33 after playing in only 85 games in 1976.

Petrocelli's post–baseball-playing career has been a roller coaster of activity. He broadcast the Red Sox games in 1979 and coached in both the White Sox and Red Sox minor league systems. He became active in the Jimmy Fund, a children's cancer charity in Boston, and eventually started his own marketing company that his son now runs. These days as one of the most popular former Red Sox players, he makes occasional appearances at Fenway Park. For many years he co-hosted a show with Ed Randall on SiriusXM radio every Saturday morning from 8:00 to 10:00 a.m. called "Remember When," where they played host to former players, authors, and more.

Rico Petrocelli has nothing but praise for the current Red Sox management and says they've been very good to him and his former teammates. "I'm really grateful that I got to play in Boston. The fans have been ... wonderful to me over the years ... all throughout New England but certainly the Boston area ... they've been just great." That is as it should be because as most Red Sox fans will agree, through the years, Rico Petrocelli has been very good to them as well.

♦ 31 ♦

Tony Conigliaro
(1964)

Brothers Billy (left) and Tony Conigliaro patrolled the outfield together at Fenway Park during the 1969 and 1970 seasons.

When my love affair with baseball began in the early 1970s, I immersed myself in learning the history of the game. I read books, magazines, and newspaper articles. Once I began to collect baseball cards, I would study and read the cards over and over, for hours on end. At some point, I came across the name of Tony Conigliaro, a slugging outfielder for the Boston Red Sox. His Italian name perked up my Italian American ears and his cruel fate engendered the empathy of my fatalistic Sicilian soul.

There were a few other things that attracted me to Conigliaro. First and foremost, he and I shared the same birthday, the seventh of January. It's true Conigliaro was almost 20 years older than I was but the year I was born was also the year Conigliaro broke into the majors. OK, so we Sicilians are a little superstitious. But then there was the smile. Conigliaro had a movie star smile that charmed all of New England in the mid–1960s. He was a guy who seemed to have the stars on his side and greatness in his future. However, instead of the story ending with an induction to Cooperstown, his was a future filled with setbacks and the ultimate question, "What might have been?"

In the summer of 1967, in the middle of the Red Sox "Cinderella season," Tony Conigliaro and the city of Boston were giddy with the excitement of the town's first pennant contender in 21 years. By the middle of August, Conigliaro had already hit 20 home runs. Then on the night of August 16, 1967, Conigliaro stepped to the plate against a pitcher for the California Angels named Jack Hamilton. Conigliaro was always known for crowding the plate and being fearless as a hitter. On inside pitches he'd wait until the last second to pull away from the pitch just to show the pitchers that he wasn't intimidated. On this night his fearlessness cost him—he was hit by a high, inside fastball that sailed in and caught him directly on his left eye. More than one player on the field that night recalled the awful sound as the ball hit Conigliaro. It was as if time stopped. In *Tony C.: The Triumph and Tragedy of Tony Conigliaro* by David Cataneo, Hall of Famer Carl Yastremzski, Conigliaro's teammate at the time, remembered it as "a deafening sound, a sickening sound." Conigliaro was face down in front of home plate as thousands of Fenway fans stood stunned and silent by what they'd just seen.

Conigliaro's friend and teammate Rico Petrocelli was the first Red Sox player to reach his comrade and encouraged him to stay calm and assured him he was going to be all right. Conigliaro was taken off the field on a stretcher and brought to the locker room where the trainers examined him as they awaited the ambulance to take him to Sancta Maria Hospital in Cambridge. His eye had swelled beyond recognition, there was blood trickling from his mouth and ear, and he was begging for something to dull the pain. Despite the severity of the injury, he wasn't fortunate enough to lose consciousness. Conigliaro was just too tough for his own good.

Many in the Red Sox organization who had witnessed the beaning were unsure that Conigliaro would live through the night. In *Seeing It Through*, an autobiography that Conigliaro wrote in 1970 with the help of journalist Jack Zanger, Tony remembered that after everyone had left the hospital that night he "wanted to have someone around to hold onto, but no one was there now. I was never so alone in my whole life." Of course, he did live through the night and as soon as the fear of death left his side, he immediately wanted to know how soon he could get back to the team and the pennant race. One of his trainers told him that although he'd be fine, he wouldn't be able to return for at least four weeks, maybe eight. Conigliaro couldn't believe his season was over. He was sure that as soon as the swelling went down and he could open his eye, he'd be right back there at Fenway helping his team win the pennant and World Series. Instead, it would be almost 20 months before Conigliaro would play baseball again.

Anthony Richard Conigliaro was born on January 7, 1945, in East Boston. He was the oldest of three boys born to Sal and Teresa Conigliaro. The Conigliaros were a tough, close-knit, Italian American working class family. In *Seeing It Through*, Conigliaro told Jack Zanger that when he was born "his father worked in a zipper factory, but that was only one of his jobs. He was always trying to make a killing in some business of his own." He goes on to describe a variety of enterprises his father attempted in his quest for success. With obvious pride Conigliaro said, "You can say one thing for my father: he was willing to try anything. He got knocked down a lot of times, but he always bounced back. He's never quit anything in his life." Sal Conigliaro would be an important source of inspiration and strength for his son when the fates challenged Tony in his own life.

Tony was a less than spectacular student in school. Once he'd decided that baseball was going to be his life, it was hard to interest him in academic pursuits. He was never terribly happy in school. He was a cocky young man and this turned off some of his school mates. He knew how good he was on the baseball field but no matter how boastful he might be, he always backed up his braggadocio with results. He wasn't lazy nor did he have any sense of entitlement. He always practiced harder than anyone else. He had a dream and he was relentless in the pursuit of that dream.

He was handsome, charming, funny, and he was a gifted athlete. Needless to say, he was never lonely. Conigliaro was the original ladies' man. He had a very serious girlfriend, Julie Markakas, when he was in high school. They talked of marriage and Conigliaro had even bought her an engagement ring but as his professional career began, his father discouraged the relationship. He didn't want his son to get tied down or lose focus of his pursuit. Conigliaro broke off the relationship with Julie shortly before he joined the hometown Red Sox. Tony Conigliaro would never marry and years later his father apologized to Julie for breaking them up.

Conigliaro signed with the Red Sox right out of high school and they sent him to a fall league in Bradenton, Florida. He was scared, lonely, and naive. Luckily he was befriended by Mike Ryan, a second year man from Haverhill, Massachusetts. Ryan would eventually become Tony Conigliaro's roommate and lifelong friend. The following February and March, Conigliaro did well and hoped to make the Double-A ball club in Pittsfield, Massachusetts, near his home. Instead, the Red Sox sent him to Single-A Wellsville, New York. Conigliaro said "It didn't take me long to find out why they're called the minors. What could be lower? We used an old school bus that should have been retired when Calvin Coolidge was President. There were no springs in it, just solid rubber tires and a lawn mower engine. Conditions are so skimpy in the minors that the manager used to drive the bus."

Conigliaro had a solid year at Wellsville and returned to the Florida fall league with much more confidence than the previous year. He impressed the coaches and management enough that they took a chance on him after a good spring and put him on the opening day roster for the 1964 Red Sox. At 19 years old, Tony Conigliaro was a Major Leaguer. And how did he mark the occasion of his first big league at-bat? By hitting a home run, of course. Tony C. seemed to be a storybook idol with destiny on his side but sometimes destiny crosses you up.

After his 1967 injury, Conigliaro reported to spring training in 1968 anxious to pursue a comeback. His eyesight still wasn't 100 percent but he didn't let on. However, as time went on he experienced more and more difficulty seeing the ball. He had trouble picking up the fly balls in the bright Florida sun. The worst damage had been done to the center of his vision; his peripheral vision was not damaged at all. For a time, he compensated as best he could by trying to look for the pitched balls by cocking his head and using his peripheral vision. However, this was not only a difficult adjustment to make but it was dangerous as well. If he couldn't quickly identify the pitch coming towards him, he could easily get hit again.

Shortly before the season was to start he went back to the eye doctor and received the bad news that a cyst had formed in the center of the eye and had burst. The doctor equated it to a burn hole in the center of a film negative. The vision in his left eye was now 20/300—he was legally blind in the eye. That was the end of his baseball career. He was inconsolable.

The next day Joe Tauro, a lawyer and family friend, helped Tony write a statement announcing his retirement. He thanked his friends, family, teammates, and fans for all their concern and support. In *Tony C.* author David Cataneo wrote, "Just like Tony, even though the doctors told him his playing days were through, he ended the statement by saying, 'And I want all these friends to know that I'm not going to quit and that somehow, some way, there will be good days again.'"

That statement in and of itself sums up the life and spirit of Tony Conigliaro. No matter what obstacle was put before him, he never gave up.

He spent the next few months depressed and frustrated. The doctors had ordered him to limit all his physical activity for a time because they didn't want the eye to worsen. Once the broken cyst had begun to heal and the doctors felt the eye was stabilized, they told Conigliaro he could go back to working out. As soon as he got the green light, he decided that if he could never hit again, why not pitch? He had done it in little league. The Red Sox told him to go ahead and try.

As with everything else he'd ever done in baseball, once Conigliaro set his mind on becoming a pitcher, he worked day and night to learn as much as he could about the mechanics and philosophy of pitching. In the off-season, Conigliaro reported to the Red Sox's instructional league in Sarasota, Florida; a veteran amidst rookies, he impressed everyone with his dedication. One of the rookies, Dennis Gilbert, recalled finding Conigliaro throwing a ball against a brick wall in the empty ballpark after everyone else had left: "The guy was a machine. He would work from early in the morning till late in the day. He was there on a mission."

Even when pitching was his goal, he continued to swing the bat and Red Sox management encouraged it. No one really wanted to believe that a hitter as great as Tony C. could really be done forever. In the instructional league Manager Billy Gardner encouraged him to take batting practice and Tony did pretty well. After a few mediocre outings as a pitcher, Gardner began to put him in for a few innings here and there as an outfielder. His hitting improved and he gained confidence. By the end of the instructional league play, GM Dick O'Connell and Manager Dick Williams told Conigliaro they looked forward to seeing him playing right field for the Red Sox in 1969.

When Conigliaro returned home he went back for another eye examination. The doctors were stunned. The hole in his eye had healed over with very little scar tissue. His vision had improved to 20/20 (although it had previously been 20/10). He had lost some depth perception but all in all the recovery was remarkable.

Tony Conigliaro played 141 games for the Red Sox in 1969. He hit 20 home runs and drove in 82 RBIs and was named Comeback Player of the Year. The following year, 1970, his numbers were even better: 36 home runs and 116 RBIs. Nevertheless, Tony was struggling to pick up the ball again, especially on sunny days or if the background was too bright. In the off-season the Red Sox traded him to the California Angels and his vision began to deteriorate even more. He was unhappy in California away from his family, friends, and hometown fans. He struggled through the first half of the season. In a game against the A's shortly before the All-Star break, Tony got into an altercation with an umpire. He exploded—the frustration and fear that had been growing inside of him was released on the field in front of thousands of jeering fans.

Back home in Boston the doctors examined the eye and found that the hole had increased in size 75 percent since the beginning of the 1969 season. If he looked straight ahead, his vision was 20/300 but if he cocked the eye one way or another, it improved to 20/30. Nevertheless, it was too difficult and dangerous for him to continue to play at this level.

Being the fighter that he was, Conigliaro attempted one last comeback in 1975. He did pretty well in spring training but couldn't keep it up. He was eventually replaced by a rookie slugger the Red Sox had just promoted from Triple A named Jim Rice.

Conigliaro would have a few more successes and challenges in his life but nothing ever satisfied him the way baseball did. In 1982 he tried out for the job as the Red Sox color commentator and was told that he won the job. As he prepared to go back to California to settle his affairs and move back East, he suffered what was originally thought to be a heart attack. In *Tony C.*, Cataneo wrote the doctors guessed that Conigliaro "had been carrying a harmless clot on the wall of the artery that ruptured, causing a blockage that stopped the heart."

Tony Conigliaro spent the next eight years a shell of his former self, barely able to speak or walk. His always devoted family took care of him until he died in February of 1990 at the age of 45. Tony C. is still remembered today as a guy who might have broken Aaron's home run record had he been given the chance.

John Greenleaf Whittier once wrote, "For all sad words of tongue and pen, the saddest are these, 'It might have been.'" The legacy of Tony Conigliaro is the ultimate "what might have been" story but it somehow seems wrong to think of Conigliaro in only those terms. If, as we're so often told, the true importance in life lies in the journey and not the destination, then Conigliaro's legacy should be one of tremendous success. He was given a gift that he respected and worked hard to improve and retain. He was confronted by numerous challenges and obstacles and faced them all with courage and a dedication to overcome all adversity. The poet Adelaide Anne Procter summed Conigliaro's life more fittingly in the line, "No star is ever lost we once have seen, we always may be what might have been."

♦ 32 ♦

Sal Bando
(1967)

The Captain, Sal Bando of the World Champion Oakland A's, 1972–1974.

32 ♦ Sal Bando (1967)

When I started following baseball as a kid more than 50 years ago, the preeminent club of the Major Leagues was known as "The Mustache Gang." They were the Oakland Athletics of the early 1970s and what a ball club they were—Reggie Jackson, Jim "Catfish" Hunter, Rollie Fingers, Bert "Campy" Campaneris, Vida Blue, and their captain, Sal Bando. You couldn't help but take notice of the Oakland A's unless, of course, you were colorblind. Their iridescent green and yellow uniforms lit up the Major Leagues and led to similarly colorful costuming from teams like the Houston Astros and Milwaukee Brewers. But while some teams were able to copy the colorful glow of the Oakland uniforms, no one could match the colorful nature of the team's players and owner.

Many baseball historians believe that had there not been so much internal, off the field strife among the players and owner of the A's, they might well have won a few more championship rings. Many of the Oakland players believed the same thing. "No telling how many championships we could have won," Sal Bando once told sportswriter Sid Bordman. "We had everything on the field—speed, pitching, defense, and power. But no management. Some of the things Charlie [Finley, the owner] did were good, helpful. But he did more destroying. He destroyed the A's. Stubbornness hurt him—a very eccentric person."

Salvatore Leonard Bando was the rock upon which Charlie O. Finley built his short-lived dynasty of the early 1970s. Bando had been born and raised in Cleveland, Ohio. In a move they'd no doubt regret for many years afterward, the Indians passed on the hometown boy, thinking him "too slow." There was, however, a semi-pro team in Cleveland sponsored by a mathematics professor from Arizona State University named Richard Lisococec who spent his time away from the ASU campus in Cleveland, Ohio. He was impressed by Bando's play and recommended him for a baseball scholarship to ASU.

At Arizona State, Bando played for Bobby Winkles. "He encouraged me to hit to all fields," Bando once told writer Ron Bergman about his college mentor. Bando made the advice pay off because in the College World Series of 1965, Sal Bando hit .480 with nine runs batted in on his way to earning the Most Valuable Player award of the series.

Bando was drafted in the sixth round of the 1965 amateur draft as the number three pick of the Kansas City Athletics. He was immediately sent to the Burlington Bees of the A level Midwest League where he played in 60 games batting .262 and hitting six home runs. In 1966 he graduated to the Double-A Mobile A's of the Southern League where he hit .277 and knocked out 12 home runs. At the end of the year he was sent to KC for 11 games and he hit a very respectable .292.

He was promoted to Triple-A Vancouver in 1967. In May, he was called up to the parent club to fill in for an injured Ed Charles at third base. Unfortunately, Bando's manager Alvin Dark wanted him to try a change to his batting stance by crouching more at the plate. Bando said, "I felt uncomfortable. I just couldn't hit at all." When he also got injured, he was sent back to Vancouver.

According to Bando, "That was the first blow I'd ever had in baseball. I was hurt that they thought I couldn't play in the majors. When I first went down, I was still trying to hit the way Mr. Dark wanted me to." Former batting champion Mickey Vernon encouraged the young Bando to return to his original stance and straighten up at the plate. He rebounded back to his original form and ended up hitting .291 and driving in 55 runs in 116 games for Vancouver.

He did so well in spring training of 1968 that he came west with the ball club to their new home in Oakland, California. Not only was Bando in the majors to stay but he also played in every game of the 1968 season. He only hit .251 but Bando had intangibles that couldn't be measured in the box scores. He had a bullet arm to throw out runners from third base, a passionate desire to win, and strong leadership qualities.

His new manager, Bob Kennedy, had only good things to say about his young 24-year-old infielder. "I think he has a wonderful future," Kennedy said. "There are a couple of little things he's going to work on, but he'll gradually start doing them himself." And then, perhaps in a nod to Bando's level of maturity for such a young man, Kennedy said, "He's smart enough to take advice. You don't have to repeat it 40,000 times."

In 1969, at the tender age of 25, Sal Bando was named captain of the Oakland A's by the new manager, Hank Bauer. It was a position he'd hold for the rest of his eight years in Oakland and beyond. They say a great leader leads by example and so, in 1969, Bando led his teammates by being the only player in all of the Major Leagues to play in every inning of every game. As rare as it was in 1969, it's a feat that would be unheard of in today's version of the game.

In the June 14, 1969, edition of *The Sporting News*, the A's slugger also credited Joe DiMaggio for encouraging the young hitter to close his stance to generate more power. The results were immediate. He went from nine home runs in 162 games in 1968 to 31 home runs in the same amount of games in 1969.

Unfortunately, the manager's position wasn't as rock solid as that of the A's third baseman. At the end of the '69 season the A's changed managers for the third time in less than two years. The new manager was John McNamara. It didn't take McNamara long to recognize Bando's value to the ball club. "He's a money ballplayer," said McNamara. "He's our leader on the field."

In a July 11, 1970, article, *Oakland Tribune* baseball writer Ron Bergman wrote that twice in one game Manager McNamara asked his cleanup hitter (Bando) to sacrifice bunt—once with a two run lead and again with a three run lead. Both times, the A's scored runs that according to Bergman, "turned out to be significant in a doubleheader sweep over the White Sox."

Bergman went on to explain, "It wasn't that Bando was having trouble connecting that day. He also hit two homers, one a 440-foot shot. But he didn't resent having to bunt, even though he was deprived of two chances to swing for homers."

"When you've got guys like Don Mincher and Felipe Alou hitting behind you,"

Bando said, "they're such good hitters you don't mind bunting to move the runners over. The only time it bothers me is when we don't score the run." That was Sal Bando, the leader. His personal glory or achievement was never his first concern. The team's success was always his primary goal.

Bando wasn't only smart and unselfish, he was tough. In a June 1970 game he was hit in the face by a pitch from the Indians' Dennis Higgins. He missed one game. Teammate Reggie Jackson said, "If Sal got hurt we'd never win without him. Sal's the most consistent player I've ever been with. Broken arm, hit in the face, hit in the head, he's there. Every day."

The A's were such a talented young ball club that even another managerial change couldn't stop their forward progress during the 1971 season. The new skipper was Dick Williams and his young crew immediately awarded him with a division title. The A's lost the playoffs to the Baltimore Orioles but they were beginning to show the baseball world flashes of the brilliance that was soon to be.

In 1972, the A's not only won the division but beat the Detroit Tigers in the American League playoffs to advance to the World Series against the Cincinnati Reds. It was a tough and tight seven game series but when all was said and done, the brash young boys from Oakland took home the trophy as champions of the baseball world.

They were also dubbed The Mustache Gang for the hirsute look they sported on the diamond. Baseball had always been a very clean shaven, all American boy kind of sport. Finley, the maverick owner, not only allowed the team's beards and mustaches but encouraged it.

The victory of the World Series championship, however, was a hollow one. When the A's began the 1973 season, the fans were nowhere to be found. In the first couple months of the season, the A's were pulling in only 3,000 to 5,000 fans a game. Soon the frustration began to show. "Nobody cares," Sal Bando told Oakland newspaper columnist Art Spander. "What else can we think? Nobody knows we're around. They came out for the World Series, and then they forgot us." Despite the apathy of the Oakland citizenry, the A's continued to win, capturing the division title for the third year in a row in 1973. This time they defeated the Orioles in the playoffs as they moved on to play the New York Mets in the World Series.

The A's would go on to win it all again but the victory would be marred by something that happened in Game Two of the series. Second baseman Mike Andrews made two errors in the game. Following his performance, Charlie Finley tried to release Andrews from the team. He told the team's doctor to say Andrews had been injured. The next day, Bando convinced his teammates to wear black armbands during warm-ups and batting practice to protest the Andrews situation. The armbands attracted the attention of Baseball Commissioner Bowie Kuhn, who in turn warned Finley that he was not allowed to drop Andrews from the Oakland roster in the middle of the series. Finley's treatment of Mike Andrews continued to bother Bando long after the series ended. "It took all the excitement and the color away," said Bando.

As the team's success continued to grow, so did the internal problems and battles with the front office and specifically with the owner, Charlie O. Finley. The players naturally assumed that as they won more and more championships, their owner would want to reward them financially. They were greatly mistaken.

Bando eventually went to arbitration over his salary dispute with Charlie Finley as did many members of the World Champion A's. Bando won his case and signed on for $100,000 for the 1974 season. Bando entered the season more relaxed and confident. "Now that I'm being paid what I'm worth," said Bando, "I don't have to try for publicity or making the All-Star team to prove anything. I used to press so hard to make the All-Star team that I tailed off in July."

Oakland Tribune scribe Ron Bergman, who would eventually author the book *The Mustache Gang: The Swaggering Saga of Oakland's A's*, wrote of Bando, "There's more to Bando's contributions than mere figures. On a team in which trouble bubbles like a live volcano, Bando, more than anyone else, keeps teammates relaxed and thinking about baseball."

The start of the 1974 season brought more problems. Dick Williams had had enough of Finley and did not return as manager. Williams suggested that Bando might be a good choice because he was one of the few people not in Finley's doghouse. While Bando expressed the desire to manage someday, he wasn't interested quite yet. He felt he had a few good years left in him as a player and wanted to stay focused on that part of his career. Even so, sportswriter Milton Richman wrote, "Sal Bando will make an excellent manager someday. He's intelligent, intensely competitive, and knows the game. He also knows how to get along with people and in this day and age that frequently becomes a primary asset."

Ironically, the new A's manager was one of the old A's managers—Alvin Dark. The A's won their division by five games over the Texas Rangers and again defeated the Baltimore Orioles in the American League Playoffs. This time they faced the Los Angeles Dodgers in the World Series and beat them in five games for their third championship in a row. In the 107-year history of the World Series, there have been only four instances of a team winning three or more championships in a row. The other three teams were all Yankee clubs of different eras.

Three championships in a row—the A's were a juggernaut that no one could stop. No one, that is, except their creator. By February of 1975, seven players were taking Finley to arbitration over contract disputes. Finley had already let Catfish Hunter escape through free agency. Within two years, the A's unstoppable team of the early '70s would be in shambles.

Bando finally escaped the Charlie O. Finley circus in 1977 when he signed a five-year deal with the Milwaukee Brewers. Once again he was "Captain Sal" on a talented but very young team. The expectations for Bando were high although he insisted that the Brewer fans should "not expect me to be a messiah."

The fans may not have expected miracles but management certainly did. Team owner Bud Selig said "He [Bando] has intangibles with which God blesses only a few of us. There's a uniqueness in him that I haven't seen in many others. It's his quiet maturity and great dedication. He knows how to win and what it takes to win. For the first time in our club's history, we're going to have an on-the-field leader."

Bando's first year with the Brewers was the only year the club finished under .500 during his five years with the team. In the strike-shortened season of 1981, the year was split into two seasons. Bando had a fabulous second half, leading his Brewers to "a playoff for the playoffs." They didn't advance but they got a taste of winning that propelled them into the World Series the following season.

Despite the rising fortunes of the Brewers, at the end of the 1981 season Sal Bando called it quits. He was 37 years old. He didn't feel he could contribute on the field any more. Management, however, felt he still had a great deal to contribute and gave him a job in the front office. He stayed on with the Brewers organization for another ten years, eventually rising to the position of general manager of the team.

Sal Bando, the business administration major at Arizona State University, went on to have a very successful career in the business world outside of baseball. He started a financial loan company with ex–NBA star Jon McGlocklin. From that venture, he eventually purchased the Middleton Doll Company and did quite well with that business as well.

Sal Bando died in 2023 of cancer. He was 78 years old. At that time, he was still a fan of the game but he'd been out of the limelight for many years. Bando was always willing to offer advice and counsel but had no desire to return to the game. That part of his career was over. A successful leader knows when to step back and let a new generation lead. When it comes to leaders, Sal Bando was one of the best.

♦ 33 ♦

Gary Gaetti
(1981)

The author with Gold-Glover Gary Gaetti.

Baseball fans, by and large, remain fans forever. However, it is the memories of our youthful fandom and the players and teams we followed in our earliest years who remain the focus of our adulation throughout our adult lives.

Let me put it to you more directly. Albert Pujols, Derek Jeter, and Randy Johnson were some of the biggest names in Major League Baseball in the new millennium, Jeter and Johnson are already in the Hall of Fame and Pujols will, no doubt, eventually join them. However, if you gave me a choice between meeting and talking with all of them or meeting and talking with three players who have yet to be voted into the Hall of Fame like Al Oliver, Al Bumbry, and Luis Tiant, all idols of my youth, I wouldn't hesitate to choose the latter group.

That may explain why I was so thrilled at the opportunity to interview former Major League slugger Gary Gaetti during the summer of 2008 when he passed through my hometown of Rochester, New York, with the Triple A Durham Bulls. As soon as I discovered Gaetti was the Bulls' hitting coach, I called an acquaintance of mine who worked for our Triple A Rochester Red Wings to ask if there was any way I could get a few minutes with Gaetti. Within a few days the details were set and I had an appointment to meet him before a Friday night game between the Bulls and Red Wings.

Next step was to do my research. The discovery of Mr. Gaetti's trip into town was last minute so I had to really crunch the numbers and do it fast. Fortunately, I remembered Gary Gaetti very well. He had been one of my favorite ballplayers of the 1980s, the second decade of my fandom. He was a hard-nosed, hard-working, blue collar ball player. A gold glove third baseman with consistent power and … he was Italian!

The day we met was an oppressively hot and humid day in Rochester. We were set to meet at 4:00 p.m. but when I arrived the press liaison asked me if I could wait until 5:00 p.m. because Gaetti was working with some of the hitters down in the cages. At around 4:30 I caught sight of Gaetti entering the field from the gates in far right field. He walked into the infield, picked up a bat, and started hitting fly balls to his outfielders. Finally, at 5:00 p.m., I was led onto the field and into the visitor's dugout where Gaetti joined me just a minute or two later after having stopped to give some advice to one of his Durham players. We spoke for about 20–25 minutes and then he excused himself while he went back out onto the field to hit grounders for infield practice. He came back about 20 minutes later and we resumed our interview. Needless to say, the "hard-working" aspect of Gaetti's personality had changed very little since his playing days.

Gary Joseph Gaetti was born in August of 1958 in Centralia, Illinois. It was a small town upbringing and sports were a way of life for Gaetti. He played basketball, baseball and was even drafted to play college football but as he grew older baseball became his central focus. His father was a welder for the Illinois Central Gulf Railroad who umpired Slow Pitch Softball games in his free time. Gaetti would wait for his dad to get home every day from work to play ball with him. "He just never

ever said no," Gaetti remembered. "I'd be sitting on the porch waiting for him to get home from work and I'm sure he was exhausted and sometimes I'd let him take a shower and sometimes I wouldn't. We'd be out in the street playing catch or go down to the field to hit some grounders ... or he'd hit me pop flies in the backyard." He credits much of his work ethic to his dad.

There were other important influences on his development as a ballplayer. A gentleman named Fred Pearson was the director of the local community recreation department. Gaetti remembered that "He was one of the original Harlem Globetrotters and he spent more time doing things with us kids ... he'd just come by in a big station wagon and honk the horn and we'd load up the car and go to different towns to play baseball, play basketball, or play football. I'd have to say he was a big influence in my life."

And then there was Jim Wassum, his college coach at Northwest Missouri State. "Jim Wassum taught me a lot about the fundamentals," said Gaetti. "How to play it the right way ... the dedication that it takes to play the game."

He was drafted in the first round of the 1979 amateur draft by the Minnesota Twins. By the end of the 1981 season he played nine games with the Twins and batted a dismal .192 while striking out six times. He did, however, hit two home runs in those nine games. His first Major League at-bat was a home run off knuckleball pitcher Charlie Hough. In fact, as of 2024, Gaetti still held the record for lifetime home runs among all players who homered in their first big league at-bat, with 360 home runs.

He made it onto the Twins' roster with a strong spring training in 1982 and never returned to the minors. Gaetti played in 145 games his rookie year hitting only .230 but pounding out 25 home runs while driving in 84 runs. He finished fifth in the Rookie of the Year voting.

In 1983 his numbers were similar as he hit 21 home runs and drove in 78 runs but he struck out 121 times while walking only 54 times. If Gaetti had one outstanding weakness as a player it was his walks-to-strikeouts ratio. He struck out 1602 times in his 20 year career while walking only 634 times with a .255 lifetime average. In almost every other facet of the game, he was a star.

Gaetti's greatest season was 1987 as he pounded out 31 home runs, drove in 109 runs and won his second Gold Glove award at third base. Most importantly, he was the MVP of the American League Championship Series as the Twins defeated the Detroit Tigers in five games. Gaetti got his Twins off to a rousing start in Game One of the Championship Series, hitting two home runs as the Twins beat the Tigers 8–5. He finished the series with two home runs, five RBIs, and a .300 batting average.

The Twins' opponents in the World Series were the St. Louis Cardinals. It was a sweet bit of baseball irony that Gaetti, who had grown up near St. Louis as a fan of the great Cardinal teams of the late 1960s, was now facing his hometown team in baseball's championship games. In the World Series, Gaetti had four extra-base hits while scoring four runs and driving in four more against his childhood team. The

Twins defeated the Cardinals in seven games to take home the first World Championship in franchise history. "The fans were always really good to us but the people will never, ever forget that [the first Championship]. It's obvious when we go back there for their functions, whether it be a reunion or anniversary, it's like we relive it all over again," said Gaetti. "Everybody's a little bit older but the stories are still the same, the fans' reaction is still the same—it's really pretty special. It's awesome."

In 1988, Gaetti won another Gold Glove for his fielding at third base and batted over .300 (.301 to be exact) for the only time in his career. He also hit 28 home runs and drove in 88 runs. He would win one more Gold Glove in 1989 (four in a row) but his offensive numbers began to decline. He was granted free agency in November of 1990 and was signed by the California Angels in January of 1991. He played 300 games in an Angels uniform but never felt completely comfortable in California. After playing 20 games for the Angels in 1993 and batting only .156, he was released.

There were some who thought that at the age of 34, Gaetti's career might be over. Instead the Kansas City Royals signed him two weeks after his release from the Angels and he finished the second half of the season with 14 home runs and 46 RBIs. He went on to have two more productive years with the Royals, including 1995 when he hit a career high 35 home runs.

In December of 1995, he signed with the St. Louis Cardinals. In the following 1996 season he hit 23 home runs, had 80 RBIs and hit .274 for the Cards. St. Louis made it into the playoffs where they swept the Padres in the NL Divisional Series but lost to the Braves in seven games in the NLCS. Gaetti hit two home runs and drove in seven runs in the postseason.

In 1998 Gary Gaetti was nearing 40 years of age. The Cardinals released him on August 14 but the Chicago Cubs signed him five days later on August 19, 1998. Cubs fans were initially wary of the acquisition of a player whose best days were obviously behind him. Nevertheless, before the summer was over, Gaetti would win the hearts of legions of Cub fans as he helped Chicago make the playoffs, hitting .320 while belting eight home runs and driving in 27 runs in just 37 games. The Cubbies lost the Divisional Series in three straight games to the Braves but Gaetti was re-signed and returned to Wrigley for the 1999 season. He played a few games in 2000 for the Red Sox before retiring at the age of 41. In over 100 years of baseball history, and roughly 23,000 players, only 57 men have played more Major League games than Gary Gaetti and only three have played more games at third base.

If nothing else, Gaetti's year and a half with the Cubs gained him a cult following—literally. It's called The Gary Gaetti Cult and it can be found on Facebook. It was started by a group of college buddies who apparently spent much of 1998–99 drinking beer and watching the Cubs on WGN. They were attracted to Gaetti's working-class values and style. They initially started the club as a joke but it took on a life of its own and continues to grow. In 2007, members of the cult drove to Minnesota when Gaetti was enshrined into the Twins Hall of Fame to meet their hero/god.

Gaetti broke into a broad smile at the mere mention of his online cult following.

"These guys are from North Dakota and it's so funny.... I just met them last year [2007] for the first time. These guys just have a lot of fun with it. We met at the Twins Hall of Fame [ceremony]. I was really glad that they made the effort ... it's really cool," Gaetti said with a laugh.

The Twins Hall of Fame was another honor in Gaetti's long career. He was the 18th inductee in the Twins Hall of Fame and the induction ceremony was the last event of a yearlong celebration of the 20th anniversary of the Twins' 1987 World Series Championship. "I really couldn't imagine ... how it could be better," Gaetti said at the ceremony. "Just the reunion is something. It's more fun to think of the team stuff than the personal stuff."

Gaetti may have played for a half dozen teams but to me, he'll always be a Twin. When I first started watching baseball in the early 1970s, the Twins were almost always in the basement despite having future Hall of Famers Harmon Killebrew and Rod Carew and Tony Oliva. So by the 1980s, drawn as I was to rooting for underdogs and players who really seemed to love playing the game, I was naturally drawn to the Twins as they put together a colorful, and under-rated, cast of ballplayers that included Gaetti, Kirby Puckett, Kent Hrbek, Tom Brunansky, and Frank Viola.

When we spoke, Gaetti had fond memories of his '87 teammates. "Kirby's in my top 10 all-time best players ... ever," Gaetti said. "Kent [Hrbek] had some injuries but he was one of the best athletes I've ever been around. He has, by far, the best hand-eye coordination of any human being I've ever known." Hrbek was known for his power at the plate but Gaetti felt that he was under-appreciated as a first baseman. When Hrbek retired, Gaetti presented one of his four Gold Gloves to Hrbek as a gift of gratitude and respect to his former first baseman.

Gaetti was out of the game for just a year before he got the itch to put the uniform back on. He recalled, "After that first summer away from it [the game] I said, 'I've got to call someone to see if I can go to Spring Training as a bullpen coach or a batting practice pitcher or something.' I called the Cardinals and it was so good to have the uniform back on and not have to worry about the pressure of competing." He enjoys teaching the game and talking to the younger guys about the secrets of the game. He told me he'd enjoy managing someday if the opportunity presents itself.

In 2012, Gaetti became the manager of the Sugarland Skeeters, an Atlantic League Professional Baseball team. He spent six years at the helm of the independent league ball club, leading them to two championship series and one title. In 2020, Gaetti returned to Centralia and opened the Gaetti Sports Academy.

Throughout our talk all those years back, the overriding aspect of Gary Gaetti's personality and philosophy was the desire to win and the dedication to hard work and constant practice that it takes to achieve that goal. When I asked him what his message would be to young ballplayers he said, "Do not cheat yourself. Be dedicated to the game, have fun, work hard, and don't cheat yourself." Gaetti is a man who's taken his own advice. He has given everything he's got to the game and his rewards have been well earned.

Immediately upon hearing that I would be interviewing a former Major Leaguer, my sons, who were then ages seven and 11, wanted to know if they could come with me. That request was denied. Then my oldest son asked if I would get him an autograph. That prompted a visit to the basement and a few hours of sifting through some of my old baseball cards to see if we had any cards of Gary Gaetti. We came up with three but I decided to bring just two with me, one for Nick and one for Frank. After all, I didn't want Gaetti to think that I needed or wanted an autograph. I'm a professional writer after all. I need to maintain my integrity and professional demeanor.

After our talk I asked him if he'd mind signing the cards for my sons, which he did gladly. I then handed him a baseball that the clubhouse man had given me while I'd been waiting for Gaetti to finish hitting infield practice. I handed him the ball and said, "This one's for me. Just make it out to Otto, O-T-T-O."

♦ **34** ♦

A. Bartlett Giamatti

Writer, columnist, and baseball fan George Will described Bart Giamatti as the Sandy Koufax of Commissioners.

There's a wonderful song written by the talented jazz musician Dave Frishberg called "The Dear Departed Past." In it, Frishberg asks the question "Can one feel a real nostalgia for a time and place one never even knew?" I love the song because it encompasses much of who and what I am. The song is about nostalgia, the longing to go back to a simpler, happier time, whether it ever truly existed or not.

The song and the feelings are apropos when I think about Bart Giamatti. Can one feel a real nostalgia, a real love, and a real void left behind by someone's passing—for a person one never even knew? The answer is yes because that's how I feel when I think of Giamatti.

I "knew" him for such a brief time—not personally, of course, but as the president of Baseball's National League and then, for a short five months, as the Commissioner of Baseball. On an intellectual level, I admired his writings, his insights into the game of baseball, and his unique ability to tie classic principles and themes from literature and history into the mythology of baseball in America. He was, at heart, a poet.

On a personal level, I liked his face. It was a friendly, open, warm, and familiar face. Bart Giamatti could have been my father or my uncle. He was only half Italian but his face was completely Mediterranean. You could picture him at home in the middle of an Italian piazza talking with the local gentry as easily as you could behind a podium at Yale lecturing to a group of eager young scholars.

For me, a grandson of Italian immigrants, Giamatti was the first Commissioner of Baseball who was accessible to me in a personal way. The first Commissioner I remember, Bowie Kuhn, was pure Mayflower America or perhaps I should say, Puritan America. The pride I felt as an Italian American upon Giamatti's ascendancy to the office of Commissioner of Baseball is indescribable. He was more than just an Italian American. He was an individual with a brilliant mind and an abundance of charm. I think it's fair to say that he was the most charismatic man ever to hold that office.

He was a man of high ideals, a romantic view of baseball, and a deep and sincere belief in his duty to uphold the integrity of the game that he felt so perfectly represented the nation that created it. Ultimately, that sense of duty required him to make an historically difficult and controversial decision for the good of the game.

Angelo Bartlett Giamatti was born in Boston, Massachusetts, on April 4, 1938. He grew up in South Hadley, Massachusetts, near the campus of Mount Holyoke College where his father, Valentine Giamatti, taught Romance Languages and Dante from 1940 until his retirement in 1973. Giamatti was named for his two grandfathers—Angelo Giamatti and Bartlett Walton. Signor Giamatti was an immigrant from a small fishing village just outside of Naples, Italy, while Mr. Walton was the son of a successful shoe manufacturer.

Valentine Giamatti met his future wife Mary (called Peggy) Walton on a trip to Florence, Italy, where he was traveling on an exchange fellowship to pursue his PhD and she was going to spend her junior year at Smith College studying the Italian language. They married in 1936 and two years later their first child was born; a son and future scholar himself.

Young Bart Giamatti grew up a happy child in the idyllic New England town where his father was a respected and much loved educator. His mother played piano and instilled a love of opera in her children. And then … there were the Red Sox. In New England, everyone loved and followed the Boston Red Sox. The dinner table was a place for discussions on Ted Williams's batting average as well as Dante.

In the 1940s, baseball was truly America's game. It was so important that when Commissioner Kenesaw Mountain Landis contemplated putting a halt to the game for the duration of World War II, President Franklin D. Roosevelt wrote to Landis, in a legendary correspondence dated January 14, 1942, "I honestly feel that it would be best for the country to keep baseball going."

Bart Giamatti chose the Red Sox second baseman, Bobby Doerr, as his childhood idol. The young Giamatti didn't have a strong arm so he chose to play second base as that was Doerr's position. From everything he read about him and learned from listening to the Red Sox radio broadcasts, Doerr was a respected and popular leader among his teammates.

Many years later Giamatti was asked the question, "Why choose to be Bobby Doerr rather than Ted Williams?" He answered, "I could imagine myself playing second base but not hitting .400. Children imagine, adults fantasize."

Sadly, Giamatti had the desire but not the skills to play ball at an advanced level. He tried out for his high school team in the spring of 1951 and caught the eye of the coach, Tom Landers, but he just wasn't good enough to make the team. In *Bart: A Life of A. Bartlett Giamatti*, by Anthony Valerio, he includes an article printed after Giamatti's premature passing that quotes the former coach of the South Hadley High School baseball team. "Oh, he played his heart out, but he just didn't have the talent necessary to make the team," said Landers. "But he was very enthusiastic and great to have around."

The coach found a way to keep the young Giamatti around—he made him the team manager. "He was a hell of an organization person," said Landers. "When I made him manager, I saw what he could do." And so it was that Bart Giamatti began his baseball career managing the day to day activities of the South Hadley High School team and eventually wound up managing the entire sport.

Before he entered the sporting world on a professional level, however, he was a gifted and celebrated scholar. He graduated from Yale University in 1960 and went on to earn his PhD there in 1964. He taught at Yale and eventually became a popular and effective president of that institution from 1978 until 1986, when he was appointed president of Major League baseball's National League. In September 1988, he was chosen to succeed Peter Ueberroth as the next Commissioner of Baseball.

As a literary scholar his focus was on Renaissance Literature and specifically on Edmund Spenser's *The Fairie Queene*. However, during his years as Yale president through his time as president of the National League and Commissioner of Baseball,

Giamatti wrote some of the most thoughtful and inspiring articles and essays ever produced on the game of baseball and its meaning for us as fans, scholars, Americans, and human beings.

Giamatti's younger brother Dino said of him, "He intellectualized about the game and analyzed it much more than the average fan, I think." The analysis and thoughtful passion of Bart Giamatti where it concerned the game is evident in his many reveries about the meaning of "home plate" or "home base"—that distinct place on the field where the action begins and ends.

"Why is home plate not called fourth base?" Giamatti asked in his book, *Take Time for Paradise*. "As far as I can tell," he wrote, "it has always been thus. 'Home' is a concept, not a place; it is a state of mind where self-definition starts; it is origins—the mix of time and place and smell and weather wherein one first realizes one is an original, perhaps 'like' others, especially those one loves, but discreet, distinct, not to be copied. Home is where one first learned to be separate and it remains in the mind as the one place where reunion, if it ever were to occur, would happen."

In an interview with Todd Brewster for an article entitled "Front-office Fan," Giamatti revealed that the musing about home plate was not a singular occurrence. "What's home?" Giamatti wondered, "Home is longing for when you were happy because you were younger. At least you thought you were happier. Home, that's what you call that thing! It's the one baseball fact that I cannot track down in all the histories that I have read. When did that pentagram where you start and where you aspire to return, when did that get called 'home?' What genius so defined the essence of what we're after by calling it home plate?"

The themes of home and nostalgia that Giamatti muses about so often when writing about baseball are themes that are of great interest and deep meaning to me. As someone who lost my father when I was still a boy, the feeling of a "paradise lost" is one that's very real to me. Unlike so many American boys, I did not share the love of baseball with my dad. He was not a sports-minded person. He cared more for music, television, and movies and, I'm sure, because they were his extra-curricular interests they became mine as well. But baseball was still important to me—perhaps, because as Giamatti liked to point out, it was so lasting, so consistent, so dependable an institution. "Baseball is one of the few American institutions to have survived since the Civil War," Giamatti said. "It represents our antiquity."

As Giamatti correctly surmises, baseball is all about childhood. When I think of baseball stars I still think of Brooks Robinson, Roberto Clemente or Rico Petrocelli, the heroes of my youth. As already stated, the modern game and the modern superstars are not nearly as important to me as those players and games of the 1970s that cultivated my love for the game of baseball.

However, as a man writing in the autumn of his years, Giamatti's insights into the game and its qualities of renewal are illuminating. He writes about the game measuring time, almost as an antidote to growing older, to make time slow down. In a piece called "The Green Fields of the Mind," Giamatti wrote, "There comes a time when every summer will have something of autumn about it. Whatever the reason, it seemed to me that I was investing more and more in baseball, making the game do more of the work that keeps time fat and slow and lazy. I was counting on the game's deep patterns, three strikes, three outs, three times three innings, and its deepest impulse, to go out and back, to leave and return home, to set the order of the day and to organize the daylight."

Sadly, the tenure of this poet-scholar as Commissioner of Baseball was too short-lived. Brief as his time in office was, Giamatti made an impact in the five months that he served. Upon accepting the position of Commissioner, Giamatti said, "Baseball is an American institution and, as the trustee of it, I will be respectful of its certain fundamental values." The columnist and writer George Will wrote that "Giamatti was to the Commissioner's office what Sandy Koufax was to the pitcher's mound: Giamatti's career had the highest ratio of excellence to longevity."

That respect for, and dedication to, its most fundamental values would lead Giamatti into conflict with one of the game's greatest players. In February of 1989, the Commissioner's office received allegations that Pete Rose, manager of the Cincinnati Reds, had not only bet on baseball games but bet on Reds games. This is an act in violation of the clearly stated, written, and posted rules of Major League Baseball. Giamatti appointed John Dowd as Special Counsel to investigate the matter. By early May, Dowd submitted a report to Giamatti. The Commissioner set a date of May 25, 1989, for Rose to answer and defend himself against the charges. Rose and his counsel asked for an extension and a new date was set for June 26, 1989. Mr. Rose never showed up to defend himself against the charges.

Ultimately, an agreement was struck between the Commissioner's office and Pete Rose wherein Rose accepted a lifetime ban from the game of baseball. Rose did not have to admit guilt and could, at a later date, apply for reinstatement although no such reinstatement was implicit within the terms of the agreement.

It was a dark day for baseball. Rose, known throughout his career as "Charlie Hustle" for the effort he put into every game and every at-bat, was the game's all-time hits leader. He possessed three World Series Championship rings. He was a legend of the sport. Bart Giamatti as a fan of the game was visibly taxed by the duties he had to perform but he would not sway from that which he thought was best for the game.

In his statement announcing the banishment of Rose, Giamatti said, "I believe baseball is a beautiful and exciting game, loved by millions—I among them—and I believe baseball is an important, enduring American institution. It must assert and aspire to the highest principles, of integrity, of professionalism of performance, of fair play within its rules.

"I will be told that I am an idealist," Giamatti went on to say, "I hope so. I will continue to locate ideals I hold for myself and my country in the national game as well as in our other institutions. And while there will be debate and dissent about this or that or another occurrence on or off the field, and while the game's nobler parts will always be enmeshed in the human frailties of those who, whatever their role, have stewardship of this game, let there be no doubt or dissent about our goals for baseball and our dedication to it."

In the end, it was the very last line of Giamatti's statement that would ring through the generations following his decision, through all ensuing labor problems, steroid controversies, collusion, and every other challenge the game would face when he said, "Let it also be clear that no individual is superior to the game." One week after he made the announcement, Bart Giamatti died of a massive heart attack.

Frank Cashen, general manager of the New York Mets, remembered Giamatti as "a brilliant man of supreme intellect. I felt he was going to be an outstanding commissioner. His handling of the Rose case certainly proved my theories I had going in. He was eminently fair, and I don't know anyone who had his passion for the game. He had as much integrity as anyone I've ever seen. When you combine that intellect with his integrity and passion, you have a rare individual."

For 14 years after the decision, Rose maintained his innocence and subtly criticized Bart Giamatti and his decision. Finally, in 2004, three days before he was releasing his autobiography, Rose admitted to having bet on baseball. He initially said he bet only on certain games. Three years later, he admitted to having bet on every game while he was managing the Reds, even the games of his own team.

On May 13, 2025, MLB Commissioner Rob Manfred succumbed to the unsolicited advice of President Donald J. Trump (a convicted felon) and lifted the lifetime ban on Pete Rose. It signifies little more than the continued erosion of public standards. Some people believe it will now assure Rose a place in the Baseball Hall of Fame. It may or it may not. Whatever the result, Rose won't be there to accept the honor as he died on September 30, 2024, at the age of 83.

No individual has ever been able to symbolically connect baseball to life and to America the way Bart Giamatti did. In a legacy of memorable quotes about the game, perhaps the most enduring thought of Giamatti's work sums up not only the game and our daily lives but also his tenure as custodian of the game:

"It breaks your heart," he wrote of baseball, "It is designed to break your heart. The game begins in the spring, when everything else begins again, and it blossoms in the summer, filling the afternoons and evenings, and then as soon as the chill rains come, it stops and leaves you to face the fall alone. You count on it, rely on it to buffer the passage of time, to keep the memory of sunshine and high skies alive, and then just when the days are all twilight, when you need it most, it stops…. And summer is gone."

The game of baseball needs someone like Giamatti now more than ever but there is no one in the on deck circle. That's too bad because the chance to reclaim the summer of our youth is almost gone.

♦ 35 ♦

Others of Note

A brief section of the Preface of this book explains how the subjects contained herein were chosen. Nevertheless, I'm confident that some people will be upset that their favorite player, or someone they felt should have been included, was omitted. I sincerely apologize for leaving out anyone's favorites but the fact is, the line had to be drawn somewhere. Believe me when I tell you, I spent far more time trying to decide whom to keep and whom to cut than you'll ever imagine.

What follows are brief career synopses for the players who were "cut" for this volume; some were profiles for *Fra Noi* magazine, some were not. The first was a gentleman named **Ping Bodie**. There was much debate over his baseball name, Ping Bodie, and his real name, Francesco Stephano Pezzolo. He took the Bodie name from a friend or relative to somewhat disguise his ethnic background. He broke into the Major Leagues in 1911 and played nine years in the big leagues, finishing up with the Yankees in 1921. While with the Yankees, one of his roommates was the young Babe Ruth, newly acquired from the Boston Red Sox. When asked what it was like rooming with the Babe, Bodie cracked, "I'm rooming with his suitcase," alluding to all of Ruth's late-night adventures.

The three best years of his career all came for different teams: the White Sox, the Athletics, and the Yanks. He was a flamboyant player who liked to socialize with the fans in the bleachers and in his Major League career, he finished with a .275 batting average and .335 on-base-percentage. He was also an above average outfielder for his time. Following his MLB years, he spent another seven years playing in the Western and Pacific Coast Leagues. He was a long-time fan favorite in his hometown of San Francisco and played in part of seven seasons for the PCL's San Francisco Seals. When his baseball career finally ended in 1928, he spent another 30 years in Hollywood as an electrician on film sets.

I never did get around to writing about **Ed Abbaticchio,** who is believed to be the first traceable Italian American to play professional baseball. There was a gentleman named Nicholas Taylor Apollonio who was of Italian extraction but he was an executive with the Boston club sometime between 1874 and 1876, not a player.

Abbaticchio also played professional football. He was a native of Latrobe, Pennsylvania, and the first American-born child of his immigrant parents. While his career statistics seem rather average today, the literature of the time shows that he was a sought after player and highly respected by his teammates. In *Beyond DiMaggio*, Lawrence Baldassaro quotes a letter written by Abbaticchio's Hall of Fame teammate, Honus Wagner, that reads, "'Batty' was one of the best of his day as a player and one of the finest of any baseball era as a man and a true friend…."

I loved discovering a little infielder named **Oscar "Spinach" Melillo** who spent 12 seasons as one of the top second basemen in the American Leagues from 1926 to 1937. Melillo was the youngest of five children born to Tuscan immigrants. He never gave baseball a thought as a career until he played on a team with his fellow workers at the International Harvester Company. He was an obvious standout and was recommended to the manager of a Winnipeg team. He eventually ended up in Milwaukee of the American Association before the St. Louis Browns bought his contract in 1925.

His minor league career turned out to be an excellent harbinger of what he would accomplish in the big leagues. He was an average hitter but an excellent anchor at the keystone base. In a 1954 newspaper article, George Schumann extolled the career achievements of the diminutive Melillo, remembering him as a fan favorite, writing, "his first name Oscar made a hit with the Germans of St. Louis, the largest foreign nationality group there, and his last name of Melillo lured the Italians, second in preponderance."

Near the end of the 1927 season, Melillo contracted Bright's disease and was told by his doctor to go on a strict diet of only spinach. He later added carrots to his regimen and enjoyed a remarkable recovery. His new diet, however, provided a new nickname as he became known as "Spinach" Melillo.

During his career he led the league in almost all defensive categories multiple times and almost assuredly would have won numerous Gold Glove Awards had they existed at the time. One newspaper account of the day by Thomas J. Connery said Melillo "glides far to his left and right to scoop up grounders and skips into the outfield for dropping flies when the occasion demands."

When his playing days were done, he spent another 20 years coaching and managing in the big leagues. His daughter Lois Melillo Maher once recalled asking her father, "Dad, how come you wake up every day so happy?" His answer was simple, "Honey, I'm a lucky guy who loves what he does for a living."

As previously stated, many of the profiled players were far from superstars, but there was almost always something, beyond just statistics, that appealed to me about them. In the case of **Sibby Sisti**, it started off with his great baseball name and the fact that he was from my little area of the world. Born Sebastian Sisti in 1920 in Buffalo, New York, "Sibby" Sisti broke in with the Boston Braves in 1939. Like so many players of that era, he lost three full years to the armed services during World War II. From 1939 to 1954, he spent the better part of 12 seasons with the

Braves organization. He became a mainstay of the Braves' infield from 1940 to 1942 although he never batted above .259 in those three seasons. He was, however, a solid fielder, an exceptional bunter, and a smart base runner.

One of baseball's greatest alliterations, Sibby Sisti.

Sisti forged a career that eventually earned him the nickname "the Supersub." In a 1997 interview with *USA Today*, Sisti recalled, "At one point I played five positions in five days." To further prove his versatility, in both 1950 and 1951, he played every position in the infield during the course of the season. The only positions he never played in his big league career were catcher and pitcher although he was known to jump into the bullpen and warm up a pitcher when needed. He was the ultimate "team player" who played for the love of the game.

In 1979 when Sisti was asked by the *Boston Herald* what his greatest thrill in baseball was, Sisti said, "Every ballplayer thinks about a big game he had. But I always said that my greatest thrills were two great honors by the Boston baseball writers—first at their dinner in 1948 after the Series, and the second [in 1967] when they brought me back as the first 'Old Brave.' It was a hell of a tribute and I'll never forget it."

In 1983, Sisti gained a different sort of fame when he served as a technical advisor for the Robert Redford film *The Natural*, shot in Buffalo. He played the bit part of the Pirate manager who goes to the bullpen to bring in a left-hander to pitch to Redford's character, Roy Hobbs. Hobbs then hits a mammoth home run off the light posts. Years after the film became a cult favorite, Sisti used to joke, "If they ever make a *Natural 2*, I'm going out there again. But this time, on the first pitch, Redford's character is going right down on his ass!"

How can you be an all-star outfielder, bat over .300 two times, have more lifetime walks than strikeouts, and play in a World Series all in a respectable ten-year baseball career, and still end up virtually unknown? Easy, play more than half of your career for the old St. Louis Browns. At least, that's how **Al Zarilla** did it.

Al Zarilla began his big league career in 1943 with the St. Louis Browns of the American League. The Browns were "the other St. Louis team" in the first half of the 20th century. They were perpetually overshadowed by the better known, and more successful, St. Louis Cardinals of the National League. In 1949, Zarilla was traded away to the Boston Red Sox. In Boston, he shared Fenway Park with the likes of Dom DiMaggio, Bobby Doerr, and Ted Williams. It's hard to get noticed in a crowd like that. It seemed that no matter where Zarilla went or what he did, stardom was not meant to be his. One baseball magazine of the 1950s called him the "Most Under-rated Player in the Majors."

He was also a streak hitter so he could go on a tear for a couple of weeks hitting over .400 and then turn cold as ice for just as long a period after that. He had an impressive sophomore season in 1944 batting .299 but then lost a year to military service. When he returned it took him a while to regain his form. There was a nervous energy that defined Zarilla. He couldn't sit still. Critics mistakenly assumed he had a less than serious attitude toward his job; however, he spent much of the latter half of the 1947 season trying to figure out how to regain success with the bat.

Al Zarilla, a streak hitter and a solid outfielder.

It paid off with his best season at the plate in 1948, hitting .329 with 74 RBIs. Early in the '49 season he was traded to the Red Sox. He had a solid remainder of the season with the Bosox and an even better year in 1950, hitting .325, before being traded to the White Sox in 1951. His last three years were mediocre at best. He played two more seasons in the PCL before retiring from the game. His old friend Ted Williams brought him back to help coach the Senators in 1971 so he could earn his full 10 year pension. He retired after the '71 season and lived out his years in Hawaii, dying in 1996 at age 77.

Southpaw **Don Mossi**'s rookie year was spent as part of the 1954 Indians, a pitching staff that included four Hall-of-Famers: Feller, Wynn, Lemon, and

Newhouser. Amazing that with a staff that good, he could even get a chance to pitch but he impressed as a reliever, finishing with a 6–1 record and a 1.94 ERA. He even carried his weight in the World Series, pitching four innings without giving up a run. The Indians lost the fall classic to the Giants but Mossi would serve as a steady Tribe reliever for five years.

In November of 1958, Mossi was traded to the Tigers and became a starting pitcher in Detroit in 1959. Once again, he excelled, going 17–9 with a 3.36 ERA with 15 complete games in his first full season as a starter. It was with the Tigers that Mossi also turned into a "Yankee Killer." He notched five straight complete game victories in a row over the Yanks giving up a total of just six earned runs. In 1960, Mossi came up with a sore shoulder that derailed his season. He started only 22 games and finished with a disappointing 9–8 record. Even so, four out of his nine victories came at the expense of the pennant-bound Yankees.

Mossi bounced back to good form in '61 but that was his last fully healthy season. He struggled on and off with shoulder problems until his retirement in 1965. Nevertheless, he finished with a lifetime record of 101–80 with 80 saves and a 3.43 ERA.

As good a pitcher as Mossi was, he was probably best remembered for his prominent ears which are on glorious display in a number of his baseball cards. He died in 2019 but would always sign anything an autograph seeker would send him in exchange for a Mossi baseball card that he would then pass on to his grandkids.

Tito Francona is another player I first learned about because of his baseball card. His last season was 1970 so I never saw him play but I got his 1963 Topps card in a trade and immediately looked up his record in my 1974 edition of *The Baseball Encyclopedia*. When I discovered what a good career he'd had I wondered why I had never heard of him. I didn't yet understand the importance of the media in creating sports stars. First of all, he had an injury-plagued career which made for an inconsistent 15 years in MLB. In addition, he played for small market teams and never saw action in the postseason.

He was signed by the St. Louis Browns for a $5000 bonus in 1954. He gave $4000 to his parents to build a house and $500 to his brother to get married. He spent two years in the minor leagues and by the time he made it to the majors in 1956, the Browns had become the Baltimore Orioles. He never quite hit his stride in Baltimore and after brief stops in Chicago (AL) and Detroit in 1958, he began a very successful stint in Cleveland in 1959. In fact, had it not been for a 1957 rule change requiring 477 plate appearances to qualify for the batting title, Francona would have won the honor in '59 with his .363 average. He finished 34 plate appearances short. At least five players in baseball history have won a batting title with less at bats than Francona had in 1959.

He enjoyed three more productive years with the Tribe before injuries caught up with him. He finished his career as a platoon player and pinch-hitter for five

The original "Tito," Terry's dad, Tito Francona enjoyed some stellar seasons in Cleveland.

different teams in the last six years of his career. He had a bit of a comeback in 1969 in 83 games but retired after the 1970 season.

It should be noted that Tito, who died in 2018, and his wife Roberta made another major contribution to baseball in their son, **Terry Francona**, who will forever be remembered as the man who ended the 86-year championship drought of the Boston Red Sox. In his eight years leading the BoSox, Terry won two World Championships. He then managed the Cleveland ball club for a franchise record of 11 seasons before retiring in 2023. In 2025, he signed on as manager of the Cincinnati Reds.

The last player cut from my original set of profiles was **Gino Cimoli**. Like so many Italian American players before him, Cimoli came out of the North Beach section of San Francisco. His dad was an immigrant but his mom was an American of Italian descent. He was a star basketball player in high school but didn't think at 6'2" he'd be tall enough for pro basketball. The Dodgers signed him to a bonus upwards of $15,000 in 1949. With the talent in the Dodger farm system, however, it took Cimoli almost eight years to make the Brooklyn ball club. His best year with the Dodgers was 1957 when he batted .293 and scored 88 runs.

He had issues with Dodger management and wanted to be played with more consistency, so after a mediocre campaign in 1958, he was traded to the Cards in 1959. There he enjoyed a bit of a bounce back to .279 and 72 RBIs. Nevertheless, to his good fortune, he wasn't in the Cardinals' plans for 1960 and ended up on the Pirates team of 1960. His key hit in the eighth inning of Game Seven of the 1960 World Series started a rally that pulled the Pirates ahead. The Yanks tied the game in the top of the ninth before Mazeroski's dramatic home run in the bottom of the ninth ended the series in Pittsburgh's favor. Cimoli was a World Champion.

Cimoli's last five seasons were stretched out over five different teams. He did well for the Kansas City A's in '62 and '63 but after just four games with the Angels in 1965, he hung up his spikes for good. He'd hoped for a career in coaching or managing after his playing days were over but it never panned out.

His last touch with fame came in a *San Francisco Chronicle* column from the fall of 1989 when Tom Fitzgerald reported that "Gino Cimoli, a delivery driver for UPS, was recently honored for completing 21 years without an accident. [Cimoli] was also credited with helping many Marina residents who were trapped in their homes during the October 17 earthquake."

Fitzgerald reported that the UPS driver never mentioned his previous life to those who honored him "because he hates tooting his own horn. As for his iron-man work as the Lou Gehrig of the parcel service, he said: 'If I could hit like Gehrig, I wouldn't be driving a truck.'"

One month I wrote about catchers of Italian American ancestry noting, among other things, the high baseball IQ that catchers must possess and relating that fact to the high number of managers who are/were former backstops.

Famed New York sportswriter Tom Meany once wrote that New York Giant catcher **Gus Mancuso** "is one of those guys who seem to have a positive genius for being inconspicuous. He has been catching excellent ball for the Giants for nearly three years and all the average Polo Grounds fan can tell you about him is that he minds his own business and is not very fast. He handles pitchers like Rockefeller does dimes—with the greatest of care."

Sportswriters often talk about leadership but the truth is, when push comes to shove, what they promote are gaudy numbers and flamboyant personalities. Gus Mancuso is a name largely forgotten to history but he spent 17 years in the Major Leagues and was one of the most respected catchers in all of baseball during the 1930s. He played on two All-Star teams, twice led the league in throwing out opposing baserunners, and was a two-time World Champion playing on five pennant winners. He finished his career with a respectable .265 average for a catcher but he was better known for his defensive skills and his outstanding ability at handling pitching staffs.

Phil Masi was one of the most reliable catchers of the 1940s. He was a four-time All Star and anchor for the 1948 pennant-winning Braves. Unfortunately, he's mostly remembered today for a controversial play from the 1948 World Series against the Cleveland Indians.

In the bottom of the eighth inning of Game One, pitcher Bob Feller twirled around and threw to shortstop Lou Boudreau in an attempt to pick off Masi from second base. Masi, who was pinch-running for Bill Salkeld, slid back to second and was called safe by umpire Bill Stewart. Cleveland players and fans were apoplectic over the call. The irony is that while the Braves won that controversial ball game by a score of 1–0, the Indians came back and won the next three games in a row before wrapping up a series victory in six games. The play proved to be unimportant to the outcome of the series but the debate eventually overshadowed Phil Masi's otherwise solid career as an All-Star catcher.

Sportswriter Ed Rumill wrote a glowing article on Masi in a 1947 edition of *The Sporting News*, touching on the challenges of a Major League catcher: "When a ballplayer happens to be a catcher and he is in there almost every day, taking the pounding a backstop has to take from enemy base-runners—running after pop flies and backing up the bases—coaxing that little extra out of the pitcher—cutting down attempted thefts, as well as taking a regular turn in the batter's box, you somehow forget what he is hitting. The percentage loses its importance. You know how valuable he is to his ball club … because you see him come up with his base-knocks when they mean something."

Phil Masi was one of those clutch hitters. In 14 seasons and more than 1,200 games, Masi finished his career with a .264 average. He rarely struck out and was remembered by teammates and members of the opposing team alike as a hard-nosed competitor. He once broke up a no-hitter by Dodger ace Whitlow Wyatt with a ninth inning pinch-hit.

The son of Italian immigrants, **Mickey Grasso** was born in 1920 and raised in Newark, New Jersey. He was a talented high school pitcher when spotted by Newark Bears' general manager George Weiss. He was encouraged to move off the mound and at the age of 21, he signed his first professional contract with the Trenton Senators of the Class B Interstate League. He was originally assigned second base but was moved behind the plate when the regular catcher sustained an injury.

When Pearl Harbor was bombed, Grasso enlisted in the Army and was sent to North Africa with the 34th Infantry Division. In February of 1943, Grasso's unit was surrounded by 10,000 German soldiers heavily armed with howitzers and tanks. Grasso and his men were captured and taken prisoner.

The prisoners were transferred to a prison camp in Furstenberg, Germany. Grasso was held captive for more than two years. He attempted to escape on three separate occasions. Each time he was caught and subsequently beaten. He succeeded in escaping on April 20, 1945, just weeks before the Germans surrendered. He was weak, frail, and 60 pounds under his playing weight. Nevertheless, he began the long fight to regain his skills on the baseball diamond.

He spent two years in Jersey City in the Giants organization and two years in Seattle of the Pacific Coast League. In Seattle in 1948, Grasso had a fan club that numbered in the thousands. One group with whom he did not easily make friends were the umpires. In 1949, Grasso was ejected 23 times, drawing more than $1,000 in fines. He said the PCL umpires were "thick-headed and thin-skinned." He didn't fare any better with the umps in the big leagues. It was believed that Grasso's attitude toward umpires was rooted in his memories of the beatings he endured at the hands of the authoritarian guards in the World War II prison camps. Nowadays, that kind of lingering issue would no doubt be recognized as a form of Post Traumatic Stress Disorder (PTSD).

Grasso never became a steady Major League hitter. Nevertheless, he was a solid defensive catcher with a strong throwing arm. He regularly cut down half the runners that attempted to steal off him. Legendary sportswriter Shirley Povich once wrote, "With Grasso in there, the Nats were never a dull team. He was a good catcher, too, a bundle of fire behind the plate and an arm that held terror for all base runners in the league."

John Anthony Romano was a hard-nosed ballplayer from a tough, blue-collar background whose nickname was "Honey," bestowed upon him by his uncle when he was a young boy. He spent 15 years in professional baseball with just about every inning of it behind the plate. The young prospect would spend five years in the minor leagues. He began as an average catcher with some encouraging power at the bat. In 1958, the White Sox made a move that would influence the future of John Romano's career when they sent former Major League catcher Walker Cooper to manage the Indianapolis Indians.

In an interview with Todd Newville in 2005, Romano said, "I played for about two or three years for former infielders as managers. You catch every day and you think you're doing it right. But, when Walker Cooper came down there (to Indianapolis) he straightened me out," Romano recalled. "The White Sox said the only thing that was holding me back from not going to the big leagues was not knowing how to catch. Walker Cooper helped me very much in that department."

The 1959 Chicago White Sox were nicknamed the "Go-Go Sox" because they were known for their speed and defense. Manager Al Lopez believed in playing veteran players so Romano had to work hard to earn a spot on the lineup card because the White Sox had an All-Star catcher in Sherm Lollar behind the plate. However, Romano's role as a pinch-hitter for the "Go-Go Sox" in 1959 was an important one. In 13 appearances as a pinch-hitter, Romano hit safely eight times for a .615 average. Romano also took part in a rare triple play that season where all three outs were recorded by applying the tag—no force-outs.

Romano had his best Major League season ever with the bat in 1961, hitting .299, belting out 21 home runs and collecting 80 RBIs for the Cleveland Indians. He was also proving to be a solid and reliable receiver as he caught 141 games accounting for over 1,200 innings behind the plate, the most ever in his career. He had such a stellar year that he was selected to play in the 1961 All-Star Game.

Romano was very proud of his two All-Star appearances (he was selected again in 1962) because he was chosen by his fellow players. "It wasn't a popularity contest in those years," Romano said. "Each ballplayer had one vote. Those guys are the ones that voted me in as the catcher. It was the actual baseball players that played against me that voted for me. And, getting voted in by your peers was a big honor."

Ernie Broglio was a promising young hurler for the St. Louis Cardinals who enjoyed three fine seasons for the Redbirds between 1960 and 1963. Unfortunately, he began to experience some elbow problems and ended up being involved in one of the best/worst trades in baseball history. On June 15, 1964, Broglio, Doug Clemens, and Bobby Shantz were sent to the Cubs for Jack Spring, Paul Toth, and a young outfielder named Lou Brock. As we all know, Brock went on to a Hall-of-Fame career with the Cards. Unfortunately, Broglio's elbow problems worsened and he won only seven more games in the rest of his shortened career.

Broglio does, however, still hold the MLB record for most relief appearances in a 20-win season with 28 relief appearances and 20 starts in 1960 when he went 21–9 for the season.

* * *

This is where, at the request of the publisher, I am supposed to include some information about the Italian American ballplayers I left out of this volume. I've struggled with this task and have concluded that it's impossible.

As I've already mentioned, when I composed the original profiles, they were not chosen merely by the success of an individual player's career. That's why you have read about less legendary figures such as Zeke Bonura, Joe Altobelli, and Jim Gentile, as well as Hall of Famers like Lazzeri, Lombardi, and Campanella. Therefore, to attempt to write a sentence or two about every Italian American player who debuted and played in the majors in just the years I've covered (roughly 1918–1981) is an impossible task. I can't mention everyone but I'll do my best to mention the ones who most readily jump to mind.

In this century alone, there have been seven Italian Americans inducted into Baseball's Hall of Fame that I know of: Ron Santo (2012), **Tony LaRussa** (2014), Joe Torre (2014), **Craig Biggio** (2015), **John Smoltz** (2015), **Mike Piazza** (2016), and **Mike Mussina** (2019). Santo and Torre are included in this volume but the others are not. Their absence quite obviously has nothing to do with their talents which were immense.

The Santos, LaRussas, and Torres, I remember from my childhood but the others came after my days of intense fandom. However, I must admit to a special feeling for Mike Mussina because he played for my hometown Rochester Red Wings and you just knew he was going to be great from what he showed us at the Triple A level.

There are many players who played long before my time who I didn't get a chance to cover like **Pete Castiglione**, an above average third baseman for some of the worst Pirate teams of the late 1940s and early 1950s. **Lou Chiozza**, who enjoyed three really solid seasons for the Philadelphia Phillies in the mid–1930s before petering out with three mediocre seasons for the New York Giants. **George Puccinelli**, who made it to the big leagues in every even year of the 1930s except 1938. The rest of the time from 1927 to 1940 he spent in the minor leagues including a couple of seasons with my local Red Wings. In fact, "Pooch" is a member of the Rochester Red Wings Hall of Fame along with fellow MLB Italian Americans **Frank Bertaina**, **Jeff Manto**, and Mike Mussina.

I love baseball nicknames and one of my favorites has always been **Frank "Creepy" Crespi**, a second baseman for the 1942 World Champion St. Louis Cardinals. The nickname supposedly came from his deep crouch as he scooped up grounders around the keystone bag. Unfortunately, he was drafted in 1943 and broke his leg playing in the service. He then ran into a string of bad luck that ultimately resulted in 24 operations on his injured leg and the end of his playing career.

And then there was **Sal "the Barber" Maglie** who earned his nickname for giving batters who crowded the plate a "close shave" with his wicked fastballs. I was always enamored of the legend of Sal Maglie and would have certainly written about him for the *Fra Noi* magazine except that at the time they employed another writer named Judith Testa who'd written an entire book about him entitled *Sal Maglie: Baseball's Demon Barber*. Quite appropriately, she was given the assignment to write about Maglie for *Fra Noi*.

One of the most fascinating aspects of Maglie's career was he was the only guy to play for the Giants, Dodgers, and Yankees in the magical 1950s before the two National League clubs fled West. From 1950 to 1957, the three teams were in the

World Series an amazing 13 times. Maglie himself pitched in three World Series, earning one ring with the 1954 New York Giants. In his 10 MLB seasons and 303 games pitched, all but 22 of those games were in the service of the three New York teams of the era, the Giants, the Yankees, and the Dodgers. He finished his career with an impressive .657 winning percentage and a 3.15 ERA.

As tough as he was in the big leagues, Maglie struggled early on in the minors. As he started to show some promise, World War II began and he tried to enlist but didn't pass the physical. He then quit baseball and worked in a defense plant for two years. He finally made it to the Giants at the end of the 1945 season and pitched well enough over 84 innings to pull down a 2.35 ERA. His pitching coach Dolf Luque convinced him to play winter ball in Cuba and when the Giants and manager Mel Ott were less than encouraging in spring training, Maglie joined a group of Major Leaguers who jumped to a new Mexican league in 1946. Commissioner Happy Chandler banned the players who fled to the Mexican league for five years so that when the new league soon folded, the players were out of baseball. When Maglie was eventually reinstated into MLB in 1950, he was essentially a 33-year-old rookie. Nevertheless, he pitched a string of three excellent seasons for the New York Giants. He had an off year in 1953 before bouncing back with a formidable campaign in 1954 as he and his Giant teammates became the World Champions of baseball.

Luque had taught him the intimidation factor and it improved his game immensely. When he finally retired from active play after the '58 season, he passed on his pitching theories as a coach and helped future Red Sox hurlers Bill Monbouquette, Earl Wilson, Dick Radatz, and Jim Lonborg.

Sadly, Maglie was widowed at 49 when his wife Kay died of cancer. They had two adopted children and while he stayed in baseball for a couple more years after his wife's death, he eventually retired back to Niagara Falls where he worked for the Niagara Falls Convention Bureau before retiring in 1979.

A memorable nickname from my generation of the 1970s was a pitcher named **John "The Count" Montefusco**. He had the bulk of his career success with the Giants in the 1970s, winning the Rookie of the Year award in 1975. He had arm troubles that plagued the second half of his career and was done by 1986. He was pitching coaching in the early 2000s for the Somerset Patriots of the Independent Patriot League.

Back when I was researching players at the HOF's Giamatti Research center in Cooperstown, I discovered a Yankee pitcher named **Marius Russo**. He pitched only six years for the Yanks and although, on paper, his career was disrupted by World War II, Russo always contended that his arm was injured by the end of 1941 due to overuse. He spent two years in the service overseas but when he returned he could never regain his form. Eventually he had bone chips removed from his elbow but it wasn't enough.

In Russo's brief career he compiled a 45–34 record with a 3.13 ERA over 680 innings pitched. He did earn three World Series rings in his short career and pitched complete game victories in the series in 1941 and 1943, giving up just one run for a lifetime World Series ERA of 0.50. He spent nearly 30 years as an executive at Grumman Aircraft following his baseball career but was always happy to participate in Yankee Old-Timer games.

The Aspromonte Brothers were closer to my time but still too early for me to have seen them play. Infielder **Ken Aspromonte** spent seven years in the big leagues from 1957 to 1963 putting in time with the Red Sox, Senators, Indians, Angels, Braves, and Cubs. His best season was spent in Cleveland in 1960 when he hit a solid .290 over 117 games. His younger brother, **Bob Aspromonte,** fared a little better as he spent 13 years with the Dodgers, Colt .45s/Astros, Braves, and the Mets. His top campaign was in 1967 batting .294 for the Astros with 51 runs scored and 58 RBIs. Bob was primarily a third baseman but played every position but pitcher, catcher, and centerfield during his career.

Did you know that one of the greatest defensive shortstops in all of baseball history was half–Italian? **Mark Belanger**'s mother was an Italian American. Belanger never struck fear into opposing pitchers with his lifetime average of .228 but opposing batters were less than thrilled to see him at shortstop when they came up to bat. The slick fielding Belanger, nicknamed "the Blade" due to his razor-thin build, earned eight Gold Gloves from 1969 to 1978 and won a World Championship with the 1970 Orioles.

There were a bunch of guys who were active in the Major Leagues when I started following the game in the early '70s. That man-about-town, blow-dryer-toting **Joe Pepitone** was finishing his career with the Cubs when I first saw him. He'd been a home run–hitting Gold Glove first baseman with the Yankees when I was born but by the time I got to see him, he was more famous for his sideburns than for his stats on the field.

Lee Mazzilli played a little first base for the other New York team, the Mets, starting in 1976. Mazzilli's was an inconsistent career. He spent the better part of 10 of his 14 seasons with the Mets with his most productive years coming from 1978 to 1980. He split the '82 season between the Rangers and the Yanks and then spent over three seasons with the Pirates before returning to the Mets midway through their championship season of 1986.

Speaking of World Series heroes, I can't forget **Bernie Carbo**. He enjoyed a great rookie season with the pennant-bound Reds in 1970, finishing second in Rookie of the Year balloting, but didn't fare too well in the World Series. That changed in 1975 when, now playing against his former club as a member of the Boston Red Sox, he hit two pinch hit home runs, one of which tied Game Six and set up Carlton Fisk's famous game winning clout in the 12th inning.

35 • Others of Note

Gene Tenace was the surprise hero of the 1972 World Series. The Oakland A's backstop hit four home runs and drove in nine runs to earn the series MVP and everlasting fame. He enjoyed a solid 15-year big league career as a respected catcher and first baseman with the A's, Padres, Cards, and Pirates.

As mentioned in a previous chapter, Italian Americans have been particularly prolific behind the plate throughout baseball history. In my time, in addition to Gene Tenace, I remember **Joe Ferguson** of the Los Angeles Dodgers. Ferguson was usually behind the dish but his moment in the sun came as a right-fielder in the 1974 World Series when he caught a fly ball off the bat of Reggie Jackson and threw out Sal Bando, who was tagging up at third, at home plate on the fly. One of the most amazing World Series throws in history.

Ray Fosse was an outstanding catcher who came up with Cleveland in the late 1960s. Unfortunately, he's mostly remembered for the 1970 All-Star collision at home plate with Pete Rose but Fosse was a fine defensive player and a decent hitter. His outstanding defense behind the plate in 1973 helped the A's to their second World Championship in as many years.

Steve Nicosia was one of the catchers for the "We Are Family" Pirates of 1979. He spent eight years in the big leagues as a utility catcher but he earned that ring. On the other side of the coin you have **Tom Pagnozzi**, one of the best defensive catchers of the 1990s who made it to a few playoffs and one World Series with the Cardinals but never won the big prize. He did, however, bring home three Gold Gloves in his 12 year career.

And then there was **Mike Scioscia**. Scioscia was one of those blue-collar, lunch bucket type of players that you just had to love. He was tough, reliable, and a leader. He was behind the plate for both Dodger championships in 1981 and 1988. His baseball IQ led him to a successful managing career leading the 2002 Angels to a World Series Championship. He did, of course, have his weaknesses. He was known to be such a slow runner that his manager Tommy Lasorda once remarked that Scioscia could race his pregnant wife to first base and finish third.

Steve Sax was a really fine second baseman for the Dodgers of the 1980s. He was the 1982 National League Rookie of the Year and he played on both the 1981 and 1988 World Series Champions. He'd been called up for the last 35 games of the '81 season and was on the postseason roster. A Silver Slugger winner and four time All Star, Sax was an iron man at second playing 150 games or more in eight out of his 11 seasons as a starter.

We can't possibly do justice to the host of really fine Italian American pitchers through the years. In the last 40 years there's been **Dave Righetti**, **Frank Viola**,

Joe Sambito, **John Franco**, **Barry Zito**, and **Jason Grilli**, to name a few. All of them appeared in World Series games but only Viola won the Series MVP for his role in the 1987 Twins victory over the St. Louis Cardinals. As a Yankee, Righetti will always be remembered for his July 4, 1983, no-hitter over the rival Boston Red Sox while in San Francisco he'll be remembered as the pitching coach of three World Champion Giant teams in 2002, 2010, and 2012. Zito had an up and down career with the A's and the Giants but finished it nicely with a strong 2012 campaign and post-season for the Giants earning his ring. John Franco, Joe Sambito, and Jason Grilli were all successful relievers in their day and chances are that Franco may still make it into the Hall of Fame someday with his 424 lifetime saves.

And how about those managers? We've already mentioned Championship managers like Altobelli, Torre, Terry Francona, and Mike Scioscia but there's a good deal more: **Joe Girardi** (2009 Yankees), **Tony La Russa** (1989 A's; 2006, 2011 Cardinals), **Tommy Lasorda** (1981, 1988 Dodgers), **Billy Martin** (1977 Yankees), and **Joe Maddon,** who ended the Chicago Cubs 108 year drought by leading the Cubbies to a ring in 2016.

There are just too many Italian American ball players to do justice to them all. The truth is I continue to discover new ones all the time. Just a few weeks ago I found a guy on BaseballReference.com named **Xavier Rescigno**. He pitched for the Pirates in the mid–1940s. Just a week later I discovered a utility infielder from the late 1940s and early 1950s named Sam Dente. I couldn't believe I'd never heard of either of these guys before. So join me and keep your eye out for the Italian American paisans that have played our great American game. Apparently, it's a neverending pursuit.

Epilogue

Sadly, the game of baseball has changed so drastically in the last 10 years I no longer watch or enjoy much of the new sport. I do, however, continue to love and need the game, the history, and the lore. Every year now with the coming of spring I turn to old games on DVD, YouTube, and classic radio broadcasts and revel in the glory of my youth when I first fell in love with this grand old game. It's as close as I can get these days to a reunion at home.

Acknowledgments

This volume has been 20 years in the making. As mentioned in the preface, most of these chapters originally appeared in the pages of *Fra Noi: Chicagoland's Italian American Voice*. To Paul Basile, their indefatigable editor, I extend my heartfelt gratitude and appreciation for his years of encouragement and guidance. A special thank-you to Mary Racila of *Fra Noi* who had the two qualities most needed when working with a writer like myself: patience and a sense of humor.

This book, I hope, has made me a new friend in Gary Mitchem, my editor at McFarland. He has been a tremendous help and resource. I thank him for his patience, encouragement, and talent.

Special thanks to John Horne of the Baseball Hall of Fame who was so kind in helping me to access the Hall's collection of photographs despite all the many other challenges with which he was dealing. I must also thank all the wonderful men and women who worked at the Baseball Hall of Fame's Giamatti Research Center and so graciously assisted me in my research at various times between 2003 and 2018.

This book, like my previous one, doesn't get done without my dear friends Jane Best and Tim Madigan. Jane helps me in all things related to computers, formatting, grammar, style, and the list goes on. Tim Madigan, despite his Gaelic roots, is my Consigliere when it comes to all things having to do with pop culture, research, writing, publishing, philosophy, etc. In addition to my counselor, he's also my conscience as, just like Jiminy Cricket, he's always on my case urging me to "get it done!"

Thank you to Scott Pitoniak for the use of certain photographs in the book as well as his inspiration as a truly talented author and columnist.

I'm grateful to Chris Hawes, Steve Taubenfeld, Dr. Joseph Tempesta, and again, Jane Best and Tim Madigan, all of whom read this manuscript at various stages and provided very helpful suggestions.

A special thank-you to Nick for all his computer and technical assistance.

On the personal side, there are all those people who helped to make me into a baseball fan at the very beginning. The top spot must go to my friend Mariano Pierleoni. Mariano, or "Mouse" as we called him in those days, not only influenced my love for the game but for baseball cards as well. Mariano is only eight months older than I am but his baseball fandom started before mine. Then there are the Ussia Brothers: Kevin and Dean. We lived across the street from each other for our entire childhoods and played baseball, wiffleball, football, hockey, and hide and seek; raced bicycles; and did whatever else caused the numerous scratches, sprains, bumps, bruises, and bloody noses that boys inevitably get along the way.

A special thank-you must go to their dad, Frank Ussia. When my dad died, both the Pierleoni and Ussia families were my lifelines outside of my own warm and loving home. However, it was Frank Ussia who continuously brought us to Silver Stadium throughout the long, hot, humid Rochester summers to catch the games of our beloved Rochester Red Wings. As with most young people, we had no idea then just how idyllic a time it was for us.

And there were so many others who were part of, and or contributed to, my being a baseball fan in those formative years: Tony DeMarco; Margaret DiFiore; Allie Di Pasqua; Mr. Hammond; Charlie Montione; Gil Morelle, Sr.; Ralph Pierleoni; my Uncle Jules Norris; Joe Rodriguez; my Uncles Gene, Bob, and Emmanuel Agnello; my Uncle Tony Murabito; "Big Nick" Agnello; and "Blackie" Agnello; and all the other adults who indulged and encouraged my passion for the game.

Thanks as well to my brother Joe Bruno; David Yockel, Sr.; David Yockel, Jr.; Marion Sokolski; Scott Schindler; Joe Hamm; the Morelle Brothers; and the countless others who've shared my passion for the game.

And finally my family—siblings Joe, Bob, and Suzanne, and especially my mom and dad—who put up with my baseball mania for so many years.

A very special thank you to Jennie for "enduring" all those trips to Cooperstown; Frank and Nick for reigniting my passion, even for a little while; and as always and for everything, my wife Mary Beth.

Bibliography

Books

Antonelli, Johnny, with Scott Pitoniak. *Johnny Antonelli: A Baseball Memoir*. Rochester: RIT Press, 2012.

Baldassaro, Lawrence. *Beyond DiMaggio: Italian Americans in Baseball*. Lincoln: University of Nebraska Press, 2011.

The Baseball Encyclopedia: The Complete and Official Record of Major League Baseball, Revised and Updated, 2nd ed. New York: Macmillan, 1974.

Baylor, Don, with Claire Smith. *Nothing but the Truth: A Baseball Life*. New York: St. Martin's Press, 1989.

Bergman, Ron. *The Mustache Gang: The Swaggering Saga of Oakland A's*. New York: Dell, 1973.

Berra, Yogi. *I Didn't Really Say Everything I Said*. New York: Workman, 1998.

Berra, Yogi, with Dave Kaplan. *Ten Rings: My Championship Seasons*. New York: HarperCollins, 2003.

Blass, Steve, with Erik Sherman. *Pirate for Life*. Chicago: Triumph Books, 2012.

Campanella, Roy. *It's Good to Be Alive*. New York: Signet, New American Library, 1974.

Cataneo, David. *Tony C.: The Triumph and Tragedy of Tony Conigliaro*. Nashville: Rutledge Hill Press, 1997.

Conigliaro, Tony, with Jack Zanger. *Seeing It Through*. New York: Macmillan, 1970.

Cramer, Richard Ben. *Joe DiMaggio: The Hero's Life*. New York: Simon & Schuster, 2000.

DiMaggio, Dom, with Bill Gilbert. *Real Grass, Real Heroes: Baseball's Historic 1941 Season*. New York: Zebra Books, Kensington Publishing Corp., 1990.

Durocher, Leo, with Ed Linn. *Nice Guys Finish Last*. New York: Simon & Schuster, 1975.

Freundlich, Larry, ed. *Reaching for the Stars: A Celebration of Italian Americans in Major League Baseball*. New York: Ballantine Books, 2003.

Garagiola, Joe, and Martin Quigley. *Baseball Is a Funny Game*. Philadelphia: J.B. Lippincott, 1960.

Giamatti, A. Bartlett. *Take Time for Paradise*. New York: Summit Books, 1989.

Halberstam, David. *Summer of '49*. New York: William Morrow, 1989.

_____. *Teammates*. New York: Hyperion, 2003.

Hughes, Pat, and Rich Wolfe. *Ron Santo: A Perfect 10*. Chicago: Lone Wolfe Press, 2001.

Kahn, Roger. *The Boys of Summer*. New York: Signet, New American Library, 1973.

Mandelaro, Jim, and Scott Pitoniak. *Silver Seasons and A New Frontier: The Story of the Rochester Red Wings*. Syracuse: Syracuse University Press, 2010.

Petrocelli, Rico, and Chaz Scoggins. *Rico Petrocelli's Tales from the Impossible Dream Red Sox*. Champaign, IL: Sports Publishing, 2007.

Pluto, Terry. *The Curse of Rocky Colavito*. New York: Fireside, 1995.

Reed, Ted. *Carl Furillo: Brooklyn Dodgers All-Star*. Jefferson, NC: McFarland, 2011.

Rizzuto, Phil, with Tom Horton. *The October Twelve*. New York: A Forge Book, 1994.

Santo, Ron, with Randy Minkoff. *For Love of Ivy*. Chicago: Bonus Books, 1993.

Talese, Gay. *Unto the Sons*. New York: Alfred A. Knopf, 1992.

Torre, Joe, with Tom Verducci. *Chasing the Dream: My Lifelong Journey to the World Series*. New York: Bantam Books, 1997.

Trimble, Joe. *Yogi Berra*. New York: Grosset & Dunlap, 1954.

Valerio, Anthony. *Bart: A Life of A. Bartlett Giamatti*. San Diego: Harcourt, 1993.

Vincent, Fay. *We Would Have Played for Nothing*. New York: Simon & Schuster, 2008.

Interviews

Altobelli, Joe. Live interview. March 2004.

Gaetti, Gary. Live interview. July 2008.

Petrocelli, Rico. Telephone interview. February 27, 2015

Periodicals

The following is a selective list of newspapers and magazines that provided information for the profiles herein. Because many were found in the form of clippings in the Baseball Hall of Fame's player files, often lacking such data as date, author and edition or issue, only the periodical titles are listed.

Bibliography

All Sports
American Legion Magazine
Associated Press
Baltimore Sun
Baseball Digest
Baseball Magazine
Boston Globe
Boston Herald
Chicago Daily News
Chicago Sun-Times
Chicago Tribune
Cleveland News
Cleveland Plain Dealer
The Daily Worker
Houston Post
Los Angeles Times
New York Daily News
New York Journal
New York Post
New York Times
Oakland Tribune
Pittsburgh Press
Il Progresso Italo-Americano
St. Louis Globe-Democrat
St. Louis Post-Dispatch
San Francisco Chronicle
San Francisco Daily News
Saturday Evening Post
SPORT
Sportfolio
The Sporting News
Sports Collectors Digest
Sports Illustrated
Super Sports
This Week
USA Today
Wall Street Journal
Washington Post
William & Mary
Yankees Magazine

Online Sources

BaseballReference.com
SABR.org

Index

Aaron, Henry 77, 117, 126, 128, 163, 195
AAU Track and Field Championship 58
Abbaticchio, Ed 16, 214, 215
Abruzzi, Italy 132, 185
Alexander, Grover Cleveland 16–18
All Sports 174
All Star appearances 41, 77, 87, 93, 115, 135, 139, 154, 173, 227
All Star Game: (1957) 154; (1959) 154; (1961) 223; (1962) 148; (1970) 227
Allen, Johnny 59
Allen, Maury 99
Allen, Mel 129
Alou, Felipe 198
Altobelli, Joe 6, 137–143, 224, 228
Altobelli, Pat 140
American Association 23, 102, 109, 139, 146, 152, 157, 175, 215
American Century 3
American Express 183
American League 16, 18, 30, 40, 59, 118, 141, 153, 154, 158, 161, 173, 204
American Legion 108
American Legion Magazine 64
American Stock Exchange 162
Amsterdam, NY 115
Anaheim, CA 173, 175
Andrews, Mike 188, 199
Anger, Lou 22
Anheuser-Busch 104
Antonelli, August "Gus" 132, 133
Antonelli, Johnny 129, 131–136
Antonelli, Josephine (née Messore) 132
Antonelli, Tony (J. Antonelli's brother) 133
Antonelli Tires 132, 135
Aparicio, Luis 187
Apollonio, Nicholas Taylor 214
Arbuckle, Fatty 22
Arioli, Pat 132
Arizona 169

Arizona Diamondbacks 105
Arizona State University 197, 201
Army Air Corps 82, 115
Arnold, Dorothy 88
Aspromonte, Bob 226
Aspromonte, Ken 226
Astoria, Queens, NY 120
Atlanta, GA 163
Atlanta Braves 164
Atlanta Braves Hall of Fame 165
Autry, Gene 164

Baer, Max 45
Baggerly, Hi 12
Baldassaro, Lawrence 16–18, 215
Ballanfant, Lee 12
Baltimore, MD 142
Baltimore Orioles 6, 57, 137, 140–142, 148, 154, 157, 175, 179, 199, 200, 218, 226
Baltimore Sun 159
Bando, Sal 196–201, 227
Banks, Ernie 158, 168
Bapchule, AZ 105
Bari, Italy 145
Barlick, Al 12
Barrow, Ed 43
Bart: A Life of A. Bartlett Giamatti (Valerio) 210
Bartlett Giamatti Research Center 2, 97, 114, 225
Baseball Digest(s) 1
The Baseball Encyclopedia 1, 218
Baseball Hall of Fame (Cooperstown, NY) 2, 16, 33, 35, 36, 37, 40, 76, 86, 89, 97, 102, 105, 111, 128, 148, 149, 161, 165, 167, 173
Baseball Is a Funny Game 5, 103
Baseball Magazine 19, 29, 31
Baseball Reference 1
Baseball World of Joe Garagiola 104
Baseball Writers of America 153

Basile, Paul 1
B.A.T. (Baseball Assistance Team) 94, 105
Battle of Okinawa 98
Bauer, Hank 110, 198
Bavasi, Buzzie 97, 138, 140, 157, 175
Baylor, Don 141, 143
Belanger, Mark "The Blade" 188, 226
Belle, Albert 59
Belmont High School 80
Bench, Johnny 96
Bennett, Chester 22
Berardino, Ann (née Mussaco; J. Berardino's mother) 80
Berardino, Ignazio (J. Berardino's father) 80
Berardino/Beradino, John 79–84
Bergman, Ron 197, 198, 200
Berra, Lawrence Peter "Yogi" 5, 6, 73, 87, 101, 102, 104, 107–111, 114, 116, 117, 132, 185
Berra, Lindsay 112
Berra, Pietro 108
Bertaina, Frank 224
Bevacqua, Kurt 6
Bevens, Bill 51, 52, 55
Beyond DiMaggio: Italian Americans in Baseball 16–18, 215
Biggio, Craig 224
Bingham, Walter 52, 55
Binghamton Triplets 115
Bisher, Furman 2
Black Sox Scandal 10
Blackwell, Ewell 93
Blades, Ray 24
Blass, Steve 179, 183
Blue, Vida 197
Bluefield Baby Birds 140
Bodie, Ping (Francesco Stephano Pezzolo) 16, 214
Bonura, Henry John Zeke "The Physique" 56–61, 114, 224
Bordman, Sid 197
Boston, MA 12, 92, 186–190, 192, 194, 209

235

Index

Boston Bees 36
Boston Braves 11, 13, 29, 30, 72, 83, 120, 133, 134, 157, 215, 216, 221
Boston Globe 147–149, 187
Boston Herald 216
Boston Red Sox 48, 72, 73, 75, 91, 99, 103, 116, 117, 120–124, 150–154, 156, 162, 173, 185–190, 192–194, 205, 210, 214, 217, 220, 225, 226, 228
Boston Red Sox Hall of Fame 154
Boudreau, Lou 83, 221
The Boys of Summer (Kahn) 96, 97
Bradenton, FL 192
Bragan, Bobby 100
Branca, Ralph 90–94, 127
Brandt, Ed 53
Braves Field 12
Brewster, Todd 211
Bright's Disease 215
Briles, Christina 182
Briles, Nelson 179, 182, 183
Brock, Lou 223
Broglio, Ernie 223
Brokaw, Tom 96
Bronx, NY 145, 151
Brooklyn, NY 46, 47, 48, 49, 53, 86, 96, 165, 185
Brooklyn/Los Angeles Robins/Dodgers 12, 19, 20, 28, 29, 33, 34, 45–49, 51, 53–55, 65, 86, 90, 92, 93, 96–100, 103, 108, 110, 117, 120, 123, 126–130, 135, 138, 140, 156, 157, 161–163, 165, 169, 200, 220, 221, 224–227
Brooklyn Royals 162
Brown, Bobby 108, 110, 134
Brown, Joe 181
Brown, Les 77, 78
Brown, Mace 123
Browne, Leo 109
Brunansky, Tom 206
Brundidge, Harry T. 23
Bryant High School 120
Buck O'Neil Lifetime Achievement Award 102
Buckner, Bill 91
Buffalo, NY 215, 216
Bumbry, Al 57, 203
Burdette, Lew 163
Burlington Bees (A) 197
Burr, Harold 51
Busch, August, Jr. 104

Cahill, Ray 81
Calabria, Italy 4
Calderone, Sam 134
California 121, 195
Cambridge, MA 191
Camerer, Dave 46
Camilli, Dolph 6, 44–49, 127

Camilli, Doug 49
Campanella, John 127
Campanella, Roy 6, 68, 96, 125, 127–130, 224
Campaneris, Bert "Campy" 197
Campbell, Frankie 45
Canadian-American League (C) 151
Candlestick Park 36
Capone, Al 70
Capra, Frank 70
Caray, Harry 104
Carbo, Bernie 226
Carew, Rod 206
Carey, Andy 42
Carl Furillo: Brooklyn Dodgers All-Star (Reed) 100
Carmichael, John 123
Carson, Johnny 104
Carter, Joe 176
Casey, Hugh 100
Cash, Dave 179
Cashen, Frank 213
Castiglione, Pete 224
Cataneo, David 191, 193, 195
Cavaretta, Phil 4, 6, 62–67, 114
Cavelli, Sgt. Vince (character) 84
Caveney, Jimmy "Ike" 39
Cedar Rapids Bunnies (D) 23
Central League 63
Centralia, IL 203
Cervi, Al 129
Chandler, Happy (Commissioner of Baseball, 1945–51) 82, 225
Chandler, Spud 118
Charles, Ed 197
Chasing the Dream: My Lifelong Journey to the World Series 161, 162
Chicago, IL 63, 67, 166, 167
Chicago Cubs 19, 23, 41, 45, 60, 62–66, 70, 91, 94, 103, 120, 121, 133, 142, 167–169, 170, 180, 205, 223, 226, 228
Chicago Daily News 123, 159
Chicago Tribune 59, 60, 65
Chicago White Sox 10, 29, 30, 58–60, 66, 97, 120, 123, 141, 158, 170, 176, 187, 189, 198, 214, 217, 218, 222, 223
Chiozza, Lou 224
Cimoli, Gino 220
Cincinnati, OH 35, 175
Cincinnati Reds 9, 10, 11, 28, 29, 34, 36, 37, 63, 122, 163, 168, 180, 183, 189, 199, 212, 220, 226
The Cisco Kid 84
Civil War 211
Claflin, Larry 187
Clason Point 151
Clemens, Doug 223

Clemente, Roberto 6, 18, 126, 127, 179, 181, 183, 185, 211
Cleveland, OH 139, 147, 197
Cleveland Indians 29, 58, 82, 83, 115, 117, 122, 136, 139, 145–147, 159, 168, 197, 199, 217–221, 223, 226, 227
Cleveland News 147
Cloninger, Tony 118
Cobb, Ty 10, 34, 59
Cochrane, Mickey 35
Colavito, Angela (R. Colavito's mother) 145
Colavito, Dominic (R. Colavito's brother) 146
Colavito, Marisa (R. Colavito's daughter) 146
Colavito, Rocco Domenico "Rocky" 6, 144–149
Colavito, Rocco (R. Colavito's father) 145
Colavito, Rocky, Jr. (R. Colavito's son) 146
Colavito, Steven (R. Colavito's son) 146
Coleman, Jerry 42, 110
Collins, Joe 110
Collins, Rip 143
Columbus Clippers (AAA) 141
Columbus Senators/Red Birds (AA) 25, 28, 102, 103
Comeback Player of the Year 194
Comiskey Park 66, 115
Commagre, Foster 57, 58
Conesus, NY 115
Conesus Lake 118
Conigliaro, Anthony Richard "Tony" 126, 190–195
Conigliaro, Billy 190
Conigliaro, Sal (and Teresa) 192
Conlan, Jocko 129
Connecticut 109
Connery, Thomas J. 215
Constantino, John 168
Cooper, Walker 222, 223
Cooperstown, NY 2, 145
Cosell, Howard 86
Covoleski, Stan 130
Craft, Harry 35
Cramer, Richard Ben 70, 71, 73
Crandall, Del 134, 163
Crespi, Frank "Creepy" 224
Cronin, Joe 121, 122
Crosetti, Frank Peter Joseph "The Crow" 4, 6, 15, 19, 36, 38–43, 132
Crotona Park 145
Cuba 225
Cuccinello, Al 120, 121
Cuccinello, Anthony Francis "Tony" "Cooch" 4, 27–31, 34, 114, 120, 123

Index

Cuccinello, Clara (née Garoselli; wife of Tony Cuccinello) 28
The Curse of Rocky Colavito 147
Cuyler, Kiki 63, 64
Cy Young Award 135
CYO Baseball 156

D-Day Invasion 109
Daily Worker 100
Daley, Arthur 34, 41
Dallas-Ft. Worth Rangers (AAA) 173
Dallas-Ft. Worth Spurs (AA) 140
Dallas Rebels 58
Daniel, Dan 71
Daniels, Special Agent Steve (character) 84
Dante 210
Danville Veterans 28
Darin, Bobby 145
Dark, Alvin 197, 198, 200
Dauer, Rich 143
Daytona Beach, FL 98
Dean, Jay Hanna "Dizzy" 5, 41
Dean, Paul "Daffy" 25
"The Dear Departed Past" 209
Derks, John C. 17
Derringer, Paul 35
Detroit, MI 138
Detroit Tigers 10, 36, 65, 76, 82, 120, 123, 138, 139, 145–148, 199, 204, 218
DeVincenzi, Cookie 53
Devlin, Art 11
DeWitt, William 83
diabetes/diabetic 168–170
Dickey, Bill 35, 59, 110
DiMaggio, Dominic 69, 72–77, 121, 122, 217
DiMaggio, Giuseppe (father) 4, 74
DiMaggio, Joseph, Jr. "Joe" 77, 88
DiMaggio, Joseph Paul "Joe" 4–6, 15, 16, 19, 36, 40, 51, 57, 68, 70–74, 76–78, 88, 96, 117, 121, 126, 132, 138, 185, 198
DiMaggio, Rosalie Mercurio (mother) 74
DiMaggio, Tom 72
DiMaggio, Vince 12, 69, 72–74, 76, 77
Divincenzi, Norma (wife of Frank Crosetti) 41
Doby, Larry 115
Dodger Coliseum 97
Dodgers Hall of Fame 49
Doerr, Bobby 74–76, 210, 217
Donlin, Mike 22
Douthit, Taylor 24
Dowd, John 212
Downs, Hugh 104

Dressen, Charlie 54, 100
Drohan, John 81
Drysdale, Don 154
Durham Bulls 203
Durocher, Grace (née Dozier; wife of Leo Durocher) 23
Durocher, Leo 13, 23, 24, 29, 40, 46–48, 51, 98, 99, 103, 134, 135
Dykes, Jimmy 59

Easter, Luke 143
Eastern League 121, 146
Eastern Shore League (D) 151
Eau Claire Braves (C) 162
Ebbets Field 48, 97
Eisenberg, John 159
Eisenhower, Gen./Pres. Dwight D. 61, 130
Elderkin, Phil 188
Elonborg, Emil 88
Emmy Awards 84
Erskine, Carl 100
Estrada, Frank 174

"The Fairie Queene" 210
Feeney, Charley 123, 182
Feller, Bob 115, 129, 133, 217, 221
Fenway Park 77, 121, 189, 190, 192, 217
Ferguson, Joe 227
Ferriss, Dave "Boo" 82
Fingers, Rollie 197
Finland 58
Finley, Charlie O. 197, 199, 200
Fisher, Showboat 24
Fisk, Carlton 226
Fitzgerald, Ray 187, 188
Fitzgerald, Tom 220
Florida 40, 121, 133, 193
Florida Fall League 193
Florida State League 146
Foley, Red 97
For Love of Ivy 167, 168
Ford, Whitey 134
Ford C. Frick Broadcasting Award 105
Forman, Ross 148
Fort Worth Cats (AA) 156, 159
Fosse, Ray 126, 227
Fournier, Jacques 80
Fra Noi 1, 2, 214, 224
Franco, John 228
Francona, Terry 220, 228
Francona, Tito 218–220
Frank, Stanley 35
Franks, Herman 94
Frazier, Joe 163
Fregosi, Jim 6, 126, 172–177
Freundlich, Larry 19
Frey, Lonny 35
Frick, Ford 12
Frisch, Frankie 13, 25, 26
Frishberg, Dave 209
"Front Office Fan" 211

Frykman, Virginia (wife of Dave Giusti) 180, 183
Furillo, Carl 6, 95–100, 114, 127
Furstenberg, Germany 222

Gaetti, Gary Joseph 2, 202–207
Gaetti Sports Academy 206
Gagliano, Phil 126
Game of the Week (TV) 5, 104, 168
Garagiola, Joe 5, 6, 101–106, 108–111
Garagiola, Joe, Jr. 105
Garagiola, John 102, 108
Gardaphe, Prof. Fred 1
Gardner, Billy 194
Garlic Gulch 167
Garner, Vice Pres. John Nance 60
The Gary Gaetti Cult 205
Gas House Gang 25
Gaven, Michael 98
Gehrig, Lou 10, 16, 18, 77, 158, 220
Gehringer, Charlie 139
General Hospital 84
Genesee Brewing Company 135
Gentile, Carol (wife of Jim Gentile) 158
Gentile, Jim 155–159, 224
Giamatti, Angelo 209
Giamatti, Angelo Bartlett "Bart" 208–213
Giamatti, Dino 211
Giamatti, Valentine 209
Gibson, Bob 143, 163
Gila River Reservation 105
Gilbert, Bill 75
Gilbert, Dennis 194
Gilbert, Larry 58
Gilbert, Wally 28
Giles, Warren 36, 38
Gionfriddo, Al 51, 55, 127
Girardi, Joe 228
Giusti, Dave 6, 178–183, 185
Giusti, Virginia 179
Gold Glove Award(s) 77, 87, 122, 148, 153, 154, 170, 173, 188, 203–206, 215, 226, 227
Gomez, Lefty 129
Gomez, Ruben 99
Goodman, Ival 36
Gordon, Joe 20, 42, 153
Goren, Herb 46
Governor's Cup Championship 140
Gowdy, Curt 5, 6, 51
Graffis, Herb 64
Graham, Frank 18, 19, 40, 60
Grasso, Mickey 222
Grayson, Harry 42
Greatest World Series Thrillers 2

Index

"The Green Fields of the Mind" 211
Greenberg, Hank 76, 138, 139, 146, 147, 158
Grich, Bob 141
Griffith, Clark 123
Grilli, Jason 228
Grimm, Charlie 63–65, 134
Gross, Milton 159
Groveland, NY 118
Grumman Aircraft 226

Hack, Stan 41
Haddix, Harvey 163
Hafey, Chick 24
Haines, Jesse 16
Halberstam, David 4, 40, 73–76, 89, 116, 117
Hamilton, Jack 191
Haney, Fred, 174
"Happy Days Are Here Again" (Jack Yellen/Milton Ager) 51
Hardy, Dr. Steve (character) 84
Harlem Globetrotters 204
Harrelson, Ken 176
Harris, Bucky 43, 73, 115
Harris, Spencer 23
Hartnett, Gabby 35, 65
Harwell, Ernie 5
Hatton, Grady 169
Haverhill, MA 192
Hawaii 121, 152, 217
Hearst All Star Game 168
Hearst National Championship 133
Hegan, Jim 117
Heinrich, Tommy 47, 117
Hemingway, Ernest 78
Herman, Babe 28
Herman, Billy 63, 64, 186
Herman, Willie 41
Hermanski, Gene 96
Hernando, FL 76
Heroes of the Major Leagues 2
Herskowitz, Mickey 181
Herzog, Whitey 164
Higbe, Kirby 100, 102
Higgins, Dennis 199
Higgins, Mike 153
Higgins, Pinky 139
"The Hill" (Dago Hill) 5, 102, 103, 108
Hirschberg, Al 133
Hoag, Myril 41
Hobbs, Roy 216
Hodges, Gil 34, 92, 156, 157
Holland, John 169
Hollywood, CA 26, 82, 83, 214
Hollywood Stars 25
Hollywood Walk of Fame 84
Holmes, Tommy 129, 157
Holtzman, Jerome 65, 66
Honig, Donald 16, 19, 20
Hopper, Clay 98

Hornsby, Rogers 16, 169
Horton, Tom 87, 110
Hough, Charlie 204
Houk, Ralph 43
Houston Buffaloes (AAA) 23, 169
Houston Colt .45s/Astros 51, 124, 159, 176, 180, 181, 197, 226
Houston Post 181
Hoyt, Waite 130
Hrbek, Kent 206
Hubbell, Carl 92
Hughes, Pat 167, 170
Hunter, Bob 25
Hunter, Jim "Catfish" 197, 200

I Didn't Really Say Everything I Said (Berra) 111
I Led 3 Lives 83, 84
Illinois Central Gulf Railroad 203
Illinois-Indiana-Iowa League 17, 28
Indianapolis Indians (AAA) 23, 146, 222, 223
insulin 169, 170
International Harvester Company 215
International League 57, 138, 143
International News Service (INS) 40
Interstate League 222
Ira Hayes Wall 106
It Ain't Over (documentary) 112
Italy 147, 161
It's Good to Be Alive (Campanella) 127
Iwo Jima (Iwo To), Japan 106

Jackson, Reggie 197, 199, 227
Japan 157
JDRF (Juvenile Diabetes Research Foundation) 170, 171
Jefferson High School 132, 133
Jenkins, Ferguson 170
Jersey City Giants 30, 222
Jeter, Derek 43, 203
Jimmy Fund 189
Joe DiMaggio: The Hero's Life 70, 73
Joe Torre Safe at Home Foundation 164
Johnny Antonelli: A Baseball Memoir (Antonelli/Pitoniak) 132, 135
Johnny Antonelli (Firestone) Tire Co. 135, 136
Johnson, Billy 89
Johnson, "Hark Rock" 168
Johnson, Pres. Lyndon B. 104
Johnson, Randy 203
Johnstown Johnnies 80, 81

"*Joltin' Joe DiMaggio*" 77, 78
Jones, Sheldon 99
Jorgensen, Spider 54
Joy, Leatrice 22
Junior League World Series 140

Kaat, Jim 88
Kahn, James M. 71
Kahn, Roger 96, 97
Kansas City Blues 41, 109
Kansas City/Oakland A's (Athletics) 43, 49, 147, 159, 194, 196, 197, 199, 214, 220, 227, 228
Kansas City Royals 205
Kaplan, Dave 110
Keaton, Buster 21, 22
Keller, Charlie "King Kong" 36
Kennedy, Bob 198
Killebrew, Harmon 123, 158, 206
Kinder, Ellis 116, 117
Kiner, Ralph 103
King, Clyde 92
Kingman, Dave 163
Kison, Bruce 179
Klaus, Billy 134
Klein, Larry 156, 158
Kleinhans, Ted 181
KMOX Radio 104
Koenig, Mark 18
Korea 152
Korean War 83
Kosher, Dave 168
Koufax, Sandy 96, 123, 208, 212
Kubek, Tony 5, 42, 104, 153
Kuenn, Harvey 147
Kuhn, Bowie (Commissioner of Baseball) 199, 209

La Guardia, Fiorello 4, 70
Laird, Tom 75
Landers, Tom 210
Landis, Kenesaw Mountain 30, 210
Lane, F.C. 19
Lane, Frank 147, 148
Lane, Joe 148
Lane Tech High School 63
Larsen, Don 14, 51
LaRussa, Tony 224, 228
Lary, Lyn 39
Lasorda, Tommy 227, 228
Latrobe, PA 214
Laurent, Lawrence 104
Lavagetto, Enrico Attilio Harry "Cookie" 46, 50–55, 122, 127
Lavelli, Dante 129
Lawing, Gene 169
Lawrence Merry Macks 28
Lazzeri, Tony 4, 6, 15–20, 40, 80, 132, 224
Lebovitz, Hal 147
Lemon, Bob 217

Liddle, Don 134
Lieb, Frederick 102
Lincoln Links 17
Linn, Edward 145, 146
Lisococec, Richard 197
Little Falls, NJ 107, 111
Lloyds of London 82
Logan Collegians 45
Lollar, Sherm 223
Lombard, Carole 4
Lombardi, Ernesto Natali "Ernie" 4, 6, 28, 32–37, 224
Lombardi, Vic 93
Lonborg, Jim 188, 225
Long Island City, NY 28, 30
Lopat, Eddie 73, 110, 116
Lopez, Al 13, 29, 34, 120, 123, 146, 158, 223
The Loretta Young Show 84
Los Angeles, CA 80, 97, 157
Los Angeles Angels (PCL) 75
Los Angeles/California/Anaheim Angels (MLB) 49, 154, 164, 170, 172–176, 191, 194, 205, 220, 226, 227
Los Angeles Coliseum 157
Los Angeles Dodgers 49
Los Angeles Times 173, 174, 176
Louisville Colonels (AAA) 121, 152
Louisville Redbirds (AAA) 176
Loyola University of the South 58
Luce, Henry 3
Luciano, Charles "Lucky" 70
Lumpe, Jerry 42
Luque, Dolf 225
Lurie, Marty 43
Lustig, Dennis 115

MacPhail, Larry 42, 46–48, 110
Maddon, Joe 228
Madison Park Hospital 161
Maglie, Sal "The Barber" 6, 99, 129, 224, 225
Maher, Lois Melillo 215
Mahoney, Neil 121
Malzone, Amy (née Gennarino) 151–153
Malzone, Frank 150–154
Malzone, James (F. Malzone's son) 152, 153
Malzone, Mary (F. Malzone's sister) 151
Malzone, Suzanne (F. Malzone's daughter) 152, 153
Malzone, Tony (F. Malzone's brother) 151
Manager of the Year 141
Mancuso, Gus 221
Mandelaro, Jim 138
Manfred, Rob (Commissioner of Baseball) 165, 213
Mangione, Jerre 1

Manhattan 4
Manhattan College 114
Manila Dodgers 102
Mantle, Mickey 114, 117, 158
Manto, Jeff 224
Mapledale Party House 129
Marconi, Guglielmo 70
Marichal, Juan 126
Maris, Roger 158
Markakas, Julie 192
Martin, Billy 42, 54, 123, 228
Masi, Phil 221
Mason, Dan 142, 143
The Match Game 104
Matthews, Eddie 163
Mattingly, Don 158
Mauch, Gene 176
Mauer, Joe 33
Maxvill, Dal 164
Mays, Willie 114, 126, 127, 134
Mazeroski, Bill 220
Mazzilli, Lee 226
McAuley, Ed 83
McCann, Gene 114
McCarthy, Bill 120
McCarthy, Joe 39, 43, 117, 122
McCarver, Tim 163
McCormick, Frank 46
McCosky, Barney 57, 121
McDougald, Gil 42
McGee, Frank 104
McGlocklin, John 201
McGraw, John 91
McMahon, Jack 40
McNamara, John 198
Meany, Tom 47, 48, 221
Medwick, Joe 24
Mele, Anna 120
Mele, Antonio 120
Mele, Sabath Anthony "Sam" 119–124
Melillo, Oscar "Spinach" 215
Mercer, Ida 127
Merkle, Fred 91
Messer, Frank 86
Metkovich, George 82
Mexican League 225
Mexico 128
Middle Atlantic League 80
Middleton Doll Company 201
Midnight Massacre 163
Midwest League 197
Miksis, Eddie 51
Milford Red Sox 151
Milosevich, Mike 42
Milwaukee/Atlanta Braves 134–136, 161–163, 176, 205, 226
Milwaukee Brewers (MLB) 197, 200, 201
Mincher, Don 198
Minkoff, Randy 167
Minneapolis Millers 23, 60
Minneapolis-St.Paul 55
Minnesota 122, 205

Minnesota Twins 55, 119, 120, 122, 123, 139, 140, 204–206, 228
Minnesota Twins Hall of Fame 205, 206
Minoso, Minnie 18
Mr. Coffee 77
Mitchell, Dale 14
Mitchell, Jerry 60
Mize, Johnny 110, 129
MLB Alumni Association 105
MLB.com 64
MLB Network 5, 145
MLB Office 165
MLBPA (Major League Baseball Players Association) 181
Mobile A's (AA) 197
Mobile Bears (AA) 156
Monbouquette, Bill 225
Monday Night Baseball 104
Montclair University 112
Montefusco, John "The Count" 225
Montreal Royals (AAA) 92, 98, 157
Moore, Donnie 91
Moore, Percy 63, 65
Moose, Bob 91
Moreno, Antonio 22
Mossi, Don 217, 218
motion pictures 22
Mount Holyoke, MA 209
"*Mrs. Robinson*" 78
Muffett, Billy 181
Munzel, Edgar 64
Murcer, Bobby 39, 88
Murderer's Row (1927) 16
Murphy, Edward T. 46, 47
Murray, Eddie 143
Murray, Jim 34
Murtaugh, Danny 182
Musial, Stan 35, 96, 101, 111, 128, 130, 143
Mussina, Mike 143, 224
Mussolini, Benito 70
The Mustache Gang 199
The Mustache Gang: The Swaggering Saga of the Oakland A's 200
MVP Award (Most Valuable Player) 33, 47, 63, 65, 75, 111, 128, 141, 152, 161, 163, 170, 173, 179, 197
Myers, Billy 35, 36
Myrra, Jon 58

Naples, Italy 209
National League 12, 13, 23, 25, 29, 30, 33, 36, 39, 53, 65, 72, 93, 103, 117, 161, 170, 210
National Youth Administration 80
The Natural 216
The Natural 2 216

Index

NBA 185
NBC 104
NEA Sports 42
Negro League(s) 105, 128
Nelson, Lindsay 5
Netflix 112
The New Breed 84
New England 189, 191, 210
New England League 28
New Jersey 110
New Orleans, LA 57
New Orleans Pelicans 58
New York, NY 16, 71–73, 135, 168, 185
New York Daily News 97, 100
New York Journal 41
New York Mets 55, 163, 170, 174, 175, 185, 199, 213, 226
New York Penn League 63
New York Post 60
New York/San Francisco Giants 12, 19, 30, 36, 48, 55, 59, 65, 91, 93, 94, 99, 103, 110, 120, 132, 134, 135, 141, 161, 176, 218, 221, 224, 225, 228
New York Sun 18
New York Times 19, 34, 41, 42, 104
New York University (NYU) 120, 121
New York Yankees 16–20, 23, 35, 36, 39–43, 47, 51, 55, 65, 70–73, 80, 86, 89, 91–93, 96, 99, 102, 109, 110, 111, 114–116, 122, 123, 126, 127, 129, 141, 156, 161, 162, 164, 167, 168, 174, 185, 186, 200, 214, 218, 220, 224–226, 228
Newark, NJ 88, 222
Newark Bears 110, 222
Newhouser, Hal 218
Newsom, Bobo 139
Newville, Todd 222
Niagara Falls 225
Niagara Falls Convention Bureau 225
Niarhos, Gus 73
Nice Guys Finish Last 48
Nichols, Max 123
Nicosia, Steve 227
Niebergall, Charlie 151
1938 Hurricane 13
1952 Bowman Sam Mele 122
1953 Topps Roy Campanella 128, 130
Norfolk, VA 109
Norfolk Tigers 109
North Africa 60, 222
North Dakota 206
Northern League (C) 162
Northwest Missouri State 204
Nothing but the Truth: A Baseball Life (Baylor) 141
Nowlin, Bill 120, 123, 124

NSTEP (National Spit Tobacco Education Program) 105
NYU Violets 120

Oakland, CA 33, 43, 52, 198, 199
Oakland Oaks 10–12, 33, 36, 53, 54
Oakland Tribune 198, 200
O'Brien, Charlie 132, 133
O'Connell, Dick 194
The October Twelve (Rizzuto/Horton) 87, 88, 110
O'Doul, Lefty 74, 75
Oklahoma 159
Oklahoma City 89ers (AAA) 180
Old-Timer's Sports Reunion Dinner 129
Oliva, Tony 123, 206
Oliver, Al 179, 203
Olympic Team (1928) 58
Omaha Beach 109
Omaha Buffaloes 23
Omaha Dodgers 138, 140
Oneonta Red Sox 151
Orsatti, Ernie 21–26
Orsatti, Ernie, Jr. 26
Orsatti, Frank (brother of E. Orsatti) 22
Orsatti, Frank (son of E. Orsatti) 26
Orsatti, Mary (née Manze; E. Orsatti's mother) 22
Orsatti, Morris (E. Orsatti's father) 22
Orsatti & Co. 25
Ott, Mel 92, 110, 225
Our Gang comedies 80
Owen, Mickey 47, 91

Pacific Coast League/PCL 10–12, 17, 19, 22, 33, 36, 39, 45, 48, 53, 54, 75, 83, 115, 152, 159, 180, 214, 217, 222
Pafko, Andy 96
Pagnozzi, Tom 227
Palermo, Sicily, Italy 57
Palmer, Jim 143
Panama 157
Pannucci, John 179, 180
Parotte, Carmen 146
Pasadena Playhouse 81
Pascual, Camilo 123
Paul, Gabe 129
PBS 51
Peabody Award 104
Pearl Harbor 222
Pearson, Fred 204
Peoria Tractors 17, 63
Pepitone, Joe 226
Perini, Lou 133, 134
periosteomyelitis 93
Pesky, Johnny 74, 76, 89, 91

Peters, Alexander 2
Peters, Hank 141
Petrocelli, Attilio (R. Petrocelli's father) 185
Petrocelli, Elsie (R. Petrocelli's wife) 188
Petrocelli, Louise (R. Petrocelli's mother) 185
Petrocelli, Rico 6, 126, 154, 184–189, 191, 211
Philadelphia, PA 142
Philadelphia Athletics 24, 30, 214
Philadelphia Phillies 13, 45, 46, 51, 65, 99, 141, 163, 174, 176
Philippines 102
Phillips, Cy 151
Phillips, Lefty 174
Phoenix, AZ 105, 135
Piazza, Mike 111, 224
Picinich, Val 11
Piedmont League 109
Pierleoni, Mariano 128
Pima (tribe) 106
Pinelli, Mabel (née McKee; wife of "Babe" Pinelli) 10, 14
Pinelli, Ray (B. Pinelli's son) 14
Pinelli (Paolinelli), Rinaldo (Ralph) Angelo "Babe" 2, 9–14, 16, 114
Pinelli, Roy (B. Pinelli's son) 14
Pirate for Life (Blass) 183
Pitoniak, Scott 107, 131, 132, 136, 138
Pittsburgh 169, 182
Pittsburgh Pirates 53, 72, 83, 103, 126, 146, 163, 169, 175, 179, 180–182, 220, 226–228
Pittsburgh Pirates Alumni Association 183
Pittsfield, MA 192
Pluto, Terry 147
PNC Park 178
Podres, Johnny 129
Polo Grounds 30, 91–94, 99, 133, 136, 168, 221
Popowski, Eddie 188, 189
Portland Beavers 10, 115
Post Traumatic Stress Disorder 222
Povich, Shirley 222
Prager, Josh 93
Procter, Adelaide Anne 195
Il Progresso Italo-Americano 16
Puccinelli, George 224
Puckett, Kirby 206
Pueblo Dodgers (A) 156
Pujols, Albert 47, 203

Quincy, MA 124

Radatz, Dick 225
Randall, Ed 189
Random House 2

Rapoport, Ron 174
Raschi, Mitje 114, 118
Raschi, Sally (wife of V. Raschi) 118
Raschi, Simon 114
Raschi, Vic 87, 110, 113–118
Reaching for the Stars: A Celebration of Italian Americans in Major League Baseball 19
Reading, PA 98
Reading Chicks 98
Reading Indians (EL) 146
Reading Red Sox (AA) 63, 188
"The Reading Rifle" 97
Real Grass, Real Heroes 75
Reardon, Beans 13
Redford, Robert 216
Reed, Ted 100
Reese, Pee Wee 34, 47, 89, 100
Reiser, Pete 20, 63
Remember When 189
Renhardt, Lena 37
Rescigno, Xavier 228
Reynolds, Allie 73, 110, 111, 116
Rice, Del 103
Rice, Jim 123, 124, 154, 194
Richard K. Polimar Productions 82
Richards, Paul 157, 158
Richardson, Bobby 42
Richman, Milton 200
Rickey, Branch 23, 48, 98, 102, 105, 108, 127, 128
Rickey, Branch, Jr. 98
Rico Petrocelli's Tales from the Impossible Dream Red Sox (w/ Scoggins) 187
Righetti, Dave 227, 228
Rigney, Bill 34, 175
Rinetti, Cesare 17
Ringolsby, Tracy 175
Ripkin, Cal 140
Ripken, Cal, Jr. 10, 77, 143
Rizzuto, Cora (née Elenborg; wife of Phil Rizzuto) 88
Rizzuto, Cynthia (child of Phil Rizzuto) 88
Rizzuto, Patricia (child of Phil Rizzuto) 88
Rizzuto, Penny (child of Phil Rizzuto) 88
Rizzuto, Phil, Jr. (child of Phil Rizzuto) 88
Rizzuto, Philip Francis Phil "The Scooter" 4, 41, 42, 85–89, 110, 111, 121, 167, 185, 187\
Roach, Hal 80
Roberts, Robin 65
Robinson, Brooks 6, 126, 127, 154, 158, 185, 187, 211
Robinson, Jack Roosevelt "Jackie" 48, 92, 93, 96, 99, 100, 127, 128, 130, 179

Robinson, Ray 2
Robinson, Wilbert "Uncle Robbie" 33
Rochester, NY 86, 129, 132, 135, 136, 138, 140, 179, 203
Rochester Community Baseball 140
Rochester Democrat & Chronicle 130
Rochester Red Wing Hall of Fame 143, 224
Rochester Red Wings 6, 57, 86, 132, 137, 138, 140–143, 179, 203, 224
Rockefeller, Nelson 126
Rockne, Knute 57, 58
Rodney, Lester 100
Roe, Preacher 117
Rofrano, Margaret 161
Rolfe, Red 39, 41, 121
Romano, John Anthony 222, 223
Ron Santo: A Perfect 10 167
Ron Santo Walk to Cure Diabetes 171
Rookie of the Year 147, 153, 169, 204, 225–227
Roosevelt, Franklin Delano/ FDR (President of the United States) 30, 48, 210
Root, Charley 23
Rose, Don 174
Rose, Pete 63, 212, 213, 227
Rosenbaum, Art 54
Rosenthal, Harold 36, 37
Rothrock, Jack 26
Rotisserie Inn 17
Rowe, Schoolboy 139
Ruffing, Red 129
Ruggeri's Restaurant 111
Rumill, Ed 120–122, 221
Russo, Marius 225, 226
Russo, Neal 181
Ruth, George Herman "Babe" 4, 13, 16–18, 39, 70, 71, 77, 114, 120, 179, 214
Ryan, Bob 187
Ryan, Mike 192
Ryan, Nolan 174, 175

Sabean, Brian 176
SABR (Society for American Baseball Research) 120, 123
Sacramento Senators/Solons 10, 45, 83
Sacred Heart College 45
Sacred Heart High School 156
St. Claire, Ebba 134
St. Francis Prep 162
St. Louis, MO 5, 102, 104, 108, 111, 154, 204, 215
St. Louis Browns (1902–1953)/ Baltimore Orioles (1954–present) 80–83, 109, 122, 215–218

St. Louis Cardinals 13, 16, 17, 23–25, 28, 65, 87, 93, 102–104, 108, 109, 117, 133, 161, 163, 181, 187, 204–206, 217, 220, 223, 224, 227, 228
St Louis Cardinals Hall of Fame 165
St. Louis Globe-Democrat 108
St. Louis Post Dispatch 25
St. Paul Saints (AAA) 92, 157, 158
St. Peter Indian Mission School 105
St. Stanislaus College 57, 58
Sal Maglie: Baseball's Demon Barber (Testa) 224
Sale of the Century 104
Salerno, Italy 151
Salkeld, Bill 221
Salt Lake City Bees 10, 17, 18, 45
Salt Lake City Tribune 17, 18
Sambito, Joe 228
Samuel Gompers High School 151
San Antonio Missions 81, 169
San Diego, CA 115
San Diego Padres (AAA) 83, 146, 159
San Diego Padres (MLB) 163, 205, 227
San Francisco, CA 4, 10, 14, 16, 17, 19, 39, 40, 43, 45, 52, 58, 72, 136, 156, 173, 220
San Francisco Chronicle 220
San Francisco Daily News 75
San Francisco Seals 12, 19, 39, 45, 74, 75, 152, 153, 214
Sancta Maria Hospital 191
Sanguillen, Manny 179, 183
Santa Barbara Dodgers (C) 156
Santo, Jeff 171
Santo, Ron 6, 166–171, 180, 224
Sarasota, FL 194
Saturday Evening Post 145, 146, 152, 153
Sax, Steve 227
Schacht, Al, "The Clown Prince of Baseball" 60
Schantz, Bobby 223
Schenz, Hank 94
Schumann, George 215
Scioscia, Mike 227, 228
Scoggins, Chaz 187
Scranton Minors/Red Sox (A) 121, 151
Scully, Vin 5, 6, 104, 105
Seattle, WA 168
Seattle Indians (AA) 12
Seattle Pilots 42
Seattle Raniers (AAA) 222
Seaver, Tom 96, 126, 163
Seeing It Through (Conigliaro/ Zanger) 191, 192
Selig, Bud 105, 200

Index

Seneca Falls, NY 179, 180
77th Infantry Division 98
Sheehan, Joseph M. 42
Shellenback, Frank 135
Shotten, Burt 99
Showalter, Buck 164
Shuba, George "Shotgun" 96
Shulte, Johnny 109
Sicilian (s) 4, 40, 127, 191
Silver, Morrie 140
Silver (Red Wing) Stadium 132, 133
Silver Seasons: The Story of the Rochester Red Wings (Mandelaro/Pitoniak) 138, 140
Silvera, Charley 110
Simon, Paul 78
Sinatra, Frank 4, 86
Singleton, Ken 88
SiriusXM 189
Sisler, George, Jr. 138
Sisler, George, Sr. 138
Sisti, Sebastian "Sibby" 215, 216
Slaughter, Enos 129
Smith College 209
Smoltz, John 224
Snodgrass, Fred 91
Somerset Patriots 225
South Carolina 123
South Hadley, MA 209
South Hadley High School 210
Southern League 58, 197
Southworth, Billy 133, 134
Spahn, Warren 93, 163
Spander, Art 199
"A Special Breed" 19
Spenser, Edmund 210
Spink, J.G. Taylor 12, 115
Spokane Indians (AAA) 157
SPORT 135, 156
Sport Collector's Digest 63, 64, 148, 152, 154
Sportfolio 103
Sporting News 19, 24, 64–66, 81, 102, 115, 123, 135, 182, 198, 221
Sports Illustrated 52, 53, 76, 175
Sportsman' Park 5, 102
Spring, Jack 223
Springfield, MA 114
Springfield Cardinals 102
Stanky, Eddie 13, 31, 40
Stanton, Leroy 174
Stargell, Willie 96, 179, 183
Steinbrenner, George 164
Stengel, Casey 36, 43, 54, 55, 76, 86, 87, 111, 116, 148
Stephens, Vern 187
Steve Blass Disease 183
Stewart, Bill 35, 221
Stirnweiss, Snuffy 42
Stockton Ports 140
Stoneham, Horace 134
Stony Creek Mills, PA 98

Strange But True Baseball Stories 2
Street, Gabby 25
Stripp, Joe 28
Stump, Al 13
Sugarland Skeeters 206
Sukeforth, Clyde 28, 98
Summer of '49 (Halberstam) 4, 40, 73, 89, 116
The Sun (New York City) 18
Super Sports 187, 188
Sutter, Bruce 135
Syracuse Stars 28
Syracuse University 180, 181

Take Time for Paradise (Giamatti) 211
Talese, Gay 3
Tampa, FL 29
Tappe, Elvis 169
Tauro, Joe 193
Teammates 74
Tebbetts, Birdie 117
Ted Williams Museum 76
Ten Rings: My Championship Seasons (Berra/Kaplan) 110
Tenace, Gene 6, 227
Terry, Bill 30, 34, 60
Testa, Judith 224
Texas League 58, 81, 140
Texas Rangers 175, 200, 226
34th Infantry Division 222
This Old Cub 171
This Week 13
Thomson, Bobby 91, 93, 94, 134, 135
Tiant, Luis 203
The Today Show 104
The Tonight Show with Jack Paar/Johnny Carson 104
Tony C.: The Triumph and the Tragedy of Tony Conigliaro (Cataneo) 191, 193, 195
Toronto Blue Jays 176
Toronto Maple Leafs (AAA) 186
Torporcer, George "Specs" 151
Torre, Ali (J. Torre's wife) 164
Torre, Frank 161–164
Torre, Joe 126, 160–165, 228
Torre, Josephine (Sister Marguerite J. Torre's sister) 161
Torre, Rae (J. Torre's sister) 161
Torre, Rocco (J. Torre's brother) 161
Torre children 164
Toth, Paul 223
Trenton Senators (B) 222
Triandos, Gus 159
Trimble, Joe 5, 148
Trosky, Hal 57
Trump, Pres. Donald J. 213
Turkin, Hy 48

Turner, Jim 115, 116
Turner, Ted 163, 164
Tuscan/Tuscany, Italy 45, 215

Ueberroth, Peter 210
U.S. Army 102, 152, 222
U.S. Marine Corps 106, 121
U.S. Navy 53, 82, 92, 94, 109, 110
U.S. Track Team 58
University of Michigan 139
University of Notre Dame 57
University of Southern California 80
Unto the Sons (Talese) 3
UPS 220
USA Preparatory School 22
USA Today 216
Ussia, Dean 145
Ussia, Frank 145
Ussia, Kevin 145
Utah-Idaho League 45

Valerio, Anthony 210
Van Nuys, CA 26
Vancouver Mounties (AAA) 197, 198
Vander Meer, Johnny 33, 35
Vaughn, Irving 59, 60
Veeck, Bill 82
Verducci, Tom 161, 175
Vernon, Mickey 198
Vernon Tigers 22, 23
Versalles, Zoilo 123
Vincent, Fay 92, 94
Viola, Frank 206, 226

Wagner, Honus 215
Walker, Dixie 100
Walker, Gee 57
Walker, Harry 143
Wall Street Journal 93
Walsh, Dee 102
Walters, Barbara 104
Walters, Bucky 36
Walton, Bartlett 209
Walton, Mary "Peggy" 209
Waner, Paul 92
Ward, John J. 29, 31
Warneke, Lon 63
Washington, D.C. 60, 73, 134
Washington Post 104
Washington Senators 49, 50, 54–56, 60, 82, 120–122, 217, 222, 226
Wassum, Jim 204
Watkins, George 24
Watson, Bob 164
The Way It Was (TV Show) 51
We Would Have Played for Nothing (Vincent) 92, 94
Weaver, Earl 141–143
Weiss, George 17, 222
Wellsville Red Sox (A) 193
Werber, Billy 39

Western Association (C) 102
Western League (A) 17, 156, 214
Westrum, Wes 55, 103
WGN 170, 205
What's My Line 104
White, Bill 86
Whitman, Dick 99
Whittier, John Greenleaf 195
"*Why Dom DiMaggio Belongs in the Hall of Fame*" (pamphlet) 76
Will, George 208, 212
William and Mary College 114, 117, 118
Williams, Billy 169, 170, 180
Williams, Dick 186, 188, 194, 199, 200
Williams, Mitch 176
Williams, Ted 57, 74–77, 87, 89, 96, 111, 114, 120–122, 128, 154, 179, 210, 217
Wilson, Earl 225
Wilson, Frank 11
Wilson, Jimmie 35, 45, 46
Winkles, Bobby 197

Winnepeg Maroons (B) 215
Winston-Salem Red Sox (B) 188
Wistert, Whitey 63
Wolfe, Rich 167
Women's Professional Baseball League 105
Woodling, Gene 110
World Series 12, 19, 23, 24, 43, 51, 71, 87, 106, 117, 142, 154, 192, 227; (1912) 91; (1926) 16, 17; (1930) 24; (1934) 25; (1935) 65; (1936) 40; (1937) 19; (1938) 65; (1939) 35, 36; (1940) 36; (1941) 12, 47, 91; (1945) 65; (1946) 103; (1947) 51, 52, 55, 110, 115; (1948) 83, 221; (1949) 117; (1954) 135; (1955) 129; (1956) 14; (1957) 162; (1959) 97; (1960) 220; (1964) 111; (1965) 123; (1967) 187; (1971) 145; (1972) 199, 227; (1973) 111, 199; (1974) 227; (1975) 189, 226; (1983) 141, 142; (1987) 204, 206; (1996) 164

World Trade Center 97
World War II 53, 60, 76, 82, 106, 139, 210, 215, 222, 225
Wrigley, Philip K. 66
Wrigley Field 63, 64, 148, 180, 205
Wyatt, Whitlow 55, 59, 221
Wynn, Early 217

Yale 121, 209, 210
Yale Playgrounds 80
Yankee Stadium 16, 40, 108
Yankees Magazine 41
Yastrzemski, Carl 186, 191
Yawkey, Tom 121, 123
YES Network 88
Yogi Berra (Trimble) 5
Yogi Berra Museum 112
York, Rudy 139
YouTube 145

Zanger, Jack 191, 192
Zarilla, Al 216, 217
Zimmer, Don 142, 169
Ziyo, Barry 228

www.ingramcontent.com/pod-product-compliance
Lightning Source LLC
Chambersburg PA
CBHW060340010526
44117CB00017B/2899